THE MODERN HISTORY OF KUWAIT

To the Memory of My Father

Mustafa M. Abu-Hakima
1896-1956.

THE MODERN HISTORY OF
KUWAIT

1750-1965

AHMAD MUSTAFA ABU-HAKIMA
M.A. (Cairo), Ph.D. (London)
Professor of Arabian Gulf History
McGill University, Montreal

LUZAC & COMPANY LIMITED . LONDON

First published 1983 by Luzac & Company,
46 Great Russell Street,
London WC1, England.

ISBN 0 7189 02599

Printed in Great Britain by
The Westerham Press.

CONTENTS

LIST OF ILLUSTRATIONS

ACKNOWLEDGEMENTS

I want to thank the many friends who have helped in various ways in the making of this book. To Christine Korah and Pat Fong goes the credit of typing the first draft. Eleanor and Elizabeth Calverley and the Duncan Memorial Centre (Hartford) supplied most of the early photographs of Kuwait.

I want also to thank Anne Melody and Sharifa (Cornelia) Dalenberg for their assistance in matters relating to the opening years of the twentieth century. Dr Robert G. Landen has read the first draft and offered invaluable criticism and penetrating comments. So did Dr. Tomas J. F. Pavlasek.

I must also acknowledge the continued cooperation of the staff of the India Office Library and Records (London); and the staff of the Sage Library of Rutgers University (New Brunswick, N.J.).

Dr. Patricia Risso Dubuisson, my student, has been extremely helpful in reading and correcting the final draft and offering very useful suggestions. Mrs. Ann Bless, by her articulate computerized typing of the final draft, produced it in its excellent form.

I am grateful to Dr. B. J. Slot, Director of the National Dutch Archives at the Hague for making available relevant historical data and also the rare collection of the Dutch East India Company's seventeenth century charts of the Arabian Gulf.

Major J. D. Lunt of Wadham College, Oxford University graciously placed at my disposal the album and private letters of the late Captain W. H. Shakespear, whose photographs of Kuwait appear in this publication.

My grateful thanks must also be given to Gillian Grant at the Middle East Centre, St Antony's College, Oxford for her help in providing old photographs.

Last, but not least, I must thank my family and my true friends in Kuwait for making this dream possible.

McGill University, Montreal, July, 1982

NOTE ON TRANSLITERATION AND ABBREVIATIONS

Since this book has been written for the benefit of the general reader, the system of transliteration, as generally agreed upon and followed by Orientalists, has not been strictly adhered to here.

Abbreviations

B.	Ibn or Bin.
B.S.	Bombay Selections.
B.M.	British Museum.
E.I/1	Encyclopaedia of Islam, first edition.
F.R.P.P.G.	Factory Records, Persia and the Persian Gulf.
J.I.H.	Journal of Indian History.
I.O.R.	India Office Records.
Sec. Com.	Secret Committee.
C. of D.	Court of Directors.

PREFACE

Relatively few people realise that the rise of Kuwait goes back to the latter part of the seventeenth century, and that the Āl-Sabāh rule began as early as 1752. To establish these facts historically, the present writer began his research on the history of Kuwait a quarter of a century ago. Most of the historical facts relating to Kuwait were established during that earlier research, and have been published for the benefit of the Western and the Arab reader in both English and Arabic. Since these facts remain unchallenged only a few dates required change in this present work.

It should be noted that this book covers nearly two and a half centuries of Kuwaīti history. The first two centuries, namely the eighteenth and the nineteenth, represent, to a certain degree, the lesser known and sparsely documented portion of that history, while the years from 1900 to the present are either fully documented or well served in twentieth century writings.

With the advent of the oil era the book market has been flooded with publications in both Arabic and European languages. Unfortunately, most of those publications which were characterised by their journalistic or narrative style lacked historical documentation and either unjustifiably distorted or completely neglected important facts concerning the early history of Kuwait. On the other hand, some writings have given adequate impressions of Kuwait in the early half of the twentieth century, a reflection perhaps on the abundance of information relating to this period, and to its greater accessibility.

For these reasons, the author has felt a need for a more accurate and in-depth study utilizing as much as possible some hitherto untouched archival materials, Arabic manuscripts (unpublished books), and contemporary sources that describe earlier events of Kuwaīti history.

The following is a brief outline of those sources used in this research.

I. Arabic Sources

Since Kuwait is a part of the Arabian Peninsula bordering on the Arabian Gulf, it was only natural to think of Arabic works as one of the sources for writing its history. Indigenous Arabic sources proved to be either of limited scope when found, or non-existent for the earlier period in the history of Kuwait. However, some valuable Arabic manuscript sources were traced in the libraries of the British Museum, Cambridge, and Oxford Universities. These had originally been purchased by representatives of the English East India Company during their stay in the Arabian Gulf region, and have since been acquired by those libraries.

Personal interviews - which constitute oral sources - held while the author was researching materials for this history in London, Bahrain, and Kuwait respectively, were used to corroborate written sources concerning the rise and rule of the Āl-Sabāh and of the Āl-Khalīfa in the 2nd half of the eighteenth century.

II. India Office Records

Perhaps the most important source of information that must be singled out is the archival materials kept at the India Office Records *(I.O.R.)* in London, England. Of special importance to the history of Kuwait are the Factory Records, classified under Persia and the Persian Gulf, *(F.R.P.P.G.)*, which commence at the turn of the eighteenth century. (It might be useful to note that the Royal Charter for the establishment of the East India Company was granted on 31st December, 1600.)

Besides the series *F.R.P.P.G.*, other unpublished India Office records were used, as may be seen from the footnotes.

The Bombay Government, which directed the affairs of the Company's Factories in the Arabian Gulf, asked some of its officials to draw on its own early records. Their research appeared in a series of books printed by the Bombay Government. Among these, three major publications stand out as containing substantial research materials relevant to the history of Kuwait. These are:

    A.   *Selections from the Records of the Bombay Government, vol. XXIV.*

    B.   Saldanha's *Precis,* listed in the bibliography.

    C.   *Gazetteer of the Persian Gulf,* by Lorimer.

III   The Egyptian National Archives (Turkish and Arabic)

Another collection, the Egyptian National Archives, (formerly 'Ābidīn Palace Archives kept in Cairo, Egypt) proved extremely helpful in shedding light on the history of Kuwait for the first half of the nineteenth century.

It was in 1810 that Muhammad 'Alī Pasha of Egypt sent a Turkish-Egyptian expedition to Arabia marking the beginning of his rule there which was to last until 1840. Though the main objective of the expedition was to drive the Wahhābīs out of the Holy Cities of the Hijāz, especially Madīna and Makka on the western side of the Peninsula, his army continued its march eastwards until it captured Wāhābi territories in Najd and al-Hasā, thus reaching the shores of the Arabian Gulf. The Shaikhdoms along the coast from Masqat in the south to Kuwait in the north are well covered in the correspondence exchanged between Muhammed 'Alī Pasha and his generals in eastern Arabia. Kuwait was not an exception, and in fact, it served towards the latter 1830's as a major support centre for the Egyptian army, where essential supplies were bought and shipped southwards to al-Hasā.

Researching the relevant archival materials in Cairo was pioneered by this author. The results proved to be extremely informative.

IV American Dutch Reformed Church Records

Supplementing the *I.O.R.* for the period from 1890 to the twentieth century were the historical archives of the Dutch Reformed Church of America, kept at New Brunswick, New Jersey, in the United States.

Researching these archives led the author to travel widely to visit the few surviving members of the American Arabian Mission who had resided in Kuwait and other parts of the Gulf from the turn of this century until very recently.

In conclusion, it is the author's hope that this book will create even greater interest in the history of the Arabian Gulf and will motivate others to pursue further avenues of investigation in this area of the world.

A. M. Abu-Hakima
McGill University
Montreal, 1979

CHAPTER I

THE RISE OF KUWAIT

Kuwait or Grane - Foundation

It has not yet been possible to fix a date for the establishment of the town of Kuwait, capital of the present State of Kuwait. Nor is it easy to accurately date the rise of the Shaikhdom of Kuwait under the ruling Sabāh family. However, earlier research,[1] based on records from the English East India Company,[2] suggests that the town was built about 1716 A D

To confirm that date, it was necessary to look into European as well as Arabic sources. The Danish traveller Niebuhr was the first to put the name Kuwait on a map dated 1765. This was accepted as the date for the rise and not the establishment of that city. Also appearing on this map was the city's other name "Grane". In 1978, on a visit to the Dutch State Archives[3] at The Hague in Holland, this writer found a seventeenth century chart of the Dutch East India Company showing the name "Grane", proving that this must be the original name of the town. Grane had been in existence before a small fortress called "Kuwait" was built by Barrāk, the Shaikh of the Banī Khālid tribe who were rulers of Eastern Arabia in the seventeenth century. The construction has been dated about 1680. However, by the end of the eighteenth century the city was mostly referred to by the name "Kuwait".

It may be interesting to point out that both names, Grane and Kuwait, are the diminutive forms (indicating smallness) of the Arabic words Qarn, meaning high hill, and Kūt, meaning castle or fort, which shows the insignificance of the place at the early stages of its history.[4] One should not omit in the present context that the Kuwaitī traditional historians, al-Rashīd and al-Qinā'ī believed that their town had existed before the establishment of Barrāk's "kuwait" or small fort. Barrāk ruled the Banī Khālid tribe from 1669 to 1682. This brings to mind the questions - who are the Kuwaitīs? and what was the place of their origin?

Origins of the Kuwaitīs

The geographical location of Kuwait in northeastern Arabia more or less dictated the tribal affiliation of its Arab population. Eastern Arabia

1. Ahmad Mustafa Abu Hakima, *History of Eastern Arabia (1750-1800), The Rise and Development of Bahrain and Kuwait*, Beirut, 1965.

2. Bombay Government, *Selections from the Records of the Bombay Government* no. XXIV, Bombay 1856. Referred to as *Bombay Selections*, XXIV. See "Historical Sketch of the Uttoobee Tribe of Arabs (Bahrein) from the year 1716 to the year 1817", by Francis Warden in *Ibid.*, pp. 361-425.

3. Records of the Dutch East India Company housed in The Hague, Netherlands.

4. Father Anistas al-Karmalī, commenting on the origin of the denomination of Kuwait, says that "al-Kuwait is the diminutive of Kūt. The word 'Kūt' in the language of southern 'Iraq and its neighbouring countries in Arabia and parts of Persia is the house that is built in the shape of a fortress or like it so as to be easily defended when attacked. This house is usually surrounded by other houses. The name 'Kūt' is given to such a house only when it lies near water, whether it is river, sea, a lake or even a swamp. Then it was applied to the village built on such a site." He gives the example Kūt al-Ifranjī, Kūt al-Zayn, Kūt al-'Amāra and Kūt Bandar. See the article "fī Tasmiat Madīnat al-Kuwait", *Al-Mashriq*, X (Bayrūt, 1904), pp. 449-458.

5. See *Bombay Selections*, XXIV, p. 361ff.

6. Four Ottoman Pashas had governed there: Fātih Pasha, who was the first Governor, 'Alī Pasha, Muhammad Pasha, and 'Umar Pasha, who surrendered to Barrāk.

7. See Ibn Bishr, *'Unwān al-Majd*, I, p. 25.

8. "Report on the Trade of Arabia etc.", in Saldanha, *Selections from State Papers*, pp. 405-409. These pages contain much information on the part played by these ports in distributing goods to central Arabia.

has been the land of the 'Adnānī division of the Arabs, or the Northern Arabs, compared to the Qahtānī or Southern Arabs, the two major sections of Arabs in their homeland. From time immemorial, the 'Adnānī Arabs inhabited, in addition to Central and Eastern Arabia, other parts of the Arabian Peninsula in the north and in the west.

The East India Company documents speak of the 'Utūb as the ancestors of the Āl-Sabāh and other large Kuwaitī families who came to live there about 1716. These 'Utūb,[5] like many Northern Arabian tribes, hail from the great Northern 'Anaza 'Adnānī tribe. Among the tribes who inhabited Kuwait or Grane before the arrival of the 'Utūb were the Banī Khālid, an 'Adnānī tribe whose Shaikh Barrāk built the *Kūt* in Grane before the turn of the seventeenth century. Since the Banī Khālid played an important role in the history of Eastern Arabia in general and Kuwait in particular, it becomes essential for this narrative to survey their history before the rise of Kuwait.

Banī Khālid, Rulers of Eastern Arabia

Before the establishment of the Banī Khālid supremacy over Eastern Arabia in the late seventeenth century, their people roamed and wandered in the territory extending from Qatar in the south to Basra in the north. During that century Eastern Arabia was a part of the Ottoman Empire which conquered Baghdad in 1534, Basra in 1546 and al-Hasa in 1555. In the last conquest, the Ottomans were helped by the 'Irāqī tribe of al-Muntafiq who had settled in the neighbourhood of Basra. The Banī Khālid had not accepted the Ottoman presence in al-Hasā, and under Barrāk, in 1670 they successfully besieged the Ottoman governor 'Umār Pasha, who surrendered and left his seat of government. He had been the fourth Ottoman ruler of al-Hasā.[6] Barrāk's rule lasted until his death in 1682 when his brother, Muhammad bin Ghurair Āl-Hamīd, took over. It is related that even in an earlier stage of their history, the Banī Khālid were powerful enough to be able to rebuff attacks sent against them by the powerful *Sharīfs* of Makka.[7]

The territory of the Banī Khālid in al-Hasā extending from Qatar in the south to Kuwait in the north was rich in agricultural produce and in pearl fisheries. In addition, the ports of 'Uqair and Qatif in al-Hasā were the major points from which the merchandise of India and other trading nations was exported to Central Arabia (Najd) in the west and the Ottoman provinces of 'Irāq and Syria.[8]

The peaceful nature of Khālidi rule together with the above-mentioned wealth were conducive to a prosperous trade in al-Hasā and its neighbouring areas. The desire to control this wealth cannot be ruled out as a factor in the Wahhābī-Khālidī wars of the second half of the 18th century.

One of the most detailed reports on the trade of Arabia bordering on the Arabian side of the Gulf can be found in the records of the English East India Company. The report is dated August 1790 and signed by Mr.

S. Manesty, the English Resident of the Company in Basra, and his assistant, Mr. Harford Jones Brydges. In other reports compiled by the agents of the same Company, the Banī Khālid are praised for their role in keeping peace along the western coast of the Gulf, hence encouraging the prosperity that prevailed in ports like Kuwait and other Arabian harbours. It might be important to mention in this connection that both the nomadic and settled modes of living of the different Banī Khālid sections promoted caravan transportation of merchandise along the coast of the Gulf from Qatar in the south to Syria in the north. Goods could not be transported across the desert without bedouin guards. The tribal nomadic sectors of the Banī Khālid thus played that part. It is also possible to claim that had it not been for this Khālidī peace in Eastern Arabia, Kuwait could not have risen to such prominence in so short a period during the early years of the second half of the 18th century.[9] This point will be taken up shortly.

From tribal headquarters of the Bani Khalid in the towns of al-Hufhūf and al-Mubarraz in the Hasā oasis, armed forces carried on wars into Najd in the west and as far as Basra in the north where they fought with rival tribes. Thus, the Banī Khālid acted as a police force amongst the unruly bedouins of the desert. It was under this umbrella of order that Kuwait began its march towards independence in the middle of the 18th century.

Arrival of the 'Utūb in Kuwait

It has been previously stated that Grane was the older name of Kuwait, and had been known to the Dutch map makers by the middle of the seventeenth century. According to local Kuwaitī historians, Grane at that time was a small fishing centre, or tiny coastal village. They mention that Barrāk built his *Kūt* in that village with the intention of keeping it as his summer residence since the weather of Kuwait was moderate when compared to the Banī Khālid's domain in the south.

The date of the arrival in Kuwait of the 'Utūb is controversial, as are the name "'Utūb" and the route they travelled. This federation of Arab families was sometimes referred to as Banī 'Utba,[10] and often as 'Utūb,[11] Ottoobee or Banī Attaba.[12] All these words derive from the Arabic root *'ataba*, meaning to travel from place to place.

Arabic sources from the second half of the eighteenth century and the early nineteenth refer to them as 'Utūb, the name which will be used throughout this book. Lieutenant-Colonel Dickson[13] felt that the name 'Utūb came from the verb *'ataba* and reported that Shaikh 'Abd Allāh al-Sālim Āl-Sabāh, the late ruler of Kuwait, informed him that his forefathers were called by that name after they had moved north: "'atabū ila al-Shamāl". Whatever the origin of their name may be, all authorities writing on Kuwait agree that the 'Utūb belong to Anaza, an 'Adnānī Arab tribe, inhabiting Najd and Northern Arabia. The Āl-Sabāh, as well as other 'Utbī families, claim to be be a division of 'Anaza. The local

9. See *ibid.*, p. 408.

10. *Sabā'ik al-'Asjad*, p. 18.

11. *Lam' al-Shihāb*, pp. 110-112.

12. Francis Warden, "Historical Sketch of the Uttoobee Tribe of Arabs (Bahrein) etc." in *Bombay Selections*, pp. 362-372.

13. Dickson, *Kuwait and her Neighbours*, pp. 362-372

14. See al-Rashīd, Vol. I, p. 12 for the origin of Āl-Sabāh. Āl-Khalīfa claim the same descent. The author was told this by Shaikh 'Abd Allāh b. Khālid Āl-Khalīfa and that they were also the descendents of the same Jumayla division of the 'Anaza.

15. Oppenheim could not fix a date for that emigration, but states that the Jumayla are still at al-Aflāj. See M. von Oppenheim, *Die Beduinen*, (Leipzig, 1939), vol. I, p. 62. He states that the 'Utūb were among them and that they migrated to Kuwait, but does not give any date for this migration. See *Ibid* and Ashkenezi, "The 'Anaza Tribes", in *South-Western Journal of Anthropology*, New Mexico, 1948, pp. 222-239.

16 'Anaza is usually divided into two groups, northern and southern. The Ruwala belong to the first. To the southern group belong Āl-Su'ūd, Āl-Sabāh, and others. Cf. A. Musil, *The Manners and Customs of the Ruwala Bedouins*, (New York, 1926), p. 46.

17. AL-Qinā'ī, *Safahāt min Ta'rīkh al-Kuwait*, p. 9; al-Rashīd, *Tar'rīkh al-Kuwait*, Vol. I, pp. 15-16.

18. Al-Qinā'ī in his *Safahāt* speaks of the Qinā's at Kuwait, Zubāra, Basra and Najd. It is not quite clear from where they came to Kuwait. According to him (p. 100), they might have come from northern 'Irāq, where they were for some time before. Genealogically, they originally belonged to the Suhūl Arabs. It seems also that some of them migrated to Zubāra during or after the emigration of Āl-Khalīfa in 1766. Soon after the desertion of Zubāra by its inhabitants in 1213/1798, some of the Qinā'āt migrated to Bahrain Islands and others to Persia (see *Ibid.*, pp. 99-100). At Manāma town in Bahrain there is a quarter called after them (*Ibid.*).

19. See "Historical Sketch of the Uttoobee Tribe of Arabs etc." in *Bombay Selections*, XXIV, p. 140. This article, by Lieutenant Kemball, depends on

tradition upheld by the Āl-Sabāh and the Āl-Khalīfa[14] states that they belong to Jumayla, a sub-division of 'Anaza, and had originally inhabited Haddār in al-Aflāj in Najd, before they migrated to Qatar, and from there sailed to Kuwait. Though it is not clear as to when the migration to Qatar took place, it may have been a part of the great 'Anaza migration late in the seventeenth century.[15] This great migration of the 'Anaza accounts for the arrival of the Ruwala in Syria.[16]

The 'Utūb were originally related families who moved from Central Arabia either as a group or separately, settling in various places on the eastern coast of Arabia before establishing themselves permanently at Kuwait. No definite date can be given for the migration of the 'Utūb.

The second half of the seventeenth century and the early years of the eighteenth century were drought years in Central Arabia. For this reason, the 'Utūb must have been among the tribes that moved to Eastern Arabia. Local tradition states that the 'Utūb lived in al-Aflāj district in Central Arabia until the drought drove them eastward to Qatar which was then under the suzerainty of the Banī-Khālid. It is not known how they finally assembled in Kuwait. They must have learned seafaring in Qatar or in al-Hasā which would explain the local historians' theory that they sailed north. In fact, tradition affirms that they had scattered into various Arabian Gulf ports before coming to Kuwait.[17] However, tribal lore suggests three possible places from which the 'Utūb must have left for Kuwait.

The first implies that they lived near Khōr al-Sabiyya, south of Basra. They were driven out by the Ottoman *Mutasallim* of Basra, because they raided desert caravans coming to that city, and attacked the shipping of the Shatt al-'Arab. Another legend is that those families living on the Persian coast of the Gulf sailed to Kuwait to escape the oppression of other Arab tribes. Others believed that they sailed from Qatar to Kuwait as a result of quarrels with Āl-Musallam Arabs of Qatar.

The late Yūsuf bin 'Isā al-Qinā'ī, the Kuwaitī historian, resolved the dilemma by saying that the 'Utūb originally inhabited Qatar after their departure from al-Aflāj. From Qatar, the families scattered into the various ports of the Arabian Gulf littorals, and eventually settled in Kuwait. He cites his own family, al-Qinā'āt,[18] which came to Kuwait about two centuries ago from the Persian littoral, 'Irāq and the south, i.e. Qatar. Thus, it is probable that the 'Utūb spent not less than half a century in the south after arriving from al-Aflāj.

The uncertainty of the date of arrival of the 'Utūb at Kuwait is another problem which faces the student of the history of Kuwait. Here we must distinguish between the coming of the Āl-Sabāh, whose chief Sabāh bin Jābir became the Shaikh of Kuwait in the 1750's, and the other 'Utbī families. The English East India Company records[19] state that in about 1716 the Āl-Sabāh along with two important branches of the 'Utūb, namely Āl-Khalīfa and Āl-Jalāhima, occupied Grane (Kuwait) and undertook to direct local affairs. There is, of course, a good bit of conjecture in the statement, since all the 'Utūb did not arrive simultaneously. Furthermore, it is an anachronism; for in the year 1716 neither Sabāh or Khalīfa were the chiefs of their families. However, this does not mean that the predecessors of Sabāh bin Jābir were not in Kuwait at the beginning of the eighteenth century.[20]

Rulers of Kuwait Between 1700-1750

Nothing definite is known about the rulers of Kuwait during the first half of the eighteenth century according to records of the English East India Company, writings of travellers, and local historical tradition. It appears that Kuwait was under the direct rule of the Banī Khālid *Amir*, Sa'dūn bin Muhammad bin Ghurair Āl-Hamīd, who ruled at the beginning of the eighteenth century.[21]) After the death of Sa'dūn, his brother 'Alī occupied the seat of government, following a struggle with Dujayn, and 'Alī became the ruler of Eastern Arabia the same year.[22]

The ruling family's struggle for succession, which started after the death of Sa'dūn in 1722, seems to have given other tributary tribes of the Banī Khālid some form of local independence. At the same time, they remained loyal to the Banī Khālid. Indeed, Kuwait's independence was not achieved until after 1750. It is interesting to note in this context that Mr. Warden of the Bombay government, in his 1817 sketch of the 'Utūb, names Sulaymān as the Shaikh of the Sabāh family as early as 1716.[23] Since no source except Mr. Warden's gives the name of any Sulaymān as the first of the Sabāh family to rule the 'Utūb in Kuwait, he must have belonged to the Banī Khālid.

It is thought that Sulaymān bin Ahmad, whom Mr. Warden believed to be the ruler of the Āl-Sabāh, was Sulaymān bin Muhammad Āl-Hamīd, ruler of the Banī Khālid tribes from 1736-1752.[24] One reason for this theory is that one might use the name Ahmad for Āl-Hamīd when mentioning the ruler's family name, so long as his first name is given, in this case Sulaymān. Secondly, the 'Utub, according to local tradition, arrived in Kuwait with permission from the Banī Khālid ruler.[25] The power of the Banī Khālid remained strong and centralized in the hands of one shaikh until the death of Shaikh Sulaymān bin Mumammad in 1752. Family disputes after the death of Sa'dūn in 1722 gave the 'Utūb a chance to practise some form of independence. This chance was enhanced after 1752, not only because of the death of Sulaymān Āl-Hamīd and the combined rivalry among the factions of his ruling tribe, but also because of the rise of the Wahhābīs, the bitter enemies of the Banī Khālid, in Central Arabia.

Sabāh bin Jābir bin 'Adhbī, First Amir of Kuwait

The absence of strong centralized rule in Eastern Arabia made it possible for the Āl-Sabāh to become totally independent of the Banī Khālid. Local tradition is not sure of the exact date for Sabāh's rise to power. However, it is related that he was chosen by the inhabitants of

previous articles written by Mr. Warden in 1817. Kemball wrote his in 1844.

20.   According to what Shaikh 'Abd Allāh b. Khalīd Āl-Khalīfa told the author, local tradition among the shaikhs of the Āl-Khalīfa says their family came to Kuwait earlier than the Āl-Sabāh, and the head of the 'Utūb was the ruler of Kuwait. Perhaps this is why the Āl-Khalīfa migrated in 1766 to Zubāra when 'Abd Allāh Āl-Sabāh became the Shaikh of Kuwait.

21.   See table of the Banī Khālid rulers in Appendix no. VII.

22.   See Ibn Bishr, I, p. 27

23.   "Historical Sketch of the Uttoobee Tribe of Arabs", in *Bombay Selections* p. 362.

24.   Cf. Ibn Bishr, I, p. 27.

25.   See al-Qinā'ī, *Safahāt*, p. 9.

26.   See al-Rashīd, II, p. 2.

27.   For an account of Khārij Island, see Dr. Ives, *Voyages*, pp. 207-216; Niebuhr, *Voyages en Arabie*, II, pp. 149-166; Parsons, *travels*, pp. 190-198.

28.   See Dr. Ives, *Voyages*, pp. 207-216.

29.   See Ives, p. 207.

30.   Khārij Island is the main terminal of Iranian oil at the present time.

31.   See Ives, p. 222.

32.   *Ibid.*, p. 224.

Kuwait, in the tribal manner, to administer justice and the affairs of the thriving town.[26] Apparently, the Āl-Sabāh were not famous before the election of Sabāh, the first to attain the shaikhship of the town. Nor were they included in contemporary traditions. Even Sabāh's name was not mentioned by the earliest European travellers. What they said was merely that Kuwait was ruled by a shaikh.

The Dutch Factory at Khārij[27] and Kuwait, 1758

The Shaikh of Kuwait who is referred to in Dr. Ives' *Voyage* of 1758, must be Sabāh, who rose to power a few years earlier in 1752.[28] One could gather from Dr. Ives' narrative, that as early as 1758, Sabāh's authority seems to have been established in Kuwait and vicinity. Because of its commercial success, Kuwait became an important port of call for desert caravans to and from Aleppo. These caravans carried goods imported by Kuwaitī vessels from India and passengers who wanted to travel from the Arabian Gulf, via the desert, to Aleppo in Syria.[29]

The story of Dr. Ives and his travels with the Shaikh of Kuwait is worth recalling here, for it is the first instance where Kuwait or Grane is mentioned in the report of a European traveller.

In March 1758 Dr. Ives, on his way from India to Europe with other travellers, anchored at Khārij Island.[30] Upon asking Baron Kniphausen, head of the Dutch settlement there, the fastest route to Aleppo, it was suggested that they should travel by *felucca* (boat) to Kuwait, whence its Shaikh would accompany them with the Aleppo caravan through the desert. This route could be covered in twenty-five to thirty days thus saving two to four weeks as compared with the time required by boat to Basra and Baghdad.

Arrangements were made for a boat to be sent to Kuwait to fetch the Shaikh on March 31st. It returned the 14th of April, bringing "the long expected Arab".[31] For the journey the Shaikh asked 2000 piastres but the Baron offered only 1000 to 1100. When negotiations failed, the Shaikh returned home while the travellers proceeded by vessel to Basra.

"The Shaikh", writes Dr. Ives, "after negotiation was broken off, waited upon the Baron, and remonstrated in this manner, 'You use me very unkindly, Sir. Pray what are these travellers to you? I and my tribe have been in friendship with you for a long time, and I could not have expected that you would thus have given the preference to strangers.' "[32]

Apparently, both the Shaikh and the Baron must have equally benefited from the conveyance of trade and people to Aleppo so as to avoid Basra and Baghdad. For the Dutch, it was a matter of hostilities with the Pasha. As for the Shaikh, his was a financial gain reaped from merchandise carried through his town.

This sea and desert trade route must have put the Shaikh in direct contact with his neighbours. Though it is difficult to define the area under the Shaikh's control during this early period of the history of Kuwait, his influence must have extended outside the walls of his town. From his dealings with Dr. Ives and because he promised the traveller a safe arrival at Aleppo, it appears that the Arabs of the desert route from Kuwait to Aleppo were on good terms with the Shaikh.

Early Boundaries of Kuwait

Though there is no written evidence to show the boundary of the 'Utūb suzerainty north of Kuwait, it must have extended to Jahra village where the wells were superior to those of Kuwait town. Off the mainland, nearby islands like Qurain, Umm al-Naml and Failaka were ruled by the Shaikh.[33] The wealth of the Shaikh (and consequently the town) could be judged by his refusal of the Baron's offer of 1,000 piastres when he had asked for 2,000, despite the fact that bargaining was desirable.

Growth of Kuwait

This rapid growth of the 'Utbī town may be attributed to the bulk of trade carried by the merchants of Kuwait and others who used that port as a station for caravans carrying goods from southern and eastern Arabia to Syria.[34] Pearl fishing was another source of wealth for which, according to the Danish traveller Niebuhr,[35] they kept a fleet of over 800 small boats. It is interesting to note that the 'Utūb sailed south to Bahrain for pearl fishing because that vicinity was the richest in pearls in the Banī Khālid territory.

It should be remembered that other 'Utbī families besides the Āl-Sabāh, the ruling family, shared the wealth brought by these occupations. These families settled in such a way that made every section of town take one family or more. Thus, the town was divided into *Hayy Sharq* [People of the East], *Qiblī* or *Jiblī* (the West, because this is the direction of Makka), and the *Wasat* [Center]. The Āl-Sabāh lived in the central quarter.[36]

The Wall

Local tradition states that the town was not walled from the beginning because the Banī Khālid authority was respected by other Bedouin tribes. No date for the building of the wall is given but it is estimated to have been about 1760, i.e. about eight years after the Banī Khālid had lost their influence among the Arab tribes. This was due to internal struggles among the ruling branch during the reign of Sabāh. The English East India Company records clearly state that the town was walled as early as the 1770's.[37] Although the wall was built of mud and could be heavily damaged by rain, it still served as an adequate defence against the Bedouin raids as recently as the early twentieth century.

33. See Niebuhr, *Description*, pp. 288 and 296.

34. The caravan by which Dr. Ives and his companions planned to travel consisted of 5,000 camels and 1,000 men. See his *Voyages*, p. 222.

35. See Niebuhr, *Description*, p. 296.

36. *Safahāt min Ta'rīkh al-Kuwait*, p. 67; "Historical Sketch of the Uttoobee Tribe, etc.", p. 362. Some of these families are living today in both Bahrain and Kuwait, e.g. Āl-Jalāhima, who are called in Kuwait Āl-Nisf. See al-Rashīd, Vol. I, p. 18.

37. *F.R.P.P.G.*, Vol. 17, dispatch no. 1152.

38.   See Al-Qinā'ī, p. 14.

39.   Cf. al-Rashīd, Vol. I, pp. 75-76, and Al-Qi'nā'ī, *op. cit.*, pp. 33-35.

40.   'Uthmān b. Sanad died in 1242/1826. See Kāzim al-Dujaylī, article on "al-Shaikh 'Uthmān b. Sanad al-Basrī" in *Lughat al-'Arab* (Baghdād, Dhul Qa'Da 1331/1913), pp. 180-186.

41.   See Ibn Ghannam, *Rawdat al-Afkār*, pp. 30-31; see also *Lam' al-Shihāb* (ed. Abu Haikma), pp. 15-16.

42.   *Safaḥāt min Ta'rīkh al-Kuwait*, pp. 35-36; al-Rashīd, *Ta'rīkh al-Kuwait*, Vol. I, pp. 75-76.

Sabāh's Government

The town's lack of protection forced the local Shaikh, Sabāh, to govern more strictly. Local tradition states that Sabāh was chosen by the different families, so his rule may not have been as despotic as expected. This was because the 'Utūb, from the beginning, were settlers, the nomadic stage having ended after their departure from Qatar early in the seventeenth century. Although the Arab shaikhs were generally powerful at the time in Arabia, the Shaikh of Kuwait consulted his people occasionally, especially regarding commercial interests.[38] If we may judge from what happened in 1775, we can conclude that the merchants of Kuwait had a voice in politics. Basra was then occupied by the Persians and many merchants moved to the 'Utbī settlements of Kuwait and Zubāra.

Administration of Justice

The Arabian shaikh saw to it that there was equal justice for all his people. In making judgments he was expected to abide by the Qur'ān and the Sharī'a law, or the traditional *'urf* or *sālifa* (custom). The two Kuwaitī historians, al-Qinā'ī and al-Rashīd, write that the Sharī'a law was not in use during the early years of Āl-Sabāh's rule, or even later.[39] It was not necessary in this case to ask the ruler to intervene. It was the custom to ask any man with the required wisdom to settle conflicts. In the case of the 'Utbī rule in Kuwait and in Zubāra, it may be assumed that the custom at al-Hasā applied to the 'Utūb. In other words, there must have been a judge (*qāḍī*) at Kuwait from the start. 'Ulamā' or learned men exerted great influence on both the people and their rulers from the seventeenth through the nineteenth centuries when almost every town in al-Hasā and Najd had its school of 'Ulamā'. 'Uthmān ibn Sanad[40], in his work *Sabā'ik al-'Asjad,* gives the biographies of twenty "Ulamā" who were mostly his contemporaries, i.e. late eighteenth and early nineteenth century. Muhammad b. 'Abd al-Wahhāb, the great Wahhābī reformer, and son of Shaikh 'Abd al-Wahhāb b. Sulaymān, the *Qāḍī* of 'Uyayna, fought hard against the other "Ulamā" to convince them of his teachings. In the 1720's he visited places in Najd and Hijāz where he listened to the "Ulamā" in Makka, Madīna and other towns of Hijāz.[41]

Shaikh Muhammad b. Fayrūz, First Kuwaitī Qāḍī

Among the biographies 'Uthmān b. Sanad lists in his above-mentioned work is that of Shaikh Muhammad b. Fayrūz and his son, Shaikh 'Abd al-Wahhāb b. Muhammad b. Fayrūz. Local tradition of Kuwait gives the name of the former as its first judge. The date given by al-Rashīd and al-Qinā'ī for the death of Shaikh Muhammad b. Fayrūz is 1722. They write that Sabāh was the first ruler and Ibn Fayrūz was the Qāḍī during his reign.[42] Since Sabāh could not have come to power before

1752, both al-Qinā'ī and al-Rashīd must be mistaken in giving Shaikh Muhammad b. Fayrūz's death in 1722. 'Uthmān b. Sanād gave the year 1733 for Ibn Fayrūz's birth in Hajar (al-Hasā) and 1801 for his death[43] and burial in Zubair, a town between Basra and Kuwait. (Ibn Sanad himself died in 1826.) It appears that Ibn Sanad was correct while the two Kuwaitī historians were not. Moreover, from the facts about Ibn Fayrūz and his duties as *Qādī*, and from the dates given by Ibn Sanad for his birth and death, it is probable that he was the first *Qādī* of Kuwait under Shaikh Sabāh.

'Abd Allāh b. Sabāh (1764-1815)

Local sources do not agree on when Sabāh became ruler of Kuwait, and differ greatly on the date of his death. However, Sabāh left five sons: Salmān, Mālij, Mubārak, Muhammad and 'Abd Allāh, the youngest. All local authorities agree that 'Abd Allāh was chosen as Sabāh's successor for his bravery, wisdom, justice and generosity, qualities an Arab admires in his shaikh.[44]

To fix a date for 'Abd Allāh's accession is not an easy task. Lorimer, in his official and comprehensive work, *Gazetteer of the Persian Gulf*, based on the East India Company records, gave the year 1762 as the start for 'Abd Allāh's rule[45] and chose the year 1812 as the year which marked the end of his rule because, according to the Company records, 'Abd Allāh ruled for fifty years. Ibn Bishr, the Wahhābī chronicler whose annals are without doubt authentic, gave the year 1815 as the end of 'Abd Allāh's rule following his death early in February.[46] Despite the fact that this end date can be considered a reliable one, it is still not possible to determine exactly when he was chosen to the shaikhship of Kuwait. The year 1764, however, can be selected for two reasons. The first is that 'Abd Allāh was said to have ruled for fifty years, and the second is the emigration in 1766 of the Āl-Khalīfa, cousins of the Āl-Sabāh, from Kuwait who were expecting to see a member of their family selected to the leadership of Kuwait after Sabāh. Kuwait under 'Abd Allāh's rule will be the subject of another chapter.

In order for the reader to understand how the Āl-Sabāh became firmly established as rulers of Kuwait in the second half of the eighteenth century and the early years of the nineteenth, the affairs in the Arabian Gulf region during that period must be reviewed. A study of those conditions will help one gain insight into how Kuwait came to occupy a prominent position among other Arab shaikhdoms by the end of the eighteenth century and how it was possible for a small shaikhdom to be built up.

43. See Ibn Sanad, *Sabā'ik al-'Asjad*, p. 96.

44. See al-Rashīd, II, p. 2 and al-Qinā'ī, p. 10.

45. See Lorimer, *Gazetteer of the Persian Gulf*, IV, Table 9.

46. Ibn Bishr, I, p. 176. See footnote 20.

CHAPTER II

POLITICAL SITUATION IN THE ARABIAN GULF PRIOR TO THE RISE OF THE ĀL-SABĀH 1700-1750

Modern Kuwait had its beginnings at least half a century before the rise of Sabāh I to power. Therefore it is necessary to sketch the political conditions in the Arabian Gulf area during that period. It is the purpose of this chapter to present and explain those factors at work before Sabāh's rule which affected the history of the area both during and after his lifetime.

Those forces or powers, which were of paramount importance to the very existence of newly rising shaikhdoms in the area, were: the Shāhs of Persia, the Ottomans in 'Irāq or Mesopotamia, Banī Khālid and the Arab tribes of Najd in Eastern Arabia, and the European trading companies.

Conditions in Persia

This was a period of constant change and unrest in Persia, when it was being invaded successively by the Afghāns, Ottomans and the Russians.[1] As a result, therefore, the Arabian Gulf remained free of the impact of Persia. Nādir Shāh's efforts to build a new fleet in the Gulf spearheaded plans to conquer Basra and establish Persian rule over Bahrain in 1736. His plans were doomed and the only visible part of that dreamed-of fleet were the rude ribs of an unfinished vessel in the shipyard of Abū-Shāhr. Nādir Shāh's naval failure is usually attributed to the fact that his Persian subjects had "invincible repugnance to the sea"[2] and he was forced to depend on Portuguese, Indians and Arabs to man his fleet. Unable to maintain necessary maritime power, the Persians could not dominate the Gulf.

Ottoman 'Irāq

Ottoman Mesopotamia, another power bordering on the Arabian Gulf, might also have exercised strong control over affairs of the Gulf, were it not for the fact that the Governor's authority was limited to Baghdād and did not extend south as far as Basra. The Wālī (Pasha) of Baghdād, as well as other governors in Mesopotamia, were in a state of almost continuous warfare with the Persians since the occupation of Mesopotamia in the 1530's.

1. For the troubled state of Persia see L. Lockhart, *Nādir Shah, A Critical Study Based Mainly Upon Contemporary Sources*, pp. 1-17.

2. Sykes, *A History of Persia*, II, p. 271.

3.   Cf. C. Niebuhr, *Voyage en Arabie et en d'autres pays circonvoisins*, Vol. II, pp. 187-188.

4.   Al-Zafīr, or al-Dafīr, originally Najdī Tribes, migrated to 'Irāq where they lived in the neighbourhood of Basra. See 'Abbās Al-Azzāwi, 'Ashā'ir al-'Irāq, Vol. I, pp. 295-304. Al-Muntafiq Tribes came from Najd and settled between Basra and Baghdād. See Ibrāhīm Ibn Sabghat Allāh Al-Haydarī, *'Unwān al-Majd fī Bayān Ahwāl Baghdād wa Basra wa Najd*, B.M.M.S. or 7567, f. 58r. See also Muhammad Al-Bassām, *Al-Durar al-Mafākhir fī akhbār al-'Arab al-Awā*khir, B.M.M.S. Add 7358, f. 43.

5.   The East India Company's Factory at Basra was established in 1643. See Longrigg, *Four Centuries of Modern Iraq*, p. 108; also A. Wilson, *The Persian Gulf*, p. 163.

In Basra, however, the *Mutasallim* (provincial administrator) ruled almost independently of the Pasha of Baghdād and his authority extended beyond town walls to the Arab tribes whom he depended upon for defense of towns and transportation of goods. The Muntafiq tribe which occupied the area west of the town were loyal to the *Mutasallim,* while the Banī Ka'b which occupied the area to the east and southeast[3] frequently changed their allegiance from the Ottomans to the Persians, sometimes paying homage to both. To these two Arab tribes bordering Basra may be added al-Zafīr[4] tribe which was usually loyal to the Pasha of Baghdād and his *Mutasallim* in Basra.

Relations between these Mesopotamian Arab tribes and those of Eastern Arabia were peaceful before the rise of Sabāh to power. Soon after, conditions turned to strife. The Pasha's policy was to develop friendly relations with these Mesopotanian Arabs, and, if possible, keep them under the direct rule of the *Mutasallim*. However, when this control weakened, Basra's trade suffered as did trade which travelled between Basra and Baghdād by water and desert caravan.

In the sixteenth century the Ottomans concentrated much of their effort at Basra as a centre for attack on the Portuguese. Their interests there continued even in the absence of the Portuguese threat during the next two centuries. The Pashas of Baghdad considered the flourishing trade of both the English and the Dutch East India Companies most important in the early years of the seventeenth century.[5]

The amount and prosperity of the Basra trade was affected by several factors. The *Mutasaallim's* greed, acumen and attitude towards the trading groups were of the greatest importance. Trade depended on peace, and this was tenuous, even in the absence of Persian aggression. Arab tribes might from time to time disrupt trade within Basra, the transit trade to Syria, or even internal trade with Baghdad and other cities of the Province.

Since time immemorial, these tribes, as well as those south of Basra, depended for their living upon the caravans travelling from central and eastern Arabia to Mesopotamia. The newly established 'Utbī town of Kuwait benefitted greatly from this desert route which passed through Jahra village for water. Jahra and other villages south of Basra were under the control of the Banī Khālid tribe in the first half of the eighteenth century.

Eastern and Central Arabia

It has been pointed out in the previous chapter how the Banī Khālid rule in Eastern Arabia which remained unchallenged until the rise of Wahhābism in Najd or Central Asia was very favourable to trade. It has also been noted that there existed the peace which was conducive to worthwhile endeavours. The situation in Najd before and after the rise of Wahhābī rule has yet to be discussed.

While Eastern Arabia was enjoying peace, Najd was being ruled by petty chiefs exercising unrestrained power over their towns or tribes. Not until 1745[6] did these towns and the *Amirs* feel the overwhelming power of the Sū'udī family of al-Dir'iyya. From time immemorial, occasional droughts in some regions of the desert forced large sections of the population to the rich outskirts of Syria and Mesopotamia. Modern recorded history suggests that such expulsions took place much later. It was customary for the Bedouins to travel with cattle to the neighbouring fertile oases when attacked by drought. Al-Hasā, with its rich oases was the refuge of the people of Najd. The attitude of the settlers and Bedouins of al-Hasā towards the immigrants seems to have been friendly. This might have been because both Najd and al-Hasā were inhabited by 'Adnānī Arabs, and the Banī Khālid, rulers of al-Hasā, belonged to Rabī'a, an 'Adnānī tribe. This attitude might be attributed to Arab hospitality. As will be seen, their blood link with the 'Adnāniyya did not prevent the Banī Khālid from later attacking the rising Su'ūdī power, primarily located at al-Dir'iyya in central Najd. The Wahhābīs were on the defensive for over twenty years (1745-1765), but changed to the offensive against the Banī Khālid until they finally defeated them in 1795.[7] Raids were carried out on towns not only in Eastern Arabia, such as Kuwait, but also in 'Irāq in the north and Hijāz in the west. These attacks subjected the Wahhābīs to counter-attacks by the Ottomans towards the end of the eighteenth century and early in the nineteenth. Reference to these wars will be made later in this history.

European Trading Companies in the Arabian Gulf

Last among the forces which had a great effect on the development of Kuwait in the second half of the eighteenth century and later, were the European powers. Though all of them will be mentioned, the British will be singled out because of their major role in the history of all the Arabian Gulf States during the era that is covered in this work.

The English East India Company

The English East India Company's trade relations with the Gulf may be viewed from two aspects. The first was competition with other European nations trading in the Gulf. The second was the East India Company's relations with the local powers. Since the English were latecomers to the Gulf, compared to other European nations (namely the Portuguese, the Dutch and the French) we shall briefly discuss the involvement of the latter powers, and then return to the English.

The Portuguese, the Dutch and the French

The Portuguese were the first European nation to find the sea route to India in 1498, a few years after Columbus had discovered the route to America. It is worth mentioning here that the Portuguese owe that

6. This year marks the beginning of the Wahhābī activities in Najd. Cf. Ibn Ghannām, *Rawdat al-Afkār*, vol. II, p. 4; also Ibn Bishr, *'Unwān al-Majd*, vol. I, p. 15.

7. See Ibn Ghannām, *op. cit.*, Vol. II, pp. 185-192. Ibn Bishr, *op. cit.*, Vol. I, pp. 100-102. *Lam' al-Shihāb*, ff. 67-72.

8. See *Encyclopaedia of Islam*, First edition, under Shihāb al-Dīn Ahmad ibn Mājid.

9. See Lorimer, I, i, p. 836.

10. See A. Wilson, *The Persian Gulf*, p. 161.

11. Both had factories in Bandar 'Abbās and Basra.

12. Gombroon Factory to the C. of D. dated 7th May 1737. See also Ives, *A Voyage*, p. 206.

13. Though the purposes for establishing these factories can be traced in most of the dispatches of the first half of the 18th century, a very clear reference to those motivations was made in a letter from Latouche on his handing over the responsibilities of the Basra Factory to his successor Mr. Manesty. See letter dated Basra 6.xi.1784 in *F.R.P.P.G.*, Vol. 18, dispatch no. 1299.

discovery to the Arab navigator Shihāb al-Dīn Ahmad ibn Mājid,[8] a native of Rās al-Khayma, who led Vasco Da Gama's fleet safely from the East African coast to India. Thus, the Portuguese were the first to establish their influence and dominate eastern waters in the sixteenth century. By the turn of the next century, however, their control began to weaken. In 1602 Bahrain slipped from their grasp; then in 1622 Hurmuz. Their last fortress in Masqat capitulated to the Arabs of 'Umān in about 1651. This political and military deterioration was followed by a decline in trade. Portuguese ships continued to frequent the Gulf for trading purposes and until 1721 their Factory at Kung Island was visited by merchant ships belonging to "Indians, both Hindus and Muhammadans".[9]

The English and the Dutch, represented by their East India Companies as early as the first half of the seventeenth century, cooperated to drive out the Portuguese. They fought a joint battle against them in the Gulf until they were dislodged.[10]

The French entered the competition after the formation of a French East India Company in 1664 but early in the eighteenth century their Factory at Bandar 'Abbās closed. It was not until 1755 that they re-established their Residency at Basra, although during the first half of the eighteenth century French ships called there and at other Gulf ports.

Holland and England were the two major European trading nations in the Gulf during the first half of the eighteenth century. Both had Factories in more than one port in countries bordering on the Arabian Gulf.[11] Relations between them seem to have been cordial during that period. The Factory Records of the English Company tell of packets and letters being conveyed from their Factory at Gombroon to Basra in Dutch ships.[12] This friendship soon ended in hostilities early in the second half of the eighteenth century when England became the largest European trader in the Gulf.

British Activities in the Gulf

A brief discussion of British interests in the Gulf during the first half of the eighteenth century helps to illustrate how their relations with Kuwait developed. These interests are reflected in the dispatches of the English factories' agents to Gombroon (i.e., Bandar 'Abbās), Isfahān, Basra and other places in Persia and Ottoman Mesopotamia. There were two main reasons for the establishment of factories. The first was to set up centres for the distribution of English materials and other goods carried by English ships to and from countries bordering on the Arabian Gulf. The second was to use these factories, especially the one at Basra, as a centre for the English Company's dispatches going east or west.[13] The English Company could depend on two fast and safe routes for doing this, either from India through the Red Sea to Europe, or the safer and more practical overland desert route through Basra and Aleppo. The overland route was safer since the only danger was from Arab tribes, whose friendship was easily bought with regular presents of money and goods. This route proved valuable not only for the Company's trade in the Arabian Gulf, but also for swift contact between Bombay, Surat and other places in India and the Court of Directors in London. It became increasingly important in the second half of the eighteenth century, before and after the Seven Years War (1756-1763) between England and France.[14]

Although the first duty of the trading companies' representatives was to expand trade, they were nonetheless unable to remain isolated from local events. As a matter of fact, the English East India Company "in less than half a century after its incorporation by a Royal Charter of 31st December 1600, assumed a political aspect".[15] Thus, politics trailed behind trade, at least until the end of the eighteenth century when the French attempted to dominate Egypt in the wake of Bonaparte's conquest of Egypt in 1798.

In 1703, the old and the new English Companies merged under the name "The United Company of the Merchants of England trading to the East Indies". The Resident who represented the Company and who had invested his personal fortune in trade was given consular power and rank from then on.[16] Thus, it was necessary for him to consider his own interests as well as those of the Company. More than once Residents quarrelled with local governments and the solution of those disputes was undertaken by the Governor at Bombay and H.M. Ambassador in Instanbul.[17]

Since Factories existed on both Ottoman and Persian territories, the governors of both countries attempted to use the Company's war vessels against each other in times of crisis. In addition, both Ottomans and Persians sought the Company's help in strengthening their naval power in the Gulf. The Company shifted its activity between them. Early in the 1720's the English East India Company decided that Basra, an Ottoman territory, might prove more beneficial for its commercial interests. Gombroon was abandoned because of Persian anarchy resulting from the Afghāns' invasion. The transfer of commercial activities from Persian to Ottoman territory was taken as a sign of enmity by the Persian Government, although the repeated transfer of the Company's chief Residency seems to have been dictated by commercial necessity. The Company wanted to show each government that the Factory could do its job in either place, and it also wished to avoid oppression by local governors.

In both situations the intended results were not always achieved. The *Mutusallims* of Basra were no less oppressive than the shaikhs of Abū-Shahr and Gombroon. To please both powers at the same time was almost impossible. However, the Residents did their best and managed to keep the Company's trade flourishing in the Arabian Gulf[18], although wars and the disturbed internal state of affairs worked against the Company's interests. Mr. Martin French of the Basra Factory wrote to the Court of Directors in London in 1732, telling them that:

14. See Chapter IX below.

15. See A. Wilson, *The Persian Gulf*, p. 169.

16. See *Ibid.*, p. 170.

17. Mr. Samuel Manesty's dispute with the *Mutasallim* of Basra and the Pasha of Baghdad in 1792 led to the removal of the Factory from Basra in 1793, and its establishment at Kuwait till 1795. Kuwait was not as satisfactory a centre as Basra for the company's trade.

18. Early in 1726, difficulties arose with the Pasha of Baghdād who hindered the progress of the Factory. In a letter from Basra, Mr. Houssaye, Basra, Chief for the Company's affairs in the Gulf of Persia, wrote to the Court of Directors in London saying that the Pasha wanted to levy customs on goods before their sale. *F.R.P.P.G.*, Vol. 14, Basra 10th April 1726, and Vol. 15, No. 2384 from Gombroon speak of the same difficulty. The letter is dated Gombroon 25th March 1727.

19. Mr. Martin French to the C. of D., Basra 19. iii. 1732/3, *F.R.P.P.G.*, Vol. 15. Another letter dated the 25th June 1732 from Basra, signed by Mr. French, is written to the same effect.

20. The consulage was collected at a rate of 2%. The consulage of the year 1725 at Basra amounted to 17,195 shāhees. *F.R.P.P.G.*, Vol. 14, dispatch no. 559. Accounts of the Factories in the Persian Gulf were given in Indian rupees or Persian Mamoodies (mahmūdīs) or Persian shāhees. Though the value of the Ottoman and Persian currency was inconsistent, some valuation can be drawn from accounts given in the Factories' records. Every Indian rupee was nearly equal to five mahmūdīs. (*F.R.P.P.G.*, Vol. 15, no. 649, dated Basra 22nd February 1736). In one pound sterling there were 80 shāhees (*F.R.P.P.G.*, Vol. 15, dispatch 2578).

The War with Persia has put so effectual a Stop to Business here that a Bale of Goods has not been sold in many Months. We do not think it advisable to unlade the Ships now here till we see how Things are likely to go.[19]

The European Companies received favourable terms from the Ottoman capitulations on the one hand, and favourable *roqoms* from the Persian Shāhs on the other. In Basra and Gombroon, the English East India Company collected the consulage from English ships.[20] The large profits realized in peace-time were often offset by the inability of the Factories to collect consulage during wars or local intervention.

In addition to threats from local governors, the Companies had to beware of sea depredations or what the reports call piracy. Factories were fortified and garrisoned by sepoys and trading ships carried guns. Because of an almost constant demand from Factories for emergency war vessels for security purposes, the Companies kept trade active in the Gulf, bringing wealth to many towns in the area.

Kuwait and Bahrain are barely mentioned in the reports of the English East India Company in the first half of the eighteenth century. During the second half of the same century, however, frequent mention of them was made, especially after Shaikh 'Abd Allāh Al-Sabāh made Kuwait one of the most thriving cities on the shores of the Gulf. This will be discussed in the chapter that follows.

CHAPTER III

POLITICAL AND ECONOMIC GROWTH OF KUWAIT IN THE SECOND HALF OF THE EIGHTEENTH CENTURY

A striking feature of the second half of the eighteenth century in Eastern Arabia was the rise of new states and the disappearance of others. During this period, the Āl-Bū-Sa'īd established their rule in Masqat and 'Umān, the 'Utūb built their states in Kuwait, Qatar and Bahrain and the Wahhābīs rose in Najd in Central Arabia. The Banī Khālid were still in control in al-Hasā but their power was being challenged by the Wahhābīs. First among those states which had more to do with the developing shaikhdom of Kuwait was the 'Utbī State of the Āl-Khalīfa in Qatar and Bahrain. Glimpses will be given of the history of each of those powers in relation to the developments in the rapidly growing 'Utbī State in Kuwait. Not to be ignored is the importance of growing British trade relations with Kuwait on one hand and, on the other, the political and military backing that was given to Kuwait by the Basra Factory of the English East India Company, especially in times of crises during the 1790's. The historian of Kuwait during this era will note that the 1750's were crucial years for the rise of Kuwait, and the years after the departure of the Āl-Khalīfa from Kuwait in 1766 and until 1775 witnessed rapid development in the political and economic life of that rising 'Utbī town.

Affairs of Kuwait (1750-1775)

Kuwait flourished in the years following 1750. By the 1760's it drew the attention of rival Arab powers in the Gulf region. The position of other powers, the Persians, the Ottomans and the English East India Company, did not hinder that growth. The Persians, as stated, had neither the sea power nor internal peace to control even their own coast of the Gulf. The Ottoman Pasha in Baghdād and the *Mutasallim* of Basra were in the same position. Neither was ready to challenge the Banī Khālid on the eastern shores of the Gulf.

Thus far the East India Company had met with no interference from the 'Utūb who, until then, did not engage in piracy. The only force that could directly affect the 'Utūb was the Wahhābī power, which was not yet consolidated. The 'Utūb had no direct contact with the maritime Arab powers in the Gulf until 1766, when some of the tribe settled south at Zubāra in Qatar. The most powerful Arabs on the Persian littoral were

1. Wilson, *The Persian Gulf*,
                        pp. 184.

2. Ibn Ghannām, *op. cit., II*,
                        p. 64.

3. Jalāhima are known today
as Āl-Nisf and are represented
both in Kuwait and Bahrain by
                rich merchants.

4. *Bombay Selections*,
Vol. XXIV, pp. 362-363.

the Banū Ka'b (whose stronghold was at Dawraq), the Arabs of Bandar Rīq, and those of Abū Shāhr.

The Arabs on the northern and eastern shores of the Gulf showed no interest in Kuwait until the 1760's when the growing trend towards piracy among the Ka'b hindered the increasing 'Utbī sea trade. The Banū Ka'b also threatened the East India Company's trade destined for its Factory at Basra. Karīm Khān Zand, Vakīl of Persia, tried unsuccessfully to subdue their Shaikh Sulaymān in 1759, and an Anglo-Ottoman expedition against the capital, Dawraq, in 1765, proved fruitless.[1]

In the west, the Wahhābīs worked hard to consolidate their power in Central Arabia and began to expand eastward at the expense of the Bani Khālid. The Wahhābī chroniclers, Ibn Ghannām and Ibn Bishr, clearly point this out in relating the events of 1757 and 1758.[2] *Lam' al-Shihāb* states that because the Wahhābīs demanded peace, the Banī Khālid did not molest them for seven years. In 1764, however, the Banī Khālid broke the pact by attacking the Wahhābīs who were fighting two strong enemies, Dahhām b. Dawwās, the chief of al-Riyād, and the 'Ajmān tribes of the Yaman. 'Abdul Azīz, the Wahhābī *Amir*, raided al-Hasā in 1762, and two years later, the Shaikh of the Banī Khālid made two attempts to occupy al-Dir'iyya, the Wahhābī capital.

The turmoil in Arabia, Persia and Ottoman 'Irāq made it possible for a large division of the 'Utūb to leave Kuwait and establish a new settlement at Zubāra in Qatar. 'Utbī historians from Kuwait give the disputes with the Banī Ka'b as a major reason behind the emigration of Āl-Khalīfa. These eventually led to the defeat of the Āl-Sabāh and the other settlers of Kuwait. The Āl-Khalīfa either refused to come to terms with the Ka'b or would not abide by the policy of the Āl-Sabāh, the ruling family, and migrated to Zubāra.

Mr. Francis Warden, of the Bombay Government, states in another explanation that Kuwait attained a high degree of prosperity in the first fifty years (1716-1766). The "accumulation of wealth rendered the mercantile branch (Āl-Khalīfa) desirous of seceding from the original league, that they might singly enjoy to add to their acquired riches". He adds that the Āl-Khalīfa, then under the leadership of Khalīfa b. Muhammad, "were obliged to have recourse to dissimulation to effect their purpose". Khalīfa told the Āl-Sabāh and the Āl-Jalāhima[3] that great wealth could be theirs if they went to the shores of the Persian Gulf where pearl-beds were located and engaged in the lucrative pearl fishery themselves. The Āl-Sabāh agreed to this plan. Thus, Khalīfa and a large part of his family left for the south.[4]

On their way south, before landing at Zubāra, the emigrants stopped at Bahrain where they hoped to settle. However, the rulers of Bahrain, the Banī Madhkūr Arabs, would not permit them to stay. Bahrain was then under the suzerainty of the Shaikh of Abū Shahr, who recognized the authority of the Shāh of Persia and paid irregular tribute on behalf of Abū Shahr and Bahrain.

5.   See above.

The departure for Zubāra was not a sudden decision. The town was well-known to the 'Utūb from their former experience at Qatar before settling at Kuwait. Although information on Zubāra is scarce, much is known about its environs. A strong Arab tribe, Āl-Musallam, controlled the Qatar peninsula and had been there when the 'Utūb left Qatar for Kuwait in the early years of the eighteenth century. They paid tribute to the Banī Khālid, who, as already mentioned, ruled al-Hasā and the east coast of Arabia, from Qatar in the south to the vicinity of Basra in the north.

Relations Between Kuwait and Other Powers in the Gulf Region (1766-1770)

It might be useful for the student of the history of Kuwait during this period to see how other powers in the Gulf fared at this juncture.

In Central (Najd) and Eastern Arabia (al-Hasā), both the Wahhābīs and the Banī Khālid were watching each other very carefully. In 1764, despite a previous peace treaty with the Wahhābīs, the Banī Khālid's shaikh took the opportunity of Dahhām ibn Dawwās' (Chief of Riyād) attack on the Wahhābī capital to invade the latter town himself, in hopes of eliminating Wahhābī influence upon Eastern Arabia. Neither the Shaikh of the Banī Khālid nor the Chief of al-Dir'iyya, Ibn Su'ūd, was able to win a decisive battle against the other. This balance of power between the Wahhābīs and the Banī Khālid, during the early period of the second half of the eighteenth century, made it possible for the rising 'Utbī towns to grow more rapidly in wealth and in military power. The 'Utūb continued to build their power in the northern and middle regions of the Gulf without fear of Wahhābī attacks or raids until the closing years of the century when the Wahhābīs managed to crush the Banī Khālid power in Eastern Arabia.

The Affairs of Persia (1750-1775)

Reference has already been made to Nādir Shāh's policy towards the Persian coast of the Gulf and how his desire to play a maritime role in the Gulf waters was not fulfilled.[5] The ten years which followed his death in 1747, until the rise to power of Karīm Khān Zand in 1757, was a period of anarchy.

Karīm Khān, whose rule lasted until 1779, brought relative peace to Persia and developed friendly relations with the Arabs to the south on the Persian coast of the Gulf. Able to gain their confidence throughout his rule, he had them help in certain wars carried out against his enemies in 'Irāq. Before studying this aspect of Karīm Khān's relations with Ottoman 'Irāq, one should try to see how the major Arab tribes of southern Persia fared during his rule.

The Arab Tribes of Southern Persia

Among the numerous Arabs inhabiting the Persian coast of the Gulf, three tribes of the northern section played major roles during the reign of Karīm Khān. These were: Al-Matārīsh who lived at Abū Shahr, the Bandar Rīq Arabs and the Banū Ka'b whose capital was Dawraq. The Huwala Arabs who lived in the southern sector and on the islands of that area, in Qishm, Qais, Hurmuz and others, did not play any significant political role during the reign of Karīm Khān as did the Qawāsim of Rās al-Khayma. However, since the Qawāsim did not have much to do with the history of Kuwait and other 'Utbī settlements, we shall not deal with them here.

The Abū Shahr Arabs

Abū Shahr Arabs invaded and captured Bahrain Islands in 1753, and remained in power for thirty years. When the 'Utūb came to Zubāra in Qatar in 1766, Bahrain was under the rule of the Matārīsh Arabs of Abū Shahr. Earlier in 1759, the French attacked and destroyed the English settlement at Gombroon (Bandar 'Abbās) after which the English East India Company moved its Factory to Abū Shahr. The Danish traveller Niebuhr, on his way home from Bombay, India in 1765, visited Abū-Shahr, describing it as the port of Shīrāz, capital of Karīm Khān Zand, Governor of Persia.

He adds that the Arabs of Abū Shahr were Huwala and had come from 'Umān. Among those Arabs were three prominent families who had formed an alliance and controlled affairs of the town before 1765. Two of these had come earlier than the Matārīsh, the third family. The Chief of the Abū Shahr was Shaikh Nasr Āl-Madhkūr, whose authority extended over Bahrain Islands in the south and the neighbouring Karmasīr on the mainland. The latter territory he governed as a representative of Karīm Khān. However, Karīm Khān did not trust Shaikh Nasr and insisted on keeping the latter's sons as hostages to guarantee the fidelity of their father.

Shaikh Nasr maintained his authority over Bahrain with the help of a strong naval fleet and a strong military garrison in the island fortresses. But this vigilance could not stop the Āl-Khalīfa and their 'Utbī allies from conquering those islands in 1782/1783.

Bandar Rīq

To the north of Abū Shahr was the shaikhdom of Bandar Rīq, whose Shaikh, like Shaikh Nasr, was from 'Umān. His territory extended to the borders of Karmasīr. While Shaikh Nasr belonged to the Matārīsh of 'Umān, Mīr Nāsir, ruler of Bandar Rīq, was of the Banī Sa'b, another 'Umānī tribe. The Governor of Bandar Rīq was killed in 1758 and his son Mīr Muhannā took over.

Both men played a major role in the affairs of the Gulf from 1753 to 1769. In 1753 Mīr Nāsir gave permission to the Dutch to establish their Factory at Khārij Island in his territory, and in 1769 Mīr Muhannā sought refuge in Kuwait as we shall see later in this chapter. Soon after Mīr Nāsir had allowed the Dutch to settle at Khārij, he found himself at odds with Baron Kniphausen, the head of the Dutch settlement. This animosity continued until his death. While Mīr Nasīr's relations with the Persians were unfriendly, he did get along very well with the Ottoman Pasha of Baghdād and the *Mutasallim* of Basra. Relations between Mīr Muhannā and the English East India Company will be discussed later on.

Banū Ka'b

As far as the history of Kuwait's relations with these Persian coast Arab tribes is concerned, the third influential power, the Banū Ka'b, are of significance to this narrative, since they had more to do with Kuwait than either the Matārīish or the Banī Sa'b. Unlike those tribes who were of 'Umānī origin, the Banū Ka'b were of Najdī extraction. According to Niebuhr, the Banū Ka'b migrated from Najd during the seventeenth century and settled at the northernmost corner of the Arabian Gulf in an area which was under the rule of the Afshār Turks. By the middle of the eighteenth century, under the leadership of Shaikh Sulaymān who ruled until his death in 1766, the Ka'b became very well-known to the Europeans due to hostile relations with the British. The Banū Ka'b were able to capture some of their vessels and keep the British out of their domains. Sulaymān's tribe also succeeded in acquiring a large segment of the Afshār Turks' lands including Dawraq and Fallāhiyya. Since the territory of the Banī Ka'b was situated between Ottoman 'Irāq and Persia, Shaikh Sulaymān and his successors shifted their loyalty between the rulers of these two countries. By keeping this balance they maintained their independence of both Ottomans and Persians. Their relations with the 'Utūb of Kuwait and Zubāra and the other powers in the Gulf area will be discussed later.

'Utbī Relations With the Other Powers in the Gulf Until 1775

The 'Utūb of Kuwait and Zubāra were forced to establish relations with each of the above-mentioned powers. On the mainland of Arabia there was no change in the balance of power between the Wahhābīs and the Banī Khālid, in spite of the fact that the Wahhābīs finally consolidated their power in Najd after the conquest in 1773 of al-Riyād, the capital of Dahhām ibn Dawwās.[6] The Wahhābīs then turned their hopes towards Eastern Arabia. The Banū Khālid, still united, were able to maintain the power to face any Wahhābī attack on their land. After the death of their Chief 'Uray'ir in 1774, war broke out between his two sons, Butayn and Sa'dūn, ending in the murder of the former in 1777. The Banū Khālid until then had carried the war into Najd, thus enabling

6. Ibn Ghannām, *op. cit.*, Vol. II, pp. 94-100. Ibn Ghannām was so greatly moved by the event that he commemorated it by a long poem. See also Ibn Bishr, *op. cit.*, Vol. I, pp. 60-61.

7. An address from Benjamin Jervis (Bushire Factory) to Charles Crommelin, President at Bombay, dated Bushire, January 5, 1765, *Factory Records*, Vol. 16.

8. Parsons, *Travels in Asia, etc.*, pp. 193-198. To carry the story of Mīr Muhannā to its end, Parsons added that, "After Mīr Muhannā had been some time at Bussoura, the Musolem acquainted the Pasha of Baghdad, that he solicited the Pasha's protection, and that he might be permitted to come to Baghdad to kiss his hands. The Pasha having been acquainted with his unnatural cruelties, thought him unworthy of life, and sent orders to the musolem of Bussoura to put him to death on the receipt of his letter...". Mīr Muhannā was killed, but his companions were allowed to live unmolested.

9. As the Persians had no fleet of their own, they depended, during the rule of Karīm Khān, on the fleets of the Banī Ka'b and Abū Shahr. See Malcolm, Vol. II, pp. 141.

10. Letter from Moore and Latouche of the Basra Factory to the Court of Directors, London, dated Basra, 13th May, 1774, *Factory Records*, Vol. 17.

Kuwait and Zubāra to continue their flourishing trade without fear of Wahhābī intervention.

The great threat to the two 'Utbī towns came from the sea. Mīr Muhannā of Bandar Rīq, who had already taken Khārij Island from the Dutch in 1765, continued his piracy, capturing any ship he could lay his hands on.[7] Bahrain, under the Arabs of Abū Shahr, was the closest area under Persian supremacy to come into contact with the 'Utūb. Because Bahrain was famous for its pearl trade, the people of these Islands felt the commercial rivalry of both Kuwait and Zubāra. The Banū Ka'b, it will be seen, represented the major menace.

Since the Dutch occupation in 1753, Kuwait had established harmonious relations with Khārij Island which continued under the rule of Mīr Muhannā. This might explain why Mīr Muhannā, after being hard pressed by Karīm Khān:

> with a few of his favourites, and men sufficient to man a swift-sailing boat, embarked in a dark night (not forgetting to carry treasure sufficient) and next evening arrived at Grane [Kuwait] in Arabia, ... From thence he and his adherents went to Bussora [Basra] where he thought himself sure of finding an asylum, having strictly conformed with the treaty made with the Pasha of Baghdād, in not molesting any ship or vessel going to or from Bussora. The musolem [*Mutasallim*] received him kindly and entertained him as the friend of his master the pasha.[8]

It might be assumed from the story of Mīr Muhannā at Kuwait and Basra, that relations between the Shaikh of Kuwait and the *Mutasallim* were friendly. What might have dictated that friendliness with Basra was the growing power of the Banī Ka'b on one hand and the Arabs of Abū Shahr on the other.

It has been pointed out how the Banū Ka'b caused the *Mutasallim of Basra and the English East India Company great trouble, and how Karīm Khān, the Vakīl* of Persia, intervened to prevent the subjugation of the Banī Ka'b. Shaikh Nasr of Abū Shahr was likewise under the protection of Karīm Khān, who made him admiral of the Persian fleet in the Gulf.[9] To lessen the impending danger of the Banī Ka'b and Shaikh Nasr, the 'Utūb, both at Kuwait and Zubāra, sought the friendship of the English East India Company and the Ottomans in Basra. The 'Utūb, who had not yet attained sufficient naval power to challenge the Arabs of the Persian coast, remained on good terms with the Banī Khālid. This friendship did not, however, prevent the Banī Ka'b in 1774 from taking and plundering al-Qatīf, the rich port of the Banī Khālid, which was "most remarkable for its pearl commerce". "The Chaub (Ka'b) *gallivats* returned to Doorack (Dawraq) with the plunder of Catiffe which is said to be very considerable."[10] Though the Banū Ka'b alone made the attack on al-Qatīf, it is worth noting that since 1770 they had worked in harmony with Shaikh Nasr of Abū Shahr. Both were used by Karīm Khān Zand as instruments to carry out his policy against the Ottomans and others in the Gulf, best exemplified in the siege of Basra in 1775.

Plague at Basra (1773)

The attack on al-Qaṭīf was carried out soon after the death of 'Uray'ir, the Chief of the Banī Khālid. At that time the town was recovering from a serious epidemic. Coming from Baghdād, where all trade and activity had come to a standstill,[11] the plague struck Basra and by April and May of 1773 had devastated the city. Members of the English Factory there had left the town before the plague reached it and went to Bombay, leaving the Surgeon Reilly in charge. At the height of the plague, many inhabitants left, carrying the epidemic to Kuwait, al-Qaṭīf, Bahrain and other towns on the Arabian coast of the Gulf. Though the loss of life was less on the Arabian coast than in Basra, the number of deaths was estimated at two million.[12] Because they took the necessary precautions to cease communications with the affected areas, the Banū Ka'b territories and the Persian littoral of the Gulf did not suffer much loss. Basra's casualties, and those of the surrounding villages, were estimated at 200,000 deaths. Mr. Moore and his colleagues of the English Factory, after returning, reported:

> Neither will this account appear to be exaggerated when it is considered that for near a month the daily deaths in the town [i.e. Basra] alone amounted from 3,000-7,000 - at length about the 25th May when least expected the disorder suddenly ceased, leaving Bussora in particular almost destitute of inhabitants.

The plague greatly decreased Basra's trade, thus giving the rival ports on the coast of the Gulf a chance to compete. Abū Shahr, on the Persian coast, was waiting for just such an opportunity. It had been the greatest emporium of trade until the English East India Company gave preference to Basra. Kuwait and Zubāra, though on good terms with Basra, attracted much of the latter's trade. Nonetheless, Basra's relations with the English Factory there continued to improve and their sea-going vessels were hired to carry dispatches to Masqat enroute to Bombay.

The shift of the English Gulf trade from Abū Shahr to Basra after 1763, making Basra the richest port in the Gulf, did not occur without Persian resistance. Karīm Khān accelerated his plans to capture Basra from the Ottomans. The Ottoman *Mutasallim* of Basra, aware of this, lost no time in strengthening his naval power in order to ward off an attack on the walled town. Thus, early in 1774 "the two Ketches of 14 guns each, which the Bashaw [Pasha] requested may be built for him at Bombay some time ago, arrived with the Revenge." They were delivered to Ottoman authorities after their cost had been paid into the Company's treasury at Bombay.

Karīm Khān, on the other hand, received naval support from the Ka'b and Abū Shahr fleets. His preparations ended in 1775 with the famous siege of Basra, in which Kuwait found itself inevitably involved. As usual, when war broke out between Persia and Ottoman 'Irāq, or other Gulf powers, it was difficult to keep out of the fray.

11. Letter from Moore, Latouche and Abraham of the Basra Factory to the Court of Directors, London, 1st April, 1773, *Factory Records*, Vol. 17.

12. Letter from Moore and his colleagues to the Court of Directors, London, dated Basra, 16th January, 1774, *Factory Records*, Vol. 17.

13. Parsons was an eyewitness
to these events and participated
in the defence of Basra against
the attacking Persians.

The establishment of the 'Utūb at Zubāra and growth of trade at Kuwait and Zubāra created jealousy among the maritime Arabs of the Gulf. Especially aroused were those on the Persian littoral, chiefly the Arabs of Bandar Rīq, Banī Ka'b and the Abū Shahr. The latter were the nearest to the 'Utūb of Zubāra since Bahrain was under its suzerainty. With the long siege of Basra and the ensuing struggle between Ottomans and Persians, the 'Utbī towns served as safe centres for trade and had another chance to accumulate more wealth and prominence. Their free trade policy drew merchants and capital. Abū Shahr grew uneasy and the tension subsequently led to a war which resulted in both Kuwait's and Zubāra's occupation of the Bahrain Islands in 1782. This naval struggle with the Arabs of the Persian coast as well as the growth of Kuwait in the last quarter of the eighteenth century will comprise the remainder of this chapter.

The Growth of Kuwait and the Rise of its Maritime Power (1775-1800)

It has been stated before that the history of the Arabian Gulf is so interrelated that any major event in one part of the region will have repercussions in almost every other part. Naturally, any rising power like the 'Utbī shaikhdom of Kuwait was going to be affected by the Persian siege of Basra, financially, militarily and politically. It seems logical, therefore, to discuss this event and the ultimate conquest of Basra by the forces of Karīm Khān.

The Seige of Basra by the Persians (16th March 1775)

To fully understand the effects of the siege and occupation of Basra on the 'Utūb in particular and Eastern Arabia in general, a brief summary of that event, which involves Ottoman, Persian and Arab forces, follows. It will be noted that the British, abandoning their policy of non-interference, fought on the Ottoman side.

No sooner had Basra recovered from the devastating plague, than rumours of a proposed Persian attack began to spread. Here we may point out again that the prosperity of Basra in the 1760's due to the shift of British trade activities from their Factory in Abū Shahr, was among the causes of "strained relations between Pasha and Regent [Karīm Khān]". In 1775 the danger became more acute; conferences were held daily between Sulaymān Aghā, the *Mutasallim*, the *Qaptān*, (naval Turkish chief), the notables of Basra and the British Agent.

"On January 15th, 1775", says Parsons,[13] "advice arrived from Bushear, in Persia, that an army had left Shiras (now the capital of Persia) consisting of upwards of fifth thousand men commanded by Sadoo Caun [Sādiq Khān] (brother to Karīm Khān, the present ruler of Persia); and that he was on his march for Bussora, being resolved to take the city." This report caused great alarm among the inhabitants.

Karīm Khān was jealous of the increased importance of Basra, and

14. See Parsons, p. 181.

was faced with discontent in his army; he decided to dispatch his expedition against the port. "Seeking pretext, he demanded the head of the *Wālī* of Baghdād as a punishment for daring to levy a tax on Persian pilgrims to Kerbela."

The Arabs inhabiting the Persian littoral of the Gulf were allied with the Persians. The Arabs of Abū Shahr, under the rule of Shaikh Nasr, supplied the attacking Persian army with ammunition and provisions, without which the Persian army was expected "soon to decamp". The Shaikh of Bandar Rīq, apparently on good terms with Karīm Khān, also assisted in the siege. The Banū Ka'b, whose boats were invaluable to both sides, and the other Arabs of the Persian littoral, put the greater part of their commercial and naval fleets at the service of the Persians. As previously stated, Sādiq Khān, with the Persian army, marched through the land of the Banī Ka'b and camped in their territory at Suwaib. It appears, therefore, that they had previously agreed to join Karīm Khān.

The Ottoman Allies

With the Ottomans, or rather on the side of Sulaymān Pasha, the *Mutasallim* of Basra, were the Arabs of the Muntafiq tribe under their Shaikhs Thāmir and 'Abd Allāh. It was hoped that they would play a major part in the defence of the besieged town, and withstand the Persian advance. During the siege, the cooperation of the parties of the Banī Khālid and the Muntafiq outside, enabled caravans to reach the city. Masqat went to the rescue of the besieged city in August 1775 at the request of the *Mutasallim*. The fleet was reported to have forced its way up the Shatt al-'Arab to Basra on October 14th, 1775, and to have been a great help. Sulaymān Aghā also succeeded in persuading the British Agent of the Basra Factory to join him in repelling the Persian aggression.

> At this time a squadron of ships of the Bombay Marine was lying in the river Shatt-ul-'Arab, near the creek of the city, consisting of the "Revenge", a frigate of twenty-eight guns, "Eagle", of sixteen guns and "Success" Ketch, of fourteen guns each; beside two other Ketches of fourteen guns each, built at Bombay for the Pasha of Baghdād.

The Pasha's ketches were "Commanded by an English midshipman in the Company's service," and had "on board, a few English sailors"; the remainder of the crew were Turks, carrying British colours. In fact, the British "gentlemen of the Factory and the English East India Company's cruisers joined the *Mutasallim's* forces wholeheartedly till their retreat from the field of battle."[14]

Kuwait Stance

Two other forces in the Gulf were expected to join either the Persians or the Ottomans, namely the Qawāsim of Rās al-Khayma and the 'Utūb of Kuwait and Zubāra. The former were not mentioned in connection with the Basra affair of 1775, though they were reported to have "become more powerful than ever, both by land and sea".

The role of the 'Utūb of Kuwait is not easy to assess or even to identify. The British traveller Parsons - an eyewitness to the siege - refers to Kuwait only twice; the first time when "the Pasha's two galliotes" were ordered to repair to its harbour in the afternoon of April 13th, 1775, and the second when the "Eagle" and one of the Pasha's Ketches, which were on their way from Basra to Abū Shahr on April 14th, "noticed two trankeys coming from Abū Shahr and going" to Kuwait. Parsons describes Kuwait as a town "dependent on Bussora". What he meant by "dependent" is not clear, yet one may gather than there must have been friendly relations between the *Mutasallim* and the Shaikh, for:

> "all the Turks and Arabs which were on board the Pasha's ketches (in number about two hundred and thirty) embarked on board these two galliotes, and their departure for Kuwait."

In a letter to the Court of Directors in London, about three months later, the Basra factors stated that:

> "the two Turkish Galivats which were sent to Grain, were demanded from the Shaikh of that Place by the Chaub [Banū Ka'b], and delivered up to him."

The same letter added that the Shaikh sent, "though unwillingly", a party of two hundred men "to the assistance of Sadoo Caun [Sādiq Khān]".

Though the position of the 'Utūb of Kuwait was vague in the Basra affair, it would not be difficult to explain their friendly attitude towards the forces of the *Mutasallim* at first, and their sending two hundred men to help Sādiq Khān three months later. Apparently, Kuwait, not sure of the victor, wanted to play both sides. Because of earlier prejudices against the Banī Ka'b and new hostilities with the Arabs of Abū Shahr, the 'Utūb of Kuwait and Zubāra were soon in conflict with these allies of the Persians.

The Effects of the Siege and Occupation of Basra on the 'Utūb (1775-1779)

The circumstances of the siege and occupation of Basra by the Persians had a far-reaching influence on Kuwait and Zubāra. In the first place, direct relations were established between Kuwait and the English East India Company's representatives in the Gulf. Kuwait became important as a centre for nearly all caravans carrying goods between Basra and Aleppo from 1775 to 1779. Because of the enmity existing between the British and the Persians, goods coming from India which could have been sent to Abū Shahr for conveyance to Aleppo via Basra, were instead unloaded at Zubāra and Kuwait. This led to the accumulation of wealth at the two 'Utbī towns, and jealousy of other Arab sea powers, especially the Banī Ka'b and the Arabs of Abū Shahr. However, they were unable to prevent the establishment of British-'Utbī relations.

"The recorded history of British relations with Kuwait," says Lorimer,[15] 'opens in 1775, when on the investment of Basrah by the Persians, the British desert mail from the Gulf to Aleppo began to be dispatched from Kuwait instead of Zubair [a town west of Basra]." The latter town was not occupied by the Persians until 1778.

The Desert Route

To the English East India Company, this desert route was of special importance, not only for forwarding mail to and from India, but for trading purposes. For the former reason, Kuwait was important to the English Factory at Basra. The Basra Factory had been sending the "desert express" from Zubair by hired messengers. About four months after the Persian attack on Basra, dispatches were received via desert mail from Kuwait. Soon after Kuwait was selected as a mailing centre and messengers were obtained there. From the start the mail service does not seem to have been efficient since the Factory had no representatives at Kuwait. To receive mail in Kuwait on time, and to arrange for the prompt departure of other mail, it was suggested that a civil officer of the Company should be stationed at that port. As there was none available at Basra in July 1776, Mr. Latouche asked Lieutenant Twiss, the captain of the "Terrible", to take charge, and arrangements were made at Kuwait. The desert mail continued to be received and sent through Kuwait during the Persian occupation of Basra.

Kuwait seems to have offered a solution to the difficulties of the English East India Company in exporting goods to the markets of the Middle East. In a letter to Mr. Latouche at Basra from the Consul at Aleppo dated June 11th, 1776, much is revealed about the situation at Kuwait and of British trade. Mr. Latouche, quoting that letter to the Court of Directors, wrote on July 14th, 1776:

> The Consul at Aleppo, in a letter to us dated the 11th inserted the following paragraph: 'India and Surat Goods continue in Demand at the Metropolis. I hear two merchant Ships arrived at Bushire from those Parts - If the Town of Grain is suffered to remain neuter, Caravans may be made no doubt to and from thence to this Place, for as long War will probably be caused by the Loss of Bussora, that City will be deserted unless Merchants can find some Method of carrying on Trade near it. Grain seems to be well situated to serve as a Substitute to Zebere [Zubair], but that can only be whilst it remains independent for should the Persians take Possession of it, it will be dangerous for Merchants to bring Goods from thence, that will probably be prohibited by the Porte even to Europeans, therefore it is in the Interest of the Merchants Your way to represent the Necessity of Grain is remaining under Benechalid [Banī Khālid] Governors independent of the Persians'.

15. Lorimer, *op. cit.*, Vol. I, i, pp. 1002.

16. Latouche, Basra, to Court of Directors, 24.vi.1776, *F.R.P.P.G.*, Vol. 17, No. 1127. Mr. Latouche's letter should not imply that before 1775 there were no caravans travelling from Kuwait to Aleppo. In 1758, Ives contemplated travelling by such a caravan.

17. Latouche and Abraham, Basra, 10.viii.1778, to C. of D., *F.R.P.P.G.*, Vol. 17, No. 1144.

Mr. Latouche adds to the Consul's letter:

We are very sensible that the thus opening a Communication with Aleppo and even Bagdat by the Way of Grain, if practicable, would be a most desirable Circumstance, especially as it might afford an Opportunity of disposing of the very considerable Quantities of Bengal and Surat goods now lying at Bombay from the Bussora merchants. We do not think however that the Merchants would attempt to send any goods across the desert, before Affairs at somewhat relieved from the Confusion which they are in at present. [16]

It was not long before the Consul's expectations came true. Kuwait remained unmolested by the Persians. Caravans transporting goods from there to Baghdād and Aleppo were unsafe in the desert and were often attacked by Arab tribes on orders from the Persians in Basra. Such a case was Shaikh Thāmir of the Muntafiq tribe, who recognized Persian suzerainty and was encouraged by them to attack caravans from Kuwait to Baghdād in April 1777. However, the Banū Khālid Arabs attacked the Muntafiq allowing the caravans to proceed. To avoid such skirmishes, caravans sometimes changed their route across the desert from Baghdād. "A large Sum of Goods which had been collecting some Time from Bushire and Muscat" was conveyed to Baghdād by a large caravan from Kuwait.

In the latter part of 1777, British trade in 'Irāq and Persia was suffering to a great extent, from the burdens imposed by the governments of Abū Shahr and Basra on the British Factories. "At Bushire," says a letter from Latouche and Abraham,

we are almost as much exposed to Oppression as we are at Bussora. The Shaiks there interfere too much in the Trade of the Place; and the few Merchants with any Property who are there, are too much in a Combination to admit of our drawing any great Commercial Advantages from it wretched indeed as is the Situation of Bussora at Present it is much superior in Point of Trade than Bushire.

The Factors at Basra now gave serious thought to the choice of their Factory. Kuwait might have been considered had it not been for fear of the repitition at Abū Shahr and Basra. Also, they feared being:

too much exposed to the Persians, who there is Reason to imagine, would regard our settling there with a jealous eye and would throw all the Impediments of their power in our way.[17]

The only other safe alternative was Khārij Island, where they hoped they might be free from "these Inconveniences".

Soon afterwards, on November 11th, 1777, Kuwait was visited by the English Company's ship, the "Eagle", to report on the site. The harbour was found suitable for anchorage, and the town

has a slight Wall calculated for Musquetry. However, it serves for the caravans for Aleppo and Bagdat to assemble with some security and free from Persian extortions.

The Factors went on to say:

In Future too it [Kuwait] might serve for Shipping bound to Bussora to take in Pilots for the River in case the port of Bushire should at any Time be shut to them or the Shaiks there continue their present Impositions with Respect to the Pilots for Your Honours Cruizers, or/as we informed the honourable the President and Council in our Letter to them dated 24th December by the "Eagle"/ should they at any Time hence occasion to send us a Packet for Your Honours, the forwarding of which required particular Dispatch, by ordering the Vessel directly to Grain, and the Captain to dispatch the original overland from thence, particularly should the wind be unfavourable for him, we might receive it many Days sooner than we otherwise should do.[18]

Messengers covered the distance between Kuwait and Basra in three days, while vessels on the river during the northwest winds, sometimes took twenty days or more. For this reason, Kuwait was of vast importance to the desert mail and helped considerably in conveying Indian goods to the markets of the Middle East and Europe. The British, however, did not establish a factory there until about fifteen years later, in 1793, when the Basra Factory moved to Kuwait.

Owing to the misfortunes of Basra and Zubair, and the wise policy of Shaikh 'Abd Allāh Āl-Sabāh in maintaining Kuwait's neutrality, the town continued to flourish and the Shaikh's relations with the English East India Company remained cordial. In fact, he was one of the Arab leaders who was presented with gifts by the Factory. Later, these relations became strained and might have been disrupted had it not been for the wise policy of the men at the Basra Factory.

Captain de Bourge, a French officer, carrying secret letters to the French in Pondicherry and Mauritius, was travelling from Aleppo to the Persian Gulf when a party of Bedouin Arabs threatened him in the desert, about fifteen days journey from Basra. After shooting one tribesman and suffering a severe sword-cut on the head, he managed to save his life by throwing himself on the "protection" of the oldest of the attackers. A sum equal to one hundred pounds sterling was promised them on condition he be transported to Kuwait in safety. On arrival there he borrowed the promised amount from an Armenian,[19] then wrote Monsieur Rousseau, the French Consul at Basra, asking transportation for his journey to Pondicherry. Because the French Consul either refused or hesitated to honour the request of his countryman, it was carried by an Arab messenger to the British Factory at Basra. In this way the staff learned of Captain de Bourge's presence in Kuwait[20] as the guest of Shaikh 'Abd Allāh Āl-Sabāh.

A difficult situation arose when a report reached Basra that war had been declared between France and Britain, and the Factors felt it the duty of British officials abroad to seize wandering French emissaries. Mr. Abraham, "one of the factors from Basra" went from Abū Shahr to Kuwait in twenty hours in the Company's cruiser, the "Eagle"[21] The British Resident, Mr. Latouche, needed to exercise caution here.

18. Latouche and Abraham, Basra, 14.i.1778, C. of D., *F.R.P.P.G.*, Vol. 17, No. 1152.

19. Armenian merchants were strongly established in the ports of the Gulf and Masqat in the eighteenth century.

20. Brydges, in his *Wahauby*, pp. 171-174, gives a detailed account of the event. He is there quoting Captain Capper's version of the story. Captain Capper met M. de Bourge at Masqat when the latter was on his way back to France via Basra. See Capper's Observations, pp. 99-104. The same story is related by Mr. Abraham in detail. See Abraham to the C. of D., Grain, 7.xi.1778, *F.R.P.P.G.*, Vol. 17, No. 1161.

21. See Brydges, p. 175.

22. *See following page.* The dispatches could not be deciphered because Captain de Bourge destroyed the key to the cypher, yet his diaries and other letters disclosed much of the French plans. For a full text of Mr. Abraham's account of the capture of Captain de Bourge and the details of his letters and diary, see Appendix I.

22.   *See previous page.*

23.   Sir Harford Jones Brydges' opinion of Shaikh 'Abd Allāh Āl-Sabāh is of interest. The Shaikh refused to hand his guest, Captain de Bourge, to Mr. Abraham and refused the presents and the bribes the Factory offered him (*The Wahauby*, pp. 175-6). Brydges comments on the Shaikh's behaviour saying: "So that it was the old Shaikh's love of justice and not his avarice, that induced him to act as he did". See *Ibid.*, p. 176.

24.   In the same letter Abraham and Latouche add: "We cannot indeed sufficiently congratulate ourselves on the good Fortune that attended the prudent Measures pursued by Mr. Abraham for the obtaining of the Packets in Question. Had not particular Expedition been used by him, Monsieur de Bourg would have escaped. He had determined to leave Grain the Morning following the Night of Mr. Abraham's Arrival and had not Mr. Abraham taken the Sheik of Grain in a manner of Surprise; had he given him the least Time for Deliberation, in all Probability, so strict are the Notions of the Arabs with Respect to Hospitality that no Consideration whatever would have induced the Sheik to suffer the Seizure." (Latouche and Abraham to C. of D., November (undated) 1778, *F.R.P.P.G.*, Vol. 17).

25.   Capper, *Observations*, pp. 99-104.

26.   Latouche and Abraham to the C. of D., Basra, 31.x.1778, *F.R.P.P.G.*, Vol. 17, No. 1161. A French Marquis de Calern arrived by a caravan from Aleppo at Kuwait at the end of September 1778, and he was planning to go to Zubāra, whence he hoped to make the journey by sea to Masqat. He seems to have been a French officer belonging to Pondicherry. See *Ibid.*.

27.   See Danvers, *op. cit.*, p. 44.

Consequences were likely to be serious if he took action against Captain de Bourge based on false rumours. The chief obstacle in the execution of his orders to Mr. Abraham was the objection of Shaikh 'Abd Allāh Āl-Sabāh to seizing a person enjoying his hospitality. He finally relented, principally, it seems, because of an assertion that Captain de Bourge was a "fraudulent debtor". Captain de Bourge and his messages were sent to the "Eagle"[22] and from Basra he was sent as a captive to Bombay.

Mr. Latouche offered an explanation to the Court of Directors:[23]

> We were well aware of the Risque we ran in attempting to intercept (the French dispatches) but we thought our Duty to our Country in General at such a critical Season extracted it from us. We doubt not but that it will be of the utmost consequence to your Affairs in India, the having thus not only sent our Honourable Superiors such early Intelligence of the War but perhaps at the same Time laid upon to them the Intentions of the French Government with respect to India...[24]

While Colonel James Capper was proceeding to India via the Persian Gulf on January 24th, 1779, he met Captain de Bourge at Masqat en route to Europe. He had been released by the Governor of Bombay and authorized to return to France overland. Capper told the story of de Bourge and the gentlemen of the Basra Factory in his *Observations*.[25]

The war between France and England brought special importance to Kuwait and Zubāra. The French sent a strong fleet to the Persian Gulf to intercept the English East India Company's mail and attack their vessels. It was safer for the Company's mail to travel on Arab vessels. Both Kuwait and Zubāra benefited from the conveyance of men and mail through the Persian Gulf and through the desert route from Masqat to Aleppo.[26]

This transfer of commercial activities from the eastern to the western shore of the Gulf did not please eastern trading centres. As already noted, a reason for the Persian attack on Basra was the transfer of the English East India Company's activity to its Factory in the latter town in preference to Bandar Rīq, Abū Shahr or Bandar 'Abbās. We have seen that the Persians depended on the Arabs of the Persian shore for their naval operations. With the death of Kārim Khān in 1779 and the absence of any other predominant political power in the Gulf, Arab chiefs had greater opportunity to pursue their independent policies. From that time may be dated the decline of Persian influence in the Gulf. About the same time the Gulf gained increased importance "for orders were issued by the Porte prohibiting Christian vessels from trading to Suez."[27] Gulf ports became the chief outlets for goods from India and the East, to Aleppo and Constantinople. There can be little doubt that Kuwait benefited from the restriction as well.

In the second 'Utbī settlement in the south, Zubāra, prosperity reached a height which made her neighbours jealous and eager to attack the town at any moment. Shaikh Nasr of Abū Shahr, who was then ruler of Bahrain, planned an attack on the town. Early disputes between the

'Utūb of Kuwait and the Banū Ka'b seem to have been revived. The Shaikh of Bandar Rīq, allied to both the Banī Ka'b and Shaikh Nasr, was ready to join them in their proposed attack on the 'Utbī towns. By 1779, however, the 'Utūb seem to have had an armed fleet that could resist their aggression. In the year 1780 the 'Utūb, both at Kuwait and Zubāra, were at war with the Banī Ka'b[28] and were expected to later join the Pasha of Baghdad in his war against them. Though the circumstances of that war are not known, one can say that enmity between the 'Utūb and the Banū Ka'b which started early in the 1760's continued to exist. These unfriendly relations with the Banī Ka'b were of less direct consequence to the success of the 'Utūb than the capture by the French of a "Muscat ship in 1781, the cargo of which is valued at 8 lacks of rupees" which was shared by the merchants of Basra, Qatīf and Zubāra.[29] The two French ships attacking other ships in the Gulf tried to intercept the English mail.[30]

The greatest threat to the 'Utūb came not from the French but from the Banī Ka'b and their allies, the Arabs of Abū Shahr and Bandar Rīq. By 1780 the 'Utūb found that they could expect an attack from the Persian coast Arabs of the Gulf and kept their fleet ready for emergency. However, the hostility between the Ottomans and the Banī Ka'b at that time may have helped postpone an attack. This was probably a result of the help offered by the Banī Ka'b to the Persians during the 1775 attack on Basra. Thus the Banū Ka'b were on bad terms with the *Mutasallim* of Basra and the 'Utūb. The latter, on the other hand, were on good terms with the *Mutasallim*, and ready to join him if he wanted war against the Banī Ka'b. Otherwise "they wait, they say, until they see that the Bacha himself is really in earnest". They were ready for battle.[31]

The rise of 'Utbī sea-power seems to have been motivated by various factors. In the first place, the 'Utūb were merchants and whenever their trade grew, they added vessels to their fleet. There can be little doubt that their trade, though its volume is not certain, grew after the siege and occupation of Basra in 1775-1779. This increase in the number of trading vessels must have been accompanied by buying and building armed vessels to protect their fleet. This was necessary after the death of Karīm Khān. Evidently he was held in such awe by the Arab pirates of Rās al-Khayma or Masqat, or suppressed them so that they made no depredations. Soon after his death, the Qawāsim and the 'Umānī tribes were at war. Depredations on Arab vessels using the Gulf became frequent and the Arab maritime states quarrelled among themselves.[32]

> Shaikh Abdoola of Ormus was at variance with Karrack [Khārij]; the Shaikh of al Haram with the Jamia people; and the Uttoobees of Zobara and Grane with the Chaab.[33]

The absence of a major power in the Persian Gulf caused the Arab maritime forces on both littorals to fight each other because of old or new grievances. Among these was the traditional enmity of the 'Utūb and the Banī Ka'b. The latter became allies of the Arabs of Abū Shahr and

28. Lorimer, *Gazetteer*, I, i, p. 1003.

29. See a letter from Latouche to the C. of D., Basra, 12.x.1781, *F.R.P.P.G.*, Vol. 17, No. 1202.

30. See a letter from Latouche to the C. of D., Basra, 20.vii. 1781, *F.R.P.P.G.*, Vol. 17, No. 1195. The attack on the Masqatī and other ships was a clear indication that the French knew that the English mail was carried by vessels other than the English.

31. In a letter from Mr. Latouche to the C. of D. dated Basra, 25.iv.1782, he speaks of "two Turkish ketches at Kuwait" which were expected to be brought to Basra "under the protection of the Grain Gallivats". And since the Pasha was at war with the Banī Ka'b it can be concluded that the 'Utbī sea power of Kuwait was in a position to defy the Ka'b's by thus escorting three ketches to Basra. See the letter in the *F.R.P.P.G.*, Vol. 17, No. 1214. Shaikh 'Abd Allāh Āl-Sabāh by the 1780's was enlisted among the influential chiefs to whom the East India Company offered presents because those chiefs had it in their power to hinder the Company's trade and mail. See a list of Abstract of charges general - Basra Factory from 1st of May, 1780 to the 31st of April, 1782, in *F.R.P.P.G.*, Vol. 17, No. 1216.

32. Of the activity of the Qawāsim after the death of Karīm Khān, says Warden: "The Ras-ool-Khyma fleet, in consequences of the decline of the Persian ascendancy in the Gulf, being constantly on the cruise, roused almost every petty chief to fit out armed boats, manned by lawless crews, under no control, but who depended solely on plunder for their maintenance, which they indiscriminately practised. This state of affairs arose out of the war between Ras-ool-Khyma and Muskat." See *Bombay Selections*, XXIV, p. 301.

33. *Bombay Selections*, XXIV, p. 301.

34. The author was told of this by Shaikh 'Abd Allāh b. Khālid Āl-Khalīfa in July 1959. Al-Nabhānī in his *Al-Tuhfa, Ta'rīkh al-Bahrain*, pp. 123-125, mentions the Āl-Khalīfa and the people of Zubāra as the only attackers of Bahrain; he does not mention the 'Utūb of Kuwait or even the Āl-Jalāhima as participants in the battle.

35. See a letter from Mr. Latouche (Basra Resident) to the C. of D., 4.xi.1782, *F.R.P.P.G.*, Vol. 17, No. 1230. See also Lorimer, op. cit., Vol. I, i, pp. 839, 1003; and "Historical Sketch of the Uttoobee", in *Bombay Selections*, XXIV, p. 264.

36. See Lorimer, *op. cit.*, Vol. I, i, p. 839.

37. See J.A. Saldanha, *Selections from the State Papers*. The author gives a selection of 1780 and leaves 1782. No. cclxxix.

38. See the document in *F.R.P.P.G.*, Vol. 17, dispatch No. 1230.

Bandar Rīq during the Basra siege. The power struggle between the 'Utūb and Arabs of the Persian littoral, which became apparent after 1779, found expression in the Bahrain affair. This ended in the establishment of the 'Utūb in the Islands and the collapse of power of the Arabs of Abū Shahr and consequently of the Persian Shāhs.

The conquest of Bahrain by the 'Utūb raises certain questions that must be addressed to both contemporary and later sources. First, the question of whether the 'Utūb of Kuwait or the 'Utūb of Zubāra were the first to occupy the Islands and secondly, the problem of fixing a date for that conquest. In addition, there are questions relating to the progress of the conquest and reasons given for it.

As for the first point, contemporary documents and local tradition clash. Local tradition preserved by the Āl-Khalīfa suggests that the 'Utūb of Zubāra, the Āl-Khalīfa and others, were the only 'Utbī element in the capture of Bahrain.[34] On the other hand, dispatches of the English Factory of Basra and others who drew on them, state that the 'Utūb of Kuwait were the first to occupy the Islands.[35] There is no doubt that the contemporary documents are correct, for in addition to stating that fact, they include convincing details of the conquest not mentioned in local tradition.

Although available sources vary as to the date of the conquest and occupation, the year 1783 is generally suggested for the occupation and transfer of power in the Islands from Shaikh Nasr of Abū Shahr to the Āl-Khalīfa of Zubāra. Lorimer, drawing on the Bombay Government records, gives the date as 1783[36] but since he does not always give precise reference to his sources, in selecting that year he may have depended on Saldanha's Selections,[37] or the Bombay Government Selections. However, after establishment of the Āl-Khalīfa at Zubāra in 1766 and with the rapid growth of 'Utbī sea trade, Bahrain must have been a port of call for the 'Utbī trading and fishing vessels earlier than the conquest. In the Factory Records of the East India Company, a document dated November 14th, 1782, clearly states that the 'Utūb had "lately taken and plundered Bahreen". This leaves little doubt that the capture of Bahrain by the 'Utūb was before 1783.[38] Perhaps the event referred to was one of a series of attacks on Bahrain that began earlier than 1782. Nonetheless, the wording of the Resident, Mr. Latouche, is clear and decisive. In fact, he states that the Shaikh of Abū Shahr tried to come to terms with the 'Utūb, preparing for a retaliatory expedition against their states at Kuwait and Zubāra.

It has been established that the 'Utūb were on bad terms with the Banī Ka'b, the Arabs of Bandar Rīq and Abū Shahr. This may have been for several reasons: rivalry for trade in the Gulf, a feeling of contempt for the Banī Ka'b and their allies because of their intermarriage with non-Arabs, a clash of Sunnī and Shī'ī creeds, or a combination of all these. Indeed, the 'Utūb were always on the alert, expecting an attack from the opposite shore of the Gulf, especially after the Persian occupation of Basra in 1776.

However, the 'Utbī expansion in Bahrain must be considered a natural phenomenon. The settlement at Zubāra which rapidly grew into a fortified and walled town could not satisfy the needs of the 'Utbī community, whose population was increased by arrivals from Kuwait and Najd[39] and who hoped to share in the water and plantations of Bahrain. The 'Utūb could not expand toward the mainland because they were allies and protegees of the Banī Khālid and it would not be easy to fight against the Arabs on land. On the other hand, with the help of their sea vessels they could defy other maritime forces and thus protect an island such as Bahrain. Whether the 'Utūb at that early period were aware of the Wahhābī danger is another factor that might have driven them to the conquest. The pearl fishery and the rich palm groves of Bahrain may have been among the attractions.

However, by the 1780's circumstances in the Arabian Gulf seem to have made an attack on Bahrain by the 'Utūb not only desirable, but necessary. The absence of a strong Persian Shāh allowed the Arabs of the Persian coast to behave independently and, the long- awaited attack of the Persian littoral Arabs became imminent and war seemed inevitable.

After diversion of much of the sea trade to Zubāra, it became an important objective of the Persian Government to then subdue it. Commencing in 1777, several unsuccessful attempts were made upon it by the Shaikh of Abū Shahr, following Persian instructions. In 1780, the Banū Ka'b were at war with the 'Utūb of both Zubāra and Kuwait, possibly in the same connection, but more probably due to piracy of the former.

According to a tradition held by the Āl-Khalīfa, perhaps from about 1780, the people of Bahrain, being Shī'īs, forbade some of Khalīfas servants to buy palm tree from Sitra, an island of Bahrain. As a result of the dispute, a servant was killed. The Zubāra inhabitants in turn attacked Sitra killing five inhabitants. The matter was reported to their Shaikh Nasr who then prepared for a retaliatory expedition against Zubāra.

Whatever the reasons for the war, by 1782 the conflicting parties were ready for the decisive battle for Bahrain. At that time, it seems each party sharing in the struggle found allies in the various maritime Arab forces of the Gulf.

On the Abū Shahr side, there were the Shaikh of the Banī Ka'b, of Bandar Rīq, of Hurmuz and the Qawāsim. On the 'Utbī sde, it is not possible to ascertain any allies. It is related that as early as 1779 the ruler of 'Umān sent a ship to Zubāra on a friendly errand. It was expected that he would side with the 'Utūb as long as his traditional enemies, the Qawāsim, were on the other side, however, the ruler is not known to have joined any party as far as the 1782 Bahrain affair is concerned. But as early as 1779, the 'Utūb did find allies in the Arabs of the Qatar peninsula.

Though the 'Utūb were on the defensive in the early stages of the fight for Bahrain, they were reported early in 1782 to have seized at the entrance of Shatt-al-'Arab "several boats belonging to Bushire and

39. The siege of Basra obliged many merchants to migrate to Zubāra. This is clearly stated in contemporary writings. See Latouche to the C. of D., Basra, 7.xi.1782, *F.R.P.P.G.*, Vol. 17. About the same time and later others migrated from Najd because of the Wahhābī threat.

40. Latouche to Court of Directors, 4.xi.1782, *F.R.P.P.G.*, Vol. 17, No. 1230.

41. *Ibid.*

42. *Bombay Selections*, No. XXIV, p. 364.

43. See report in *Bombay Selections*, XXIV, pp. 27-29. See also the same source, pp. 364-365.

Bunderick". Shaikh Nasr of Abū Shahr was reported to have been:

> collecting a marine, as well as a military force, at Bushire, Bunderick, and other Persian ports - he gives out that he intends to revenge these hostilities by attacking Zebarra.[40]

He was reported also to "have wrote [sic] for a supply of money to Aly Morat Caun" at Isfahān. Mr. Latouche commented on these preparations thus:

> Notwithstanding this Show of Vigor, however, it is said, that he [Shaikh Nasr] has lately sent to Grain to request a Peace, but that the Shaik had refused to grant it, unless Shaik Nassir pays him half the Revenues of Bahreen and a large annual Tribute also for Bushire.

Mr. Latouche goes on to say in the next paragraph:

> It is not many Years since Grain, was obliged to pay a large Tribute to the Chaub, and that the Name of Zebarra, was scarcely known. On the Persians attacking Bussora, one of the Shaiks of Grain, retired to Zebarra, with many of the principal People. Some of the Bussora Merchants also retired thither. A great Part of the Pearl and India Trade, by this means entered there and at Grain, during the Time that the Persians were in Possession of Bussora, and those Places have increased so much in Strength and Consequence, that they have for some Time past set the Chaub at Defiance, have gained very considerable Advantages against him, and is now under no Apprehensions from the Force Shaik Nassir threatens to collect aginst them.[41]

However, Shaikh Nasr found it necessary to proceed against Zubāra to avenge those 'Utbī depredations, especially after the capture of a "Bushire Gallivat that had been sent to Bahreen to receive its annual tribute" by the 'Utbī vessels. He prepared an expedition for the destruction of his powerful rival; in this he was helped by the Shaikhs of Bandar Rīq, Ganāvuah, Dushistān and other areas on the Persian coast. The fleet sailed from Abū Shahr for Bahrain with two thousand Arabs under the command of Shaikh Muhammad, a nephew of Shaikh Nasr. This fleet–

> though deemed sufficient to attack Zobara, it appeared to be Shaik Nassir's object to bring the Arabs to terms by blockading their port, for which purpose the Persian fleet kept constantly cruising between Zobara and Bahreen.[42]

Though the conquest of Bahrain by the 'Utūb of Kuwait and Zubāra may be of interest to this study, the details of that feat belong to the history of Bahrain. Hence, it suffices to say that the role which Kuwait played in the conquest was decisive as clearly stated in contemporary reports of the English East India Company.[43]

This commercial and political success brought with it many rivalries that had not existed before 1782. Added to the list of old enemies were Shaikh Rāshid of Rās al-Khayma, his son, and Shaikh 'Abd Allāh of Hurmuz. A more dangerous threat to the 'Utūb at Bahrain was from the ruler of Masqat, who had earlier claimed sovereignty over Bahrain but who did not become a threat to the 'Utūb until the closing years of the eighteenth century. He was reported to have "preserved strict neutrality" towards the struggle that ensued between the 'Utūb and their enemies both during and after the time of the conquest.[44] This attitude of the ruler may be explained by the fact that Masqat was not in a position to interfere in Bahrain. The 'Utūb who were struggling for supremacy in Bahrain had so far no grievances against the Masqatī. Other Arabs of the Persian coast, including the Qawāsim, the traditional enemies of Masqat, were his enemies. If he were to join the 'Utūb, he would lose his claim to Bahrain as a former tributary to Masqat, and he would not join the others because they were his enemies. The 'Umānī ruler, Ahmad b. Sa'īd, moreover, was by 1780 too old to start a war. His death on December 15th, 1783 was followed by a struggle for the throne by three of his sons.

The fact that the ruler of Masqat could not intervene did not stop the Arabs of the Persian coast from planning a reoccupation of Bahrain, and other 'Utbī territory at Kuwait and Qatar. But it seems that by the 1770's the 'Utūb had a strong naval power that could withstand any attack on their territories.

> During the latter part of the year 1783 preparations were on foot for an expedition on a large scale by the Shaikhs of Būshīr and Hormuz, assisted by Persian troops and by the Shaikh of the Qawāsim, against Zubārah and Kuwait; but no armament actually sailed.[45]

Preparations for that purpose were renewed at the close of the following year. On 12th February, 1785, Shaikh Nasr proceeded by land to Kungūn, and the Abū Shahr and Bandar Rīq fleets sailed for that area on the 21st; there to be rejoined by the Shaikhs of Hurmuz and Rās al-Khayma. A small force from Shīrāz had already arrived at Kungūn to join the expedition.

> But the death of 'Alī Murād Khān of Shīrāz dispelled the danger which thus threatened the Āl-Khalīfa of Bahrain during the next few years, while the Shīrāz Government laboured under domestic difficulties, the Shaikhs of Bahrain remained unmolested.[46]

This may also be attributed to the Shaikh Nasr on the 11th April, 1789.

In Kuwait, the 'Utūb were having difficulties with Sulaymān Pasha of Baghdād. Sulaymān lost his control of Basra in 1787 when its *Mutasallim* Mustafā Aghā tried to govern the town independently of orders from Baghdād. Sulaymān Pasha, who had been the *Mutasallim* of Basra before the Persian occupation of the town in 1776, still hoped to direct the affairs of the place after becoming Pasha of Baghdād in 1780. Thus, he started an expedition to reduce Basra, when Thuwaynī, the Shaikh of the strongest Arab tribe near Basra, joined hands with the *Mutasallim*. In 1787, Thuwaynī established himself as governor of the town and sent the Mutfī of Basra to Constantinople to persuade the

44. See "Report on the Trade of Arabia", in Saldanha, *Selections from State Papers*, p. 409.

45. *Bombay Selections*, XXIV, p. 365, and Lorimer, *op cit.*, I, i, p. 840. In a letter from Basra to the Secret Committee dated 17th December, 1783, Mr. Latouche speaks of the Banī Ka'b's preparations for an attack on Kuwait and Basra. He speaks as well of Shaikh Nasr of Abū Shahr as an ally of the Banī Ka'b. See *F.R.P.P.G.*, Vol. 17, No. 1262.

46. Lorimer, *op. cit.*, I, i, p. 840.

47. See a letter from Mr. S.
Manesty, the Resident, and his
Joint Factor, Mr. H. Jones, to
the Secret Committee, 29.
vi.1789, *F.R.P.P.G.*, Vol. 18,
No. 1532. It is interesting to note
that Mr. Manesty and Mr.
Jones observe that the Kaya was
not really in earnest in asking the
Shaikh to deliver Mustafā Aghā
because he deemed him a great
rival, if he was pardoned by the
Pasha and if he stayed in
Baghdād. See *Ibid.*

48. Manesty to Shaikh 'Abd
Allāh b. Sabāh, *F.R.P.P.G.*,
Vol. 18, No. 1532.

49. Shaikh 'Abd Allāh to
Manesty, 30.iv.1789,
F.R.P.P.G., Vol. 18, No. 1532.

50. See text of the above letters
in Appendix I.

51. Manesty and Jones to the
Secret Committee, Basra,
29.vi.1789, *F.R.P.P.G.*, Vol. 18,
Nos. 1520, 1535.

authorities to install him as governor of Basra and its neighbourhood.

As a result of Sulaymān's expedition, Mustafā Aghā, his brother Ma'rūf Aghā, Thuwaynī and many others who took part in the insurrection against the Pasha of Baghdād, sought refuge in Kuwait with its Shaikh, 'Abd Allāh b. Sabāh. The Pasha and his Kaya demanded they be turned over to them. On the Shaikh's refusal to do so, the Pasha asked the Resident of the English Factory at Basra to intervene, but the latter refused to share in the expedition which the Pasha was planning against Kuwait.[47]

Mr. Manesty in a letter to the Shaikh 'Abd Allāh b. Sabāh, dated 17th April, 1789, informed the latter of the Pasha's plan to march against Kuwait unless the refugees were handed over.[48] Shaikh 'Abd Allāh, in his reply to Mr. Manesty, said that he was ready to fight against the Pasha to protect his guests if the latter were to attack Kuwait.[49] In the meantime, Shaikh 'Abd Allāh assured the Resident and Sulaymān Pasha that they need not fear an attack on Basra as long as they remained in Kuwait under his protection.[50] The fears of the Pasha were not without foundation, for—

> In the beginning of the month of July, Shaikh Twiney assembled a Force at Jarra [Jahra village], a Place in the Vicinity of the Town of Grain where he was joined by Mustafa Aga the late Mussaleem, and about one hundred and fifty Turkish Horsemen.

Their small united army advanced towards Basra and "on the 10th July encamped at Saffwan [Safwān] a hill at about 30 miles distance from it." They were met there by Hamūd b. Thāmir, the new Shaikh of the Muntafiq, and the new *Mutasallim* of Basra. Thuwaynī and Mustafā Aghā were defeated. The former sought refuge with Shaikh Ghuthbān of the Banī Ka'b, while the latter, accompanied by his brother and some Turks, fled to Kuwait. There they sold their horses and proceeded to Masqat "with the intention of repairing to Mecca".

The determined behaviour of the Shaikh of Kuwait shows plainly that the power he could exert against any meditated attack on his territory was strong enough to repel any aggressor. It has already been seen how he defied the Banī Ka'b and Shaikh Nasr of Abū Shahr in 1782, and how his fleet led the attack on Bahrain at the end of the same year. The established authority of Shaikh 'Abd Allāh b. Sabāh and his "excellent character" gained him the respect of the English Factory at Basra. Mr. Manesty and Mr. Jones, when difficulties arose with the *Mutasallim* of that town and Sulaymān Pasha, thought that Kuwait could replace Basra as a centre for the English Factory. Friendship between the Factory and the Shaikh "has long subsisted".[51]

Before dealing with Kuwaitī relations with the British, let us examine the latter's position and attitude towards the struggling Arab forces in the Gulf.

That position was one of neutrality dictated mainly by orders from Bombay. What mattered to the English East India Company so far, was that her trade with the Gulf should go unmolested and her ships should not interfere with pirate ships as long as the British flag was respected. The Resident at Basra, after the Qāsimī attack and capture of an English vessel in 1778, waited for the moment when he would receive orders and vessels to destroy their power. However, when that power was at hand, the Company's directions to the Basra Factory in the 1780's were to continue on friendly terms with the "several powers" of the Gulf, i.e., with the Banū Ka'b,

> with the Bunderick, the Grain people, and other tribes of Arabs on the Persian and Arabian coasts, who have it in their power to annoy our trade ... for the security of the Company's dispatches, of the English trade, and of English travellers, passing between Basra, Aleppo and Bagdat.

The Company found that "timely presents are often of great use in preserving this good understanding."[52]

As stated, Shaikh 'Abd Allāh was on good terms with the representatives of the English East India Company. Friendly relations continued through the 1780's. This appears natural because of the benefit to both. For some time past, the Company had depended on Kuwait for her dispatches. The Shaikh derived substantial gains from the traffic. We have seen in the case of Captain de Bourge how those good relations almost collapsed over the question of the "protection of the guest", and how they were again exposed to strain when Mr. Manesty tried to intervene in the question of Shaikh Thuwaynī and Mustafā Aghā. Whenever entanglements arose between the Basra Factory and the Pasha of Baghdād, Kuwait was mentioned by the Factors as a substitute for Basra.[53] These disputes lingered on from 1780, when Sulaymān was appointed Pasha of Baghdād, till 1792, when a final and decisive step was taken by Manesty and Jones to move the Factory from Basra to Kuwait.

But by this time, the danger that threatened the 'Utūb both at Kuwait and Zubāra, and later at Bahrain, came neither from the Arabs of the Persian coast of the Gulf nor from the Pasha of Baghdād. It came from Central Arabia. Here a new overwhelming power was forcing its way to the Arabian coast of the Gulf - the Wahhābīs.

52.　Latouche to Manesty, Basra, 6.xi.1784; a letter from Manesty to the Secret Committee, *F.R.P.P.G.*, Vol. 18, No. 1299.

53.　Mr. Jones was in Kuwait for the "change of air" on 7th March 1790. See a letter from Manesty and Jones to the Court of Directors, 27.vi.1790, *F.R.P.P.G.*, Vol. 18, No. 1551. The preference was given to Kuwait as a substitute for Basra, when Khārij Island was thought of as a possible solution. See Manesty and Jones to Secret Committee, Basra, 29.vi.1789, *F.R.P.P.G.*, Vol. 18, No. 1520.

CHAPTER IV

THE WAHHĀBĪS IN EASTERN ARABIA AND THEIR RELATIONS WITH BANĪ KHĀLID AND KUWAIT

Reference to the Wahhābīs has been made several times in the previous chapters of this book. However, a study has not yet been made of the Wahhābīs' occupation of the Banī Khālid's territory in Eastern Arabia and their relations with Kuwait. Despite the importance of the Wahhābī-Khālidī struggle for the history of the region, it seems best to deal with it briefly rather than to discuss it in detail. Since Kuwait is the focus of this book, this chapter will also examine Wahhābī-Kuwaitī relations.

The Wahhābiyya[1]

A short summary of the basic Wahhābī doctrines is essential here, because the Wahhābī wars with the Banī Khālid were to a large extent based on the Wahhābīs' interpretation of Islam. In their wars with the former, the Wahhābīs were aware of the fact that they were not merely fighting against the petty chiefs of Najd. It must be recalled that the Wahhābīs did not carry war into the heart of al-Hasā till the late 1790's. They remained well aware of the power of the Banī Khālid Shaikh. However, those tribes who fought under the leadership of the Āl-Su'ūd did so primarily because of their zeal for the teachings of Muhammad b. 'Abd al-Wahhāb, founder of the movement.

The Unitarianism of Muhammad b. 'Abd al-Wahhāb was founded on the concept of unimpaired and inviolate Oneness of God.[2] There was nothing original in Shaikh Muhammad's creed, nor did he intend there should be. As a reformer, he wanted to rid his people of their sinfulness when they departed from the law laid down in the Qur'ān and led a life that violated the Moslem creed, as he interpreted it. He wanted them to go back to the Qur'ān and to put into practice the Words of the Prophet and his pious companions. This was in essence the aim of Shaikh Muhammad's preaching.

In Shaikh Muhammad's life one can clearly see three distinct phases. The first was his early religious education by his father, Shaikh 'Abd al-Wahhāb who was a *Qādī* at 'Uyayna in Najd, and by other 'Ulamā in Najd; the second was the period of his wide travels; and the third began with his return to 'Uyayna where he started to propagate Wahhābism,

1. Arabic rather than European writings are the main sources used here for the Wahhābī-Khālidī struggle, while the Factory Records and other European sources form the main authorities on the development of the 'Utbī States.

2. European and Moslem writings contemporary to the Shaikh are very misleading. Their erroneous statements were criticized by later European writers like Burckhardt in his *Notes on the Bedouins and Wahabys*, p. 277. Another example can be traced in Shaikh Mansūr, the Italian physician and commander of the forces of Sayyid Sa'īd, the Sultan of Masqat, in his *History of Seyd Sa'īd*, p. 36.

3. The following is a list of the Khālidī rulers in the second half of the 17th century and the first half of the 18th. For a full table of the Banī Khālid Shaikhs, see Appendix VII.
1. Barrāk b. Ghurair of the Āl-Hamīd (1669-1682).
2. Muhammad b. Ghurair (1682-1691).
3. Sa'dūn b. Muhammad b. Ghurair (1691-1722).
4. 'Alī b. Muhammad b. Ghurair (1722-1736).
5. Sulaymān B. Muhammad b. Ghurair (1736-1752).

4. The first expedition that was sent against the Wahhābīs on Ottoman instigation was that of Thuwaynī in 1787. Thuwaynī's second expedition about ten years later, ended by his assassination at the hands of a Wahhābī fanatic, Tu'ayyis by name. Tu'ayyis was slave of Barrāk b. Muhsin of the Banī Khālid. Ibn Ghannām, *op. cit.*, II, pp. 266-271, in a poem of 88 verses expressed his and the Wahhābī joy and blessings at the death of Thuwaynī.

which led to his expulsion from 'Uyayna and final settlement at al-Dir'iyya. The man chiefly responsible for his expulsion was Sulaymān b. Muhammad Āl-Hamīd of the Banī Khālid. The ruling family of Āl-Hamīd was divided after the death of Sa'dūn in 1135/1722 and its chiefs were struggling for the succession.[3]

The rival parties were 'Alī and Sulaymān, the brothers of the deceased Sa'dūn, against the two sons Dujayn and Munay'. At first the brothers defeated the sons of Sa'dūn, who had sought the help of al-Zafīr and al-Muntafiq tribes. Hostilities were renewed in 1136/1723, but Dujayn was again unsuccessful; he returned in 1139/1726 to the al-Zafīr and al-Muntafiq who attacked al-Hasā but were defeated by 'Ali b. Muhammad and then went back to their own land. This internal strife among the Shaikhs of the Banī Khālid was resumed upon the death of 'Alī in 1736. Sulaymān continued to rule the Banī Khālid from 1736 to 1752.

During the reign of Sulaymān, the first clash with the Wahhābīs occurred. Shaikh Muhammad b. 'Abd al-Wahhāb and his followers at 'Uyayna ordered an adulterous woman stoned to death. Consequently, the enemies of the movement tried to suppress it before it spread to other parts of Najd. But because Shaikh Muhammad b. 'Abd al-Wahhāb was under the protection of 'Uthmān b. Mu'ammar, the chief of 'Uyayna, the chiefs of the weak neighbouring towns turned to the Shaikh of the Banī Khālid, who had the power to command Ibn Mu'ammar to do whatever those chiefs wanted. Shaikh Sulaymān's power was so great that Ibn Mu'ammar yielded instantly to his orders. Thus, Shaikh Muhammad left 'Uyayna for al-Dir'iyya where he allied himself with its chief Muhammad b. Su'ūd in 1158/1745, an alliance destined to bring about a clash between the rising Wahhābī power in Arabia and the already established power of the Banī Khālid.

The history of the Banī Khālid tribe during the second half of the eighteenth century was characterized by internal feuds and bloodshed. Since this is not within the confines of this book, it will not be investigated further. It should be mentioned that because of those feuds the Banī Khālid, by the year 1789 and for the next six years, were unable to fight against the advancing Wahhābī forces. In 1795 the Wahhābīs overran al-Hasā.

With the conquest of the Banī Khālid, the Wahhābīs won more than a military victory. The fight resulted in political, religious and economic gains. Their expansion was one of the reasons for the eventual overthrow of the Wahhābī power not only in Eastern Arabia, but also in Najd itself, by provoking the Ottoman expeditions sent against them.[4]

Politically, Wahhābī influence was established in Eastern Arabia in such a way as to make other forces who had interests in the area feel their impact. The latter resorted either to appeasement or elimination. To the first group belonged the English East India Company, whose interests in Eastern Arabia were commercial. Consequently, they avoided any clash with the Wahhābīs. The British cared only that their desert mail remained unmolested and were insured of this through gifts to the

Wahhābī chief. Other Arab forces faced the following alternative: either succumb to the Wahhābī teachings, or else expect the same fate as had befallen the Banī Khālid. This concerns only the Qawāsim who became adherents of Wahhābīsm, and the 'Utūb who did not. The Ottomans, who had occupied al-Hasā[5] before the Banī Khālid and who had religious interests in Arabia, were alarmed by the spread of Wahhābī influence to the borders of Basra.

As for the religious gain, the Wahhābīs imposed their tenets on Eastern Arabia. According to their policy of eradicating what they considered *shirk* (idolatry or pluralism), they devastated monuments in the towns of al-Hasā and installed their exponents in the mosques. It would have been easier for the Wahhābīs to promote their teachings, if it had not been for the fact that certain towns in al-Hasā, especially al-Qatīf, were Shi'ite. This proved to be a factor working against Wahhābī domination and control of the area and gave them considerable trouble soon after their occupation of parts of that country in 1792 and later on.

Economically, the Wahhābīs gained much from conquering territory richer than their own. Musil may be right in assuming that the Wahhābīs in their rush to the East aimed at acquiring an outlet to the sea.[6] But this was not the main economic outcome of the acquisition of al-Hasā. The house of Al-Su'ūd did not merely divide the riches of the conquered country among their warriors. They acquired fabulous wealth by adding much of the Khālidī territory to their own. The farms of al-Hasā were known for their rich produce, and its harbours had long supplied Najd and inner Arabia with Indian and European goods. The only places of consequence to withstand Wahhābī attacks were in the 'Utbī territory north and south of al-Hasā.

But before studying the relations of the 'Utūb with the Wahhābīs, it is necessary first to study developments in the 'Utbī states between 1790 and the close of the century.

Development in the 'Utbi States (1790-1800)[7]

The long peaceful rule of Shaikh 'Abd Allāh Āl-Sabāh continued in Kuwait. In the south, at Zubāra and Bahrain, Shaikh Ahmad Āl-Khalīfa ruled till his death in 1796. He was succeeded by his son, whose reign lasted until 1825.

During the 1790's the prosperity of the 'Utūb of the north continued. They were fortunate in escaping subjugation by the Wahhābīs, the real danger to all forces in Eastern Arabia. It is true that though the Wahhābī impact on Eastern Arabia was strongly felt at Kuwait, various factors contributed to keeping Kuwait out of danger.

The 'Utūb benefited from the misfortunes of other ports and states in the Gulf, and especially from the Persian siege and occupation of Basra in 1775-1779. In the early 1790's difficulties with Ottoman officials[8] compelled the staff of the British Factory at Basra to withdraw; on the 30th April, 1793,[9] they established themselves at Kuwait[10] remaining

5.   In 1555.

6.   See *Northern Negd*, p. 160.

7.   The major source of information on the development of the 'Utbī states in the 1790's, and which also throws some light on their history, is the Factory Records of the East India Company. Contemporary Arabic sources, especially the Wahhābī writings, are very meagre on the subject of the 'Utūb. Ibn Ghannām and Ibn Bishr merely record two Wahhābī attacks on Kuwait and others on Zubāra, but no details are given about other activities in the 'Utbī states. *Lam' al-Shihāb* is invaluable for the siege of Zubāra by the Wahhābīs in 1798, but this work also does not give any other information on the development of the 'Utbī towns. The records themselves do not give much information on the southern part of the 'Utbī states in Qatar and Bahrain.

8.   Detailed accounts of those difficulties are given in the letters of Manesty and Jones to the Court of Directors in London and the British ambassador, Sir Robert Ainslee, at Constantinople. See *F.R.P.P.G.* in numerous dispatches of the year 1792.

9.   Early in 1792, Manesty and Jones left Basra for Ma'qil, a place about five miles to the north of Basra, where the Company had built a resort for its men. From there most of the letters of the Factory were sent and thus Ma'qil or Maghil, as it was called by Manesty, was the place from which they retired to Kuwait. Their stay at Ma'qil was a preliminary threat to the Pasha of Baghdād of their intention of going farther to Kuwait or Khārij if he did not come to terms with them.

10.   The departure took place by vessels from Ma'qil on the 30th of April and they arrived at Kuwait on the 5th of May. See Manesty and Jones to the S. Com., Grain, 18,vii.1793, *F.R.P.P.G.*, Vol. 19, No. 1652.

11.   Cf. Lorimer, I, i, p. 1004. Buckingham writing in 1816 in his *Travels in Assyria*, pp. 462-3: "The next port above El Kateef of any note on this coast is that of Graine, as it is called in our English Charts, though known among the Arabs by the name of Koete only...It seems always to have preserved its independence too...and they still bear the reputation of being the freest and the bravest people throughout the Gulf."

12.   They arrived on May the 5th 1793, as given in a letter from Manesty to the Sec. Committee from Grain dated 18.vii.1793, No. 1692. The first letter sent from Qurain was addressed to Harford Jones and it is dated 7th May, 1793, No. 1654. In this letter, Mr. Manesty asks Mr. Jones to proceed to Abū Shahr carrying important dispatches which arrived at Qurain from the British Ambassador and they were addressed to the Bombay Government.

until the 27th of August, 1795. The head of the Factory was Samuel Manesty, assisted by Harford Jones, the Joint Factor, and John Lewis Reinaud.

The selection of Kuwait as a place of refuge from the Ottomans implies that it cannot have been in any way an Ottoman dependency.[11] Various reasons dictated this choice. First, Kuwait had served well as a centre for the East India Company's dispatches during the period of the Persian occupation of Basra (1775-1779). Thus, one of two purposes behind the maintenance of the Factory at Basra would not be affected by its removal to Kuwait. Moreover, Manesty could safely assert "that the Charges for a Factory at Grain would be more moderate than those of the Hon'able Company's Factory here (at Basra)". Shaikh 'Abd Allāh Āl-Sabāh was on good terms with the British and it is reported that on their arrival, he received them with great hospitality. The town was known to Harford Jones, who spent some time there in 1790 when he was in bad health. Manesty may have thought that Kuwait's harbour was suitable for the Company's vessels and, therefore, goods could be unloaded there (although this hope, if it existed, was futile). Apart from these advantages, Manesty had virtually nowhere else to go when his threat to the Pasha of Baghdād failed. He was compelled to leave Basra or withdraw his threat. Manesty had already made known his intentions to the Bombay Governor, the British Ambassador at Constantinople and the Company's headquarters in London. The India mail was dispatched from Constantinople to Kuwait on 19th March, 1793 before the Factors' departure from Basra, and arrived at Kuwait before the staff.[12] The withdrawal of Manesty and the staff from Basra did not mean the closing of the Factory. An agent was retained there to look after the Company's commercial interests. At the same time, Manesty was careful to inform the Captains of the English ships to call and unload their goods at Kuwait instead of Basra, whenever possible. Letters to this effect were sent to the *Mutasallim* of Basra and to Mr. Nicholas Hankey Smith, the Resident at Abū Shahr. The Company's captains, however, were unwilling at first to risk anchoring in an unknown harbour. Later some ships called at Kuwait and unloaded there. Negotiations between the Pasha and Manesty continued. Manesty does not seem to have insisted that English ships unload at Kuwait while the Factory was there.

A year after the establishment of the new Factory, Manesty seems to have realized that his calculations about the facilities Kuwait had to offer as a substitute for Basra were not entirely accurate. In the first place, Kuwait was menaced by the Wahhābīs who attacked it more than once between 1793-1795 and secondly, Shaikh 'Abd Allāh was growing too old to continue to meet the responsibilities of his position.

It became clear to Manesty that Kuwait could not replace Basra. As a result of negotiations with the Pasha, the Factory returned in August, 1795, after two years and four months residence at Kuwait. Mr. Manesty, in a letter to the Court of Directors dated 8th Juy, 1795, showed his delight at the re-establishment of the Factory "in the most Honourable

Manner" at Basra. On the 27th August, 1795, he embarked at Qurain on board an Ottoman vessel escorted by other Ottoman ships and the "Viper" of the East India Company. They arrived at Basra on 2nd September, and on the 4th September Mr. Manesty made his public entry into Basra. From the Factory's point of view, the stay in Kuwait had the desired effect of bringing the Pasha round to the English terms. From the Shaikh's viewpoint, the stay of the British Factory greatly enhanced the prestige and income of Kuwait. Nothing is stated in local tradition about the British Factory at Kuwait and Arabic chroniclers make no mention of its stay. Its importance, however, can be gathered from events recorded in the English dispatches from Kuwait and from the information related by Brydges in his *Wahauby* and Dr. Seetzen in *Monatliche Correspondentz*.[13]

The town profited greatly from ships' cargoes unloaded there. Though no exact estimates are given as to the amount of this cargo, it must have been considerably more that that which had previously entered the town.

Kuwait must also have realized profit from the Company's mail which was usually transported by the Arab desert express. The latter consisted of camel riders chosen from the Arab inhabitants of the town, or those who lived there in order to earn a livelihood in this manner.

Manesty's personal contacts with the Shaikh undoubtedly strengthened and may well have extended to other Kuwaitī merchants whose boats were sometimes used by the Basra Factory to carry dispatches to India. This was done to avoid interception of British vessels by the French fleet in the late 1790's. The Shaikh also allowed British factors to intercept French emissaries and their dispatches carried by Kuwaitī boats.[14]

The 1790's saw considerable French activity in the Persian Gulf area. In 1793, war was declared between England and France, and the French increased their activities in India and the Indian Ocean. At the same time, more use was made of the overland route via the Syrian desert and the Gulf to India. French emissaries and dispatches became liable to interception by the British Factors' staff in the Gulf. To discuss in full detail the Anglo-French rivalry in the Persian Gulf is beyond our scope here. Suffice it to say that this rivalry was not without repercussions in Eastern Arabia, and the 'Utūb became involved in it.

In their struggle against the British in India, the French attempted to render the Persian Gulf route useless to the British, at the same time hoping to use it for conveying their own dispatches to India. To achieve this, French emissaries were sent to the various states bordering the Gulf to try to win them to their side.[15] A French fleet was also sent to police the Indian Sea and the Gulf. Simultaneously, the French sent several dispatches overland to Basra and tried to send others by Arab boats to India.

It was in this phase of French activities in the Gulf that the northern 'Utūb became involved. The friendship of Mr. Manesty and Shaikh 'Abd

13. In a letter from Burckhardt, the traveller, to Sir Joseph Banks, the secretary of the Association for promoting the Discovery of the Interior Parts of Africa, dated Malta, April 22, 1809, he gives the following about Dr. Seetzen:
"Dr. Seetzen is a German physician, who was sent five or six years ago by the Duke of Saxe-Gotha into the Levant, to collect manuscripts and Eastern curiosities. He has resided for a considerable length of time at Constantinople for the last eighteen months at Cairo, from whence his letter to Mr. Barker (the brother of the English Consul at Malta) is dated on the 9th February last. After sending from Cairo to Gotha a collection of fifteen hundred manuscripts and three thousand different objects of antiquity he planned to travel to Suez and the eastern coast of the Red Sea and enter Africa to explore its interior." See Burckhardt, *Travels in Nubia*, London 1822, p. vi. Burckhardt also speaks of Dr. Seetzen's travels in Syria and the Holy Land in his work *Travels in Syria and the Holy Land* London, 1822, p. v.

14. Several examples of this interception of French emissaries can be located in the Basra Factory dispatches of the years 1794, 1795, 1796, 1797, and 1798. There were earlier French activities such as the mission of M. de Bourge in 1778.

15. Sir Richard Worsley, Minister Resident at Venice to the Principal Factor or Agent at Basra, Venice, 15.iii.1796, *F.R.P.P.G.*, 19, No. 1803.

16.   Shaikh Ibrāhīm Ghānim on whose vessel two Frenchmen were travelling from Masqat to Basra is an example of this. He refused to allow these two men to be captured by the English though he was offered a large amount of money as a bribe. He finally agreed because he was shown a letter signed by the Shaikh of Kuwait telling him to deliver the Frenchmen to the English. See the details of this event in Manesty to Reinaud, Grain, 10.vii.1795, *F.R.P.P.G.*, 19, No. 1754.

17.   Mr. Manesty speaks of the substantial armament of Arab ships in general in a letter from Grain, 23.viii.1795, *F.R.P.P.G.*, 19, No. 1763, sent to the Sec. Committee and thinks that they will be a great danger to the British trade in the Gulf. In another letter from Grain, 17.i.1795, *F.R.P.P.G.*, 19, No. 1723, to the Sec. Committee, he speaks of Kuwaitī vessels being heavily equipped for war.

18.   Manesty to Reinaud, Grain, 17.i.1795, *F.R.P.P.G.*, 19, No. 1723. The reference to the indignation of Shaikh 'Abd Allāh Āl-Sabāh is reported in another letter; Manesty to the Sec. Committee, 18.i.1795, *F.R.P.P.G.*, 19, No. 1722. Signor Visette did not have any French dispatches and he continued his travel to India.

19.   The Āl-Ghānim family is now one of the richest trading families in Kuwait.

Allāh Āl-Sabāh helped curb French plans for using 'Utbī vessels to convey emissaries and dispatches. The chief reason for using Arab boats was that neither the English nor the French had regular mail service in the Gulf and it was necessary to keep the dispatch of important information as secret as possible. That secrecy could be secured via Arab dhows or gallivats, whose *nōkhadhas* (captains) were noted for their honesty.[16]

British influence in the Gulf expanded in the second half of the eighteenth century, but the sending of dispatches was not limited to the British Persian Gulf Factories. The majority of mail went to India, where the ocean was always endangered by French vessels during any crisis with the British in Europe or elsewhere. It could be argued that the French and English might intercept Arab boats as well, but apparently this did not happen unless emissaries or dispatches were reported to be travelling by a known boat. It would have been a difficult and impracticable task for either fleet to stop every Arab vessel. They might also have encountered difficulties with the Arab shaikhs who would not have allowed it. In addition, Arab vessels were well-equipped with guns which would have made interception difficult.[17]

The 'Utūb were in a difficult position although the British Factory rendered Kuwait invaluable services by its establishment there in 1793. The Shaikh was well-disposed towards the British, but did not approve their position in regard to Kuwaitī ships carrying French dispatches and citizens. This was the situation in January, 1795, when Manesty directed Reinaud to seize Signor Gulielmo Vicenzo Visette, son of the Venetian Pro-Consul at Aleppo, in a gallivat at Kuwait.[18] It is worth noting that Manesty, who was not sure of intercepting Visette at Kuwait, gave Reinaud letters to the Shaikh of Bahrain and Ibn Khalfān, the Governor of Masqat, to facilitate Reinaud's call. What the response of both might have been to the letters remains unknown because Visette was seized earlier at Kuwait. Yet writing to Shaikh Ahmad Āl-Khalīfa of Bahrain suggests that he was amicable towards the British.

Later that year, Shaikh 'Abd Allāh changed his attitude concerning the interception of French dispatches. On July 10th, intelligence reached the British Factory at Qurain that a Kuwaitī vessel sailing from Masqat to Basra carried two Frenchmen who might possibly have dispatches from Mauritius. At Manesty's request, Shaikh 'Abd Allāh reluctantly wrote to the Kuwaitī *nōkhadha* asking him to allow Reinaud to confiscate these. However, because Reinaud fell ill soon after his departure from Kuwait, the order failed to materialize.

Three months later, under similar circumstances, the Shaikh's attitude changed considerably, for reasons unknown. On October 25th, Manesty, after receiving intelligence that a Monsieur Guirard left Basra enroute to Surat in a Kuwaitī dhow owned by Shaikh Ibrāhīm b. Ghānim,[19] directed Reinaud to capture the French dispatches carried by Guirard. Manesty gave Reinaud a letter to Shaikh 'Abd Allāh asking him to write Ibrāhīm to permit Reinaud to seize the dispatches. Shaikh 'Abd Allāh complied, but it was uncertain whether Ibrāhīm, the *nōkhadha*, would allow the seizure. To ensure this, Reinaud carried 4,000 piastres to be given to Ibrāhīm if he agreed.[20] Ibrāhīm agreed after he had seen the letter from Shaikh 'Abd Allāh. It is interesting to note here that the vessel involved in the last incident was also owned by Ibrāhīm.

By the 13th of November of the same year, Shaikh 'Abd Allāh had granted the British Resident at Basra the right to search every 'Utbī vessel that called there for foreign dispatches and emissaries.[21] This grant proved valuable to the British, for they found it easier not only to intercept dispatches before the carriers landed and contacted the French Consul, but also to carry out their activities in Ottoman territory.

The French apparently became aware of the British talent for interception and in the last four years of the century, no more was heard of 'Utbī boats carrying French agents, emissaries or dispatches. Another deterrence may have been the agreement of the Tartar Aghāsi[22] to deliver to Reinaud all French dispatches sent to M. Rousseau, the French Consul at Baghdād. Since the French diplomatic manoeuvres at Constantinople, Baghdād, Persia and Masqat during the period 1793-1798 did not include the 'Utbī states, one may infer that with the establishment of the British Factory at Kuwait from 1793-1795 and the favourable policy of the Shaikh towards the British, the French could not hope to win his support.[23] With the French occupation of Egypt and the British diplomatic successes at Masqat and in the Persian court in 1798, there was no place in the Persian Gulf for French dispatches or emissaries.

Apart from this European activity, another aspect of the 'Utbī episode scarcely dealt with by historians is their relation with the Wahhābīs.

'Utbī-Wahhābī Relations (1793-1800)

Against this background of the general state of affairs in Eastern Arabia and of the 'Utbī states in particular, the study of 'Utbī-Wahhābī relations will be divided into three parts. The first deals with conditions in the 'Utbī states and how they invited Wahhābī action against themselves. The second concerns the actual military operations. The third shows how and why the 'Utūb were able to stay free of Wahhābī control until the close of the eighteenth century.

It must be remembered that the 'Utbī states, which formed part of Eastern Arabia, started as small towns under the protection of the Shaikhs of the Banī Khālid. When those towns grew in importance and new territory was conquered in Bahrain, no change was reported in the attitude of the Banī Khālid Shaikhs towards the 'Utbī chiefs of both Kuwait and Bahrain. Friendly relations continued with the 'Utūb offering help at certain critical periods in the history of the Banī Khālid.

This may be seen in the temporary stays of Zayd b. 'Uray'ir at Kuwait in 1793, when he succumbed to the Wahhābī attack on his territory of al-Hasā, and Barrāk b. 'Abd al-Muhsin in 1795, when he fled from al-Hasā for the same reason. Many inhabitants of al-Hasā who fled

20. Manesty to Reinaud, Basra, 25.x.1795, *F.R.P.P.G.*, 19, No. 1773. It should be remembered that the British Factory returned to Basra on 27th August, 1795. For the local and foreign currency in the Gulf in the second half of the eighteenth century, the best information can be traced in an anonymous pamphlet in the British Museum, *An Account of the Monies, Weights and Measures*, etc., London, 1789.

21. This grant came after a request from Manesty to the Shaikh which Reinaud carried with him on his last mission. See Reinaud to Manesty, Basra, 13.xi.1795, *F.R.P.P.G.*, 19, No. 1773. In this letter Reinaud gives interesting details concerning his mission and how Ibrāhīm was at first reluctant and how he finally helped in the seizure of the dispatches.

22. Dispatches from Kuwait and Basra to Aleppo were usually carried by the Arab express while those coming from Constantinople were carried by Tartars. The Tartars were the imperial Ottoman couriers, referred to as Ulak.

23. When M. Beauchamp and other French emissaries arrived at Aleppo from Turkey on their proposed journey to Masqat, Robert Abbot, the British Agent at Aleppo, wrote to Manesty at Basra, telling him that they might travel through Persia to Masqat and not through Kuwait, al-Hasā and Zubāra. See Abbot to Manesty, Aleppo, 27.i.1798, and 1.ii.1798, *F.R.P.P.G.*, 19, No. 1871.

24.   Ibn Ghannām, *op. cit.*, II.
p. 105, states that many of the
inhabitants of the towns of
al-Hasā were allowed to leave
their forts safely on condition
that they would leave the
country, which they did, and
after taking boats in the harbour
of al-'Uqair, they sought refuge
with the Zubāra people and told
them about the situation in
al-Hasā.

25.   The Wahhābīs were
efficient warriors on land, but
not at sea, for they dared not
attack the islands which belonged
to the Banī Khālid. Even in the
first one that they conquered,
al-'Amāyir, the island was near
the shore and people could reach
it by swimming or wading out to
it. Even then the Wahhābīs were
helped by al-Mahāshir, a
division of the Banī Khālid. Cf.
Ibn Ghannām, *op. cit.*, II,
pp. 225-226.

26.   *Lam' al-Shihāb* in treating
the Wahhābī attacks on Zubāra
says that it was one of the richest
ports and included some of the
wealthiest Arab merchants, such
as Ibn Rizq, Bakr Lūlū and
others of the Āl-Khalīfa.
See p. 111.

27.   Cf. Ibn Ghannām, *op. cit.*,
II, p. 273 and Ibn Bishr, *op. cit.*,
I, p. III.

28.   See Manesty and Jones to
the C. of D., Grain, 15.vii.1794,
F.R.P.P.G., 19, No. 1700.

from the Wahhābīs found shelter in the fortified 'Utbī town of Zubāra.[24] It seems that Bedouin tribes of the Banī Khālid, whenever defeated by the Wahhābīs, travelled northward to the region of Kuwait, while the settlers took to their boats and remained at Zubāra and on the coastal islands which the Wahhābīs had not yet conquered.[25] The 'Utūb, probably alerted to the dangers by these refugees, assumed the role of protector while at the same time gaining strength. In doing this, the 'Utūb clearly showed the Wahhābīs that there was no alternative but to bring the 'Utbī states under their control.

Offering shelter to refugees from the Wahhābī yoke was not the only reason for the 'Utbī-Wahhābī struggle. In their teachings, the Wahhābīs were pledged to carry war to wherever *shirk* (pluralism) and *bida'* (innovation) existed. The 'Utbī territory, therefore, could not be excluded because the 'Utūb, like other non-Wahhābī Moslems, practised Islām in a manner unacceptable to the Wahhābīs. Moreover, Bahrain was one of the territories proclaimed by the Wahhābīs as a land of *shirk* and *rafada* (rejectionist) and Shī'ites. The subjugation of such lands was vital to upholding essential Wahhābī doctrines.

It appears that the Wahhābīs were also attracted by the substantial wealth which the 'Utbī towns had accumulated through trade. Whatever their motive in attacking Eastern Arabia, they would have done their cause no harm by seizing the property of the 'Utūb who were classified, in the Wahhābī teachings, as *mushrikīn*.[26]

The actual armed clash between the 'Utūb and the Wahhābīs did not take place until 1208/1793, when the latter had almost annihilated the strength of the Banī Khālid in several raids on the various towns of al-Hasā. The 'Utūb seem not to have presented a unified front in their fight against the raiders. While the Al-Sabāh in Kuwait had to face the earlier Wahhābī raids in 1793, it was not till 1795 that the Āl-Khalīfa were exposed to direct Wahhābī attacks on Zubāra and vicinity. Even if the Āl-Khalīfa or their cousins the Āl-Sabāh were aware of a Wahhābī attack, the long distance between Kuwait and Bahrain and Zubāra made it impractical for 'Utbī forces to go to their aid by land or sea. In addition, the Wahhābī warfare technique of rapid raids and withdrawals would not permit it. The Wahhābīs, in their attacks, depended on their great mobility. Chroniclers give accounts of two such raids directed against Kuwait. The first in 1208/1793 was led by Ibrāhīm b. 'Ufaysān, who had already won battles against the Banī Khālid in al-Hasā. His army was composed of Najdī Arabs from al-Kharj, al-'Ārid and Sudayr; there was no mention of al-Hasā Arabs by either Ibn Ghannām or Ibn Bishr.[27] In this first attack, the Wahhābī chroniclers state that the people of Kuwait faced the Wahhābīs outside the town and in the booty captured were "famous and precious weapons". Ibn 'Ufaysān and his men returned with their booty after killing thirty inhabitants of Kuwait.

The second Wahhābī raid on Kuwait, which included people from al-Hasā among the invaders, according to the chroniclers, took place in 1212/1797. It can be inferred from a Basra Factory dispatch[28] and

Brydges' *Wahauby*[29] that these attacks on Kuwait continued throughout the factory's stay at Kuwait. Brydges gave an interesting description of one of the more serious assaults in which he revealed how Shaikh 'Abd Allāh Āl-Sabāh "and his brave townsmen" repelled the onslaught. This apparently took place before his departure to Baghdād in 1794, and from there to Constantinople and England. From the two Wahhābī chroniclers and the English sources, it is difficult to believe that the 'Utūb were ever on the offensive. The only reference to an 'Utbī attack on the Wahhābīs may be traced to Ibn Ghannām who, when relating the events of 1212/1797, states that a certain Mashārī b. 'Abd Allāh al-Husayn attacked a Wahhābī party near Kuwait. The attacking party consisted of the 'Utūb mounted on horses and twenty camels. Mashārī was killed in this battle.

Earlier that year, the Wahhābīs attacked Kuwait, led by Mannā' Abū Rijlayn. The 'Utūb met the enemy outside their town, but eventually retreated from the battlefield, leaving much armour and twenty dead behind.[30]

The Wahhābīs might have intended warning the 'Utūb, that those who helped enemies of the Wahhābīs were open to attack. Their pre-occupation with the expeditions of Thuwaynī and 'Alī Pasha, incited by the Ottomans, seems to have saved the 'Utūb of Kuwait who apparently played some part in supporting the Ottomans. In 1211/1796, upon their retreat to Iraq Thuwaynī's forces spent about three months at al-Jahra in the neighbourhood of Kuwait.

Earlier in 1795, after the failure of what the Wahhābī chroniclers called the "Conspiracy against the Wahhābīs in al-Hasā", many of the Banī Khālid and inhabitants of al-Hasā escaped to Basra and Baghdād. There they persuaded Sulaymān Pasha to send Thuwaynī against the Wahhābīs who would soon be attacking his territory in Basra. Although the role of the 'Utūb in Thuwaynī's expedition is not clear (because reference is always made to the Banī Khālid and their supporters), they must have sided with Thuwaynī because they were under constant Wahhābī threat and were also supporters of the Banī Khālid.

However, this support led the Wahhābī commander, Ibrāhīm b. 'Ufsaysān, chosen by Su'ūd as Governor of al-Hasā after its annexation in 1795, to write to 'Abd al-'Aziz Āl-Su'ūd seeking permission to subdue the 'Utbī settlement of Zubāra and its neighbourhood.[31] Zubāra was used as a shelter for refugees fleeing from Wahhābī occupation; its inhabitants continued to plot against the new regime in al-Hasā. It is not clear from the text of *Lam' al-Shihāb* why Ibn 'Ufaysān made his demands from 'Abd al-Azīz in secret. Neither is it clear why he did not wage war against the town when he had 'Abd al-'Azīz's sanction to attack. Ibrāhīm, however, dispatched raiders to the vicinity of Zubāra, instructing them to cut off the town on the land side and thus prevent the inhabitants from obtaining water and wood. The town of Zubāra depended for its water on wells about one-and-a-half *farsakhs* (ca. 7 miles) from the town. These were protected by a citadel. Between the citadel and the town were a

29. See Brydges, *The Wahauby*, pp. 11-12.

30. Ibn Bishr, *op. cit.*, I, p. III, says that this attack on Kuwait was carried out by order of 'Abd al-'Azīz Āl-Su'ūd. The fact that the attackers were from al-Hasā may indicate that 'Abd al-'Azīz wanted to test the fidelity of the people whose land he had subjugated two years before, in 1795.

31. It is odd that Wahhābī chroniclers do not mention the reduction of Zubāra in their works. The only source of information is *Lam' sl-Shihāb*, pp. 76-78 and 110-112.

32.   *Lam' al-Shihāb*, p. 77, states that the building of the citadel and the fortresses was effected after Ahmad Āl-Khalīfa gathered a council of the rich merchants of the town and consulted them, when he realized the approaching Wahhābī danger.

33.   Ahmad died in 1796 and Salmān, his son, was chosen as his successor.

34.   According to *Lam' al-Shihā*b, p. 78, the 'Utūb thought the Wahhābī Government would not last forever, and eventually they would return to their homes.

35.   Details of the equipment of this expedition, its march against the Wahhābīs to al-Hasā instead of al-Dir'iyya, and reasons for its failure, can be traced in the writings of three contemporaries and eyewitnesses. The first is Brydges in his *Wahauby*, pp. 19-24; the second is the anonymous work of *Lam' sl-Shihā*b, pp. 126-133; the third is Ibn Sanad who gives a detailed account in his *Matāli' al-Su'ūd*, ff. 170-175.

36.   *Lam' al-Shihāb*, p. 127, The man who arranged this was 'Abd Allāh Aghā, the Mutasallim of Basra. He seems to have been on good relations with the 'Utūb because he himself, when hearing of the approach of 'Alī Pasha and because of earlier animosity with him, took to one of the 'Utbī vessels going to Kuwait. 'Alī Pasha, however, promised not to allow previous grievances to affect him and so he returned to Basra. See *Ibid.*, p. 126.

37.   It is stated in *Bombay Selections*, p. 429, that the Arabs of Kuwait were supposed to take part in the expedition together with the Arabs of Basra and the Muntafiq, but no details are given there of the manner in which the 'Utūb participated. It appears that they offered marine help.

number of fortresses *(kūts)*, which enabled the 'Utūb to reach the water under guard. It seems clear that Ibrāhīm had hoped to capture the town without opposition, but because of its strength, position and water supplies, his expectations proved futile, thus compelling him to take it by force. The citadel fell after heavy Wahhābī losses, but the fortresses *(kūts)* did not.[32] Shaikh Salmān Āl-Khalīfa, the ruler of Zubāra, ordered his men to leave the *kūts* after rendering them useless. Zubāra was cut off from the mainland and the siege began. The 'Utūb mistakenly thought the assailants would tire and depart. Meanwhile the Wahhābīs were conquering other towns in Qatar, such as Furayha, al-Huwayla, al-Yūsufiyya, and al-Ruwayda. Boats from the latter towns were directed by the Wahhābīs against the 'Utbī vessels. It is reported in *Lam' al-Shihāb* that the 'Utūb of Zubāra attacked these newly occupied towns and scattered their forces, but were unable to meet the Wahhābīs in an open land battle. Ibrāhīm came to the rescue of the other towns and maintained a strong siege of Zubāra; its inhabitants, under the rule of Shaikh Salmān b. Ahmad Āl-Khalīfa,[33] hoped the enemy would leave their town after they themselves migrated to Bahrain.[34] Once there, they settled at al-Jaw, on high ground in the south of the largest island where a citadel and homes for the immigrants were built.

The date of this departure is uncertain and there is no evidence to indicate that the Wahhābīs, on finding Zubāra abandoned, asked the 'Utūb to return. All that is revealed by *Lam' al-Shihāb* is that Ibn 'Ufaysān, on entering the deserted town, regretted his act conceivably because he had occupied a town known to be wealthy, but had acquired no booty *(ghanā'im)* to distribute among his soldiers or to enrich the state treasury of al-Dir'iyya.

Soon after the failure of Thuwaynī's expedition of 1796, Su'ūd led the Wahhābī forces northwards and attacked the outskirts of 'Irāq. With the Wahhābī danger at his door, Sulaymān Pasha fitted an expedition against them, under the leadership of his *Kaya*, 'Alī Pasha, a Georgian slave. The calvary rode to al-Hasā. The infantry, artillery and ammunition were transported by water to Bahrain and other ports at al-Hasā, where they were warmly welcomed.[35] *Lam' al-Shihāb* reports that artillery and provisions were transported by vessels, 200 of which were hired from the 'Utūb of Kuwait.[36] This landing at Bahrain indicates that the Āl-Khalīfa was also on the side of the Ottomans.[37] The detailed account of this incursion belongs mostly to Ottoman and Wahhābī history, and thus has been discussed only to the extent that it throws light on the history of the 'Utūb.

One last point concerning 'Utbī-Wahhābī relations is the maintenance of 'Utbī independence while most of Eastern Arabia was conquered by the Wahhābīs. In this matter, it is wise to consider separately the northern and southern 'Utbī domains in their resistance to Wahhābī aggression.

Both areas shared the same geographical factors. They lay on the coast of the Gulf, protected from Wahhābī influence by the Banī Khālid lands on their western border. After 1792-1793, with the decline of the Banī Khālid, the subjugation of the 'Utūb seemed likely. However, with the rise of Zayd. b. 'Uray'ir to power in 1789 and the rise of Barrāk b. 'Abd al-Muhsin in 1793, the establishment of direct Wahhābī rule over Eastern Arabia was postponed for some years. Even though they subjected Kuwait to frequent attacks, the Wahhābīs failed to capture the town in the 1780's and 1790's.

The fall of Barrāk in 1795 marked the beginning of the end of Khalīdī rule in Eastern Arabia. With that decline, the difficulties the 'Utūb faced became greater.

Reference has already been made to the growing power of the 'Utbī fleet and its high standard of arms equipment. From 1793 onwards it was necessary to make use of these weapons for defense. The 'Utūb, who were among the Arabs trading with India, were able to arm themselves with weapons superior to those of the Wahhābīs. This might explain Ibn Ghannām's comment of the "famous weapons" which the Wahhābīs won from the 'Utūb after their attack on Kuwait in 1793.

The Role of the British Factory

The presence of the British Factory at Kuwait from 1793-1795 may have been another reason for the safety of Kuwait and its escape from the Wahhābī yoke. There is no evidence in the Basra Factory records to show that the Factory supported the 'Utūb in their struggle against the Wahhābī raids. On the contrary, Brydges, the Joint Factor at Kuwait, in his *Wahauby* gives the impression that Kuwait was defended by its own courageous people who had full confidence in Shaikh 'Abd Allāh b. Sabāh, a venerable old man of commanding appearance, regarded more as a father than a governor. He reports that the Factory, on orders from the Company, did not risk intervention for fear the Wahhābīs might intercept the Company's mail in the desert.[38]

However, this is not in accord with what Mr. Reinaud, a remarkable figure in the history of the Factory, wrote to Dr. Seetzen from Aleppo in 1805.[39] Brydges represented the grand attack of the Wahhābīs as having been made by 500 men, who were driven off by a single shot from an old gun that had been brought ashore by the Shaikh from one of his vessels. Mr. Reinaud, instead, places the strength of the enemy at 2,000 camels, each carrying two men, the front rider armed with a gun and the other with a lance to protect his companion while re-loading. He alleges that, under Manesty's orders, two guns were landed from the British cruiser protecting the Factory, and that the sepoy Factory guard participated in repelling the attack, in which the Wahhābīs suffered heavy losses as they fled the beach to avoid the fire of the cruiser. Reinaud adds that the resentment of the Wahhābīs, with resultant raids on the Company's desert mail, was the cause of his own mission to al-Dir'iyya.[40]

No fixed date is given for the attack by either authority, except that it took place during the sojourn of the Factory at Kuwait. It seems likely

38. According to Corancez, p. 50, the Wahhābī Amīr undertook to protect the British mail only so long as he should be at peace with the Pasha of Baghdād. He once put a man to death for tampering with it.

39. See *Monatliche Correspondentz*, pp. 234-235.

40. He gained fame by that mission as the first European to visit that town; see *Gazetteer of the Persian Gulf*, I, i, p. 1004.

41. See extract of a letter from Brydges to Jacob Bosanguet, Chairman of the Court of Directors, dated Baghdād, 1.xii.1798, in *F.R.P.P.G.*, Vol. 21.

42. Mr. Warden in his historical sketch on the rise of Masqat, *Bombay Selections*, p. 174, states that on the conquest of Bahrain in 1801 by the ruler of Masqat, the latter demanded of the Shaikh of Kuwait that he would personally pay him homage. This, according to Warden, the Shaikh must have complied with, as the Masqatī shortly after dismissed all his troops. However, there is no reference to Kuwait in the Wahhābī chronicles, which refer only to Bahrain and give the name of Shaikh Salmān Āl-Khalīfa as "Amīr 'Abd al-'Azīz 'alā al-Bahrain wal-Zubāra". Cf. Ibn Bishr, *op. cit.*, I, p. 129.

that Mr. Reinaud's version of the Factory's role, which has more evidence to support it, is not entirely false or fabricated. In the first place, the Factory was responsible for the Company's goods at Kuwait. The Wahhābīs presumably would not have spared the infidels if the town had been taken. In addition, it is doubtful whether Manesty would have been so ungrateful as to refuse aid to the people of Kuwait who had previously received him with hospitality. At the same time, Manesty could not explain in letters to his superiors the role he played against the Wahhābīs, for the policy of the Company had so far been one of neutrality towards the Gulf powers. It is interesting, that in the dispatches from Kuwait, there is no mention of any Wahhābī attacks, although it is indisputable that they took place.

After the subjection of Zubāra, Kuwait was no longer under the influence of the Wahhābīs who were busy repelling attacks by the *Sharīfs* of Makka on the one hand, Thuwaynī of the Muntafiq in 1797 and 'Alī Pasha in 1798-1799 on the other. Moreover, the 'Utūb represented no threat to the strongly established Wahhābī regime in Eastern Arabia, which could at that time put 50,000 men mounted on camels in the field.[41] In this way, the repression of the 'Utūb seems to have been postponed.

In 1799, the ruler of Masqat attacked Bahrain on the complaint that 'Utbī ships refused to pay tribute for passing the Straits of Hurmuz. He failed to capture its capital, Manāma, and returned to Masqat. In 1800, in another expedition, the Islands were occupied and twenty-six 'Utbī families were taken as hostages to Masqat. Others fled to their deserted homes at Zubāra, where they sought help from the Wahhābīs who readily cooperated. The 'Utūb re-occupied Bahrain in 1801, but now the influence of the Wahhābīs was established in their islands.

It is not clear how much Wahhābī influence existed in Kuwait. According to Lieutenant Kemball, the British Assistant Resident in the Persian Gulf, by 1800-1802 Wahhābī influence was established throughout the whole Persian Gulf coast from Basra in the north to the territories of the Qawāsim in the south. This suggests that the 'Utūb of Kuwait must have recognized the Wahhābī suzerainty.[42] We shall turn to this matter in the following chapter.

CHAPTER V

GROWTH AND DEVELOPMENT OF KUWAIT 1800-1815

We have already seen in the previous chapter how Kuwait came into being early in the eighteenth century, how it began to play a political role in the affairs of the Gulf region and how it established its relations with the major powers, local and/or foreign. The planner and executor of that strategy was Shaikh 'Abd Allāh ibn Sabāh, the second ruler from the Al-Sabāh family. 'Abd Allāh's rule in Kuwait lasted more than fifty years. The turn of the century saw him still in complete command of the ever changing political affairs in the region.

This chapter addresses itself to the last fifteen years of the prosperous rule of Shaikh 'Abd Allāh. His treatment of the political affairs of the Gulf and relations with the various powers followed the patterns of his earlier policies. We will seek to investigate the relations of Kuwait with those powers during the aforementioned fifteen years, and hope also to find out the nature of the relationship which developed between the Kuwaītī 'Utūb in the north, and their kinsmen, the 'Utūb of Qatar and Bahrain in the south.

From all that has been said, it should by now be quite evident that the affairs of the Gulf shaikhdoms and states were so inter-related that events which took place in any part of that region affected the others.

First to be considered will be the most influential forces in the Gulf, and Kuwait's relations with them. This has not been an easy task to accomplish because of the scarcity of information on Kuwait in both Arabic and European sources. Lorimer, for example, stated that Kuwait was not mentioned in the correspondence of the English East India Company after the return of its Factory from Kuwait to Basra in 1795.[1] For the student of the history of Kuwait, this is disheartening. However, the search has not been futile. Useful information on the 'Utūb of the north was discovered in some European and Arabic sources as well as in the Records of the English East India Company itself.

The major forces with which Kuwait had to deal during this period were the Wahhābīs in Central and Eastern Arabia, the Qawāsim at sea, the ruler of Masqat and the English East India Company. No mention is made here of the Ottomans and Persians, the two powers that had played major roles in the affairs of the Gulf during the eighteenth century. This

1. *Gazetteer*, I, i. p. 1006.

2. For the murder of Sulaymān
Pasha in 1802, see Ibn Bishr,
'Unwān al-Majd, I, p. 122.

3. See *Lam' al-Shihāb*, pp.
126-133, for details on that
expedition, and also Brydges'
Wahauby, pp. 23-27, and
Matāli' al-Su'ūd, ff. 170-175.

is due to the fact that the latter had been in constant internal turmoil and
the former was totally occupied with its wars against Russia on the one
hand and with the French who had attacked Egypt in 1798 on the other.
The last situation did end with the expulsion of the French from Egypt in
1801, and the rise of Muhammad 'Alī to power in Egypt in 1805.
Muhammad 'Alī was an ambitious *Walī* who had plans aimed at
expanding his authority beyond the borders of his province. Reference
will be made to him later when relations between Kuwait and Egypt in
the 1830's are discussed. The only hope for a predominant Ottoman
presence in the Gulf was the province of Baghdād, but after the decease of
Sulaymān, Pasha of Baghdād in 1802, no one of his calibre succeeded to
the seat of the Governorship. Subsequent governors were weak and
unable to establish Ottoman rule in the Gulf.[2]

A better understanding, therefore, of the state of affairs in Kuwait
and the other 'Utbī settlements in the south can be achieved by examining
the state of affairs of the four powers: the Wahhābīs, the Qawāsim, the
ruler of Masqat and the English East India Company.

The Wahhābīs

The Wahhābīs have been referred to several times in previous
chapters in dealing with their rise to power in Central Arabia during the
second half of the eighteenth century and especially with the onset of their
conquests of Banī Khālid territories in Eastern Arabia. The total collapse
of the Banī Khālid in the last decade of the eighteenth century marked the
success of the Wahhābī campaign which was aimed at the seizure of
al-Hasā, the richest territory in Eastern Arabia. Since 'Utbī territories in
Kuwait, Qatar and Bahrain had been exposed to their raids, it is
important at this point to study Kuwait's relations with the Wahhābīs.
Since Wahhābī history as such is not our major interest, we shall deal
with it only in as much as it affects the growth of Kuwait between 1800
and 1815. It was during this period that the Ottomans and the East India
Company, two powers who had special interests in the Arabian
Peninsula, changed their attitude towards the Wahhābīs noticeably. Until
the end of the eighteenth century, both powers were not willing to wage
substantial attacks on the Wahhābīs. The situation changed by the turn of
the century when the Wahhābīs captured the holy cities of Madīna and
Makka and the shores of the Arabian Gulf in the first decade of the
1800's.

A chronological look at the events of the latter part of the eighteenth
and the first decade of the nineteenth centuries might be pertinent here. In
1787, the Pasha of Baghdād commissioned Thuwaynī, Chief of the
Muntafiq tribes, to lead an expedition to al-Hasā against the Wahhābīs
who were attacking that province. But neither this campaign, nor the one
in 1796 in which Thuwaynī lost his life, met with any success. Again in
1798-1799, the Pasha of Baghdād sent his *Kaya,* 'Alī Pasha, against them,
but to no avail.[3] His forces were routed in al-Hasā, and pursued by the

Wahhābīs as far north as the outskirts of Kuwait. These failures resulted in the intensification of Wahhābī raids on 'Irāqī towns and cities between 1801 and 1810.[4] Basra, Karbālā, Najaf, Samāwa and Baghdād were subjected to severe losses and damage. Another major reason for these savage attacks was the murder of Amīr 'Abd Azīz ibn Muhammad ibn Su'ūd, Chief of the Wahhābīs, by an 'Irāqī of the Shī'ī sect,[5] believed by some, however, to be a Kurd.

The reign of Su'ūd ibn 'Abdul Azīz (1803-1815) could be considered the golden era of the Wahhābī rule in Arabia for it was during the first decade of the nineteenth century that Hijāz, with its holy cities of Madīna and Makka, was conquered, thus placing the holy pilgrimage at the mercy of the Wahhābīs. With the interruption of the pilgrimage from 1808 to 1810, the Ottoman Sultan in Istanbul sought the help of the strongest among his Governors, the Pasha of Egypt, for putting an end to Wahhābī control over these cities. Under the leadership of Tūson Pasha, son of the Pasha of Egypt, Muhammad 'Alī, the holy cities were recaptured in 1811 and the Wahhābīs driven out of Hijāz. Nevertheless, the complete victory over the enemy was not achieved until Ibrāhīm Pasha, son of Muhammad 'Alī, led his army deep into Najd, occupied most of its towns and finally captured and destroyed al-Dir'iyya, the Wahhābī capital, in 1818.[6] For the sake of this narrative, however, these wars and Wahhābī relations with the Egyptians need not be further explored. It is their occupation of certain territories in Eastern Arabia that are of most concern here. One such area is that of 'Umān al-Sīr,[7] held by the Qawāsim who had considerable sea power. Another area which fell to the Wahhābīs was that of the Banī Khālid under whose protection the 'Utbī states thrived. Kuwait was thereafter going to be subjected to Wahhābī pressures and threats, as were Bahrain and the other 'Utbī settlements in Qatar.

Al-Qawāsim

The role of al-Qawāsim during this period was complementary to the Wahhābīs, under whose control they played the part of a forceful sea power. The Wahhābīs themselves maintained a large land force which enabled them to subdue the islands adjacent to the coast of al-Hasā. Al-Qawāsim, after accepting the Wahhābī teachings, became more daring in their sea raids. Certain questions relating to al-Qawāsim will be taken up in this book. Were they, for example, pirates as they are depicted in contemporary English sources? If so, what was their role in Wahhābī-'Utbī relations? These questions and others, in relation to the history of Kuwait and other 'Utbī towns, have been unanswered until now.[8]

Masqat and 'Umān

Another sea power equally strong, and able to challenge the Qawāsimī naval power, was that of Masqat. Masqat and 'Umān, during

4. Ibn Bishr, I, pp. 123-132; and Musil, *Northern Negd*, p. 26 FF.

5. Ibn Bishr gives the details of that event in *'Unwān al-Majd*, I, pp. 121-129. See also *Longrigg, Four Centuries of Modern 'Irāq*, p. 229.

6. For a detailed account of the conquest of the lands of the Wahhābīs in Arabia, Dr. 'Abdul Hamīd El-Batrik's Ph.D. thesis, entitled *Turkish and Egyptian Rule in Arabia, 1810-1840*, is by far the best source of information. It is unfortunate that this thesis is still in typescript form and not published.

7. Trucial 'Umān or the United Arab Emirates was known to the Arabs as 'Umān al-Sīr.

8. For the rise of al-Qawāsim in the early years of the nineteenth century, see: Buckingham, *Travels in Assyria*, *etc.* pp. 204-227 and also Low, *History of the Indian Navy*, pp. 315-366.

9.   Rulers of 'Umān from the
Āl-Bū Saʿīdīs during this period
were all immediate descendants
of Ahmad ibn Saʿīd:
Ahmad ibn Saʿīd (1749-1783),
Saʿīd ibn Ahmad (1783-c.1811),
Hamad ibn Saʿīd (1789-1792),
Sultān ibn Ahmad (1793-1804).

10.   Saldanha, *Selections*, p.
444, paragraph 26.

the first two decades of the 19th century, were attacked by Wahhābī land forces, who forced the rulers, the Āl-Bū-Saʿīd, to pay tribute, a sign of political allegiance resulting from internal weakness. From 1803, they paid tribute to the Wahhābī Amīr until the destruction of al-Dirʾiyya, the Wahhābī capital in 1818.[9]

As far as Kuwait is concerned, Masqat had been at odds, not only with Kuwait, but also with the 'Utūb of Zubāra and Bahrain. It should be pointed out that Masqat's relations with Kuwait at the time had so much to do with both Wahhābī and Qāsimī relations that they could hardly be subjected to individual studies. Hence, they will be treated simultaneously.

The Bombay Government and the East India Company

British trading activities in the Arabian Gulf continued uninterrupted throughout the eighteenth century and their relations with Kuwait, as was pointed out in the previous chapter, helped to advance the political understanding between the 'Utūb and the British. Despite the fact that the British won the Seven Years War, French presence in the Arabian Gulf continued. The British remained as merchants and tradesmen in the region but without any binding treaties or agreement with the Arabian Gulf States. It was not until 1798 that the British, in order to forestall an attempt by the French to sign a treaty with the ruler of Masqat, signed their first treaty with an Arab Gulf State. This agreement was reinforced by another in 1800. French attempts continued into the nineteenth century. This struggle between the two European powers in the Indian Ocean and the Arabian Gulf, and also in Persia and 'Irāq, must have had indirect effects on Kuwait and the other 'Utbī towns in the south.

Having given a brief survey of the powers influencing the state of affairs in the Gulf region, the discussion will now focus on how Kuwait reacted to the power interplay during the first fifteen years of the nineteenth century.

Kuwait at the Beginning of the Nineteenth Century

The position of Kuwait at the turn of the century seems to have been very strong indeed. In a report compiled by Mr. Malcolm in 1800, Kuwait was referred to as a head of the 'Utūb with a thriving prosperity.[10] Sultān bin Ahmad of Masqat, in 1799, attacked Bahrain, the 'Utbī land in the south, capturing it in 1801. A number of the Bahrain 'Utūb fled to Zubāra in Qatar, while others sought refuge with their kinsmen in Kuwait. Masqat's forces seemed to be at the point of attacking both Zubāra and Kuwait, however, Zubāra under Wahhābī protection at that time was saved. Because the Masqatīs attacked Bahrain in order to settle a claim for an overdue financial toll and failed to collect it at the island, they found it expedient to follow the Bahrainī refugees to Kuwait. Masqat also claimed that Kuwait had refused to pay a certain toll when its merchant fleet crossed the Straits of Hurmuz, passing by the Cape of

Musandam, a Masqaṭī and 'Umānī territory. According to Lorimer,[11] an authority on the subject, the Masqaṭī-'Umānī attack on Bahrain was actually motivated by greed. Both Bahrain and Kuwait prospered as a result of the interruption of trade in Qaṭīf and 'Uqair, major seaports of al-Hasā and Najd which were being subjected in 1800 to a major Wahhābī offensive. No details of the attack on Kuwait are available and sources vary regarding the question of whether Sulṭān bin Ahmad had collected any tribute from her.[12] According to all reports, the 'Umānī forces sailed back to Bahrain and later to Masqat after they had placed a member of the Āl-Bū-Sa'īd family as head of the government of Bahrain. Soon after, the 'Utūb of Bahrain drove the 'Umānī forces out of the Island, depending heavily on Wahhābī support. Sulṭān bin Ahmad tried to recapture the Island in 1802, but was forced to withdraw, this time because the Wahhābīs were raiding his territories in 'Umān itself and Masqat, the capital city, was in danger.[13]

It appears that the Masqaṭī attack on the territories of the 'Utūb in Bahrain and Kuwait was a challenge to the supreme authority of 'Abd Allāh bin Sabāh, Chief of the 'Utūb in general. Though the Wahhābīs had succeeded in occupying Zubāra in 1798, they failed to conquer Bahrain to which most of the settlers of Zubāra had fled during the battle for their town. It should be noted that Kuwait had successfully withstood the Wahhābī attacks of the 1790's and not only retained its independence from the Wahhābīs and other Gulf forces, but was adding to its commercial prosperity and accumulation of wealth when most of the trade of al-Qaṭīf and 'Uqair in al-Hasā was diverted to it in 1800, as previously stated. The Masqaṭī threatened attack on Kuwait was, therefore, an attempt to subdue Kuwait and force its Shaikh to acknowledge the supremacy of 'Umān over Bahrain. This could be achieved only if Kuwait, the head of the 'Utūb as Malcolm called it, was brought to its knees. Masqat failed in the end to achieve its objective because its territory was under attack by the major land power in the Arabian Peninsula, the Wahhābīs.

Kuwait and the Wahhābīs (1800-1815)

This chapter will address itself to several questions that relate to Wahhābī-Kuwaitī relations during this fifteen year period. Did Kuwait pay any tribute to the Wahhābīs in order to avoid losing its independence, especially when most of the Arabian Peninsula was paying such a tribute, or had even been absorbed by the Wahhābīs? It might seem that Kuwait must have paid such a tribute, but contemporary sources, Wahhābī and others, do not support this. And if it is assumed that Kuwait did not pay tribute to the Wahhābīs in any form, then one must argue this point and prove that it was possible.

The blood relationship between the ruling families in Kuwait and al-Dir'iyya being both of the 'Anaza tribe, could have been accepted had it

11. Cf. Miles, *Countries and Tribes*, II, p. 292, and Lorimer, I, i, p. 841.

12. Cf. for these different points of view, Lorimer, I, i, p. 948, and p. 1007, and Miles, II, p. 292.

13. For Wahhābī aid to the Āl-Khalīfa, see Ibn Bishr, I, p. 122, and Lorimer, I, i, p. 842 and pp. 1056-7. For the Wahhābī danger getting nearer to Masqat, see Miles, II, p. 197.

14.   See Lorimer, I, i, p. 1006. Kuwait was able to muster that number of fighters around 1800. See how Kuwait was able to defend itself against the numerous attacks after 1793 when the Wahhābī power was at its prime.

15.   Lorimer, I, i, p. 842 and also page 1057.

16.   Ibn Bishr, I, p. 123.

17.   See Ibn Bishr, I, pp. 146-148, 154-155. For Wahhābī activities in 'Umān, see Ibn Razīq, *Al-Fath al-Mubīn*, ff. 196, 197 ff.

not been for the example of the rulers of Zubāra and Bahrain. For the Āl-Khalīfa, in their turn, were cousins of both the Āl-Sabāh and the Āl-Su'ūd. This blood link did not, however, stop the Al-Su'ūd - the Wahhābīs - from capturing Āl-Khalīfa's territories in both Zubāra and Bahrain.

It has already been pointed out how Kuwait was able to successfully resist the Wahhābīs in the 1790's. There are several reasons for this. Until the late 1790's, the Banī Khālid were powerful enough to forestall Wahhābī occupation of Eastern Arabia. This, along with the continued presence of the British Factory in Kuwait from 1792 to 1795 served to discourage Wahhābī attacks. But by 1800, neither of these conditions existed. As to whether this success could be related to neighbouring Muntafiq tribes of southern Irāq or the Pasha of Irāq who were open to Wahhābī attack, it is a question best answered in the negative since neither were able to ward off Wahhābī raids staged between the years 1801 and 1811. What saved Kuwait during this period must have been the ability of its strong fleet to withstand any premeditated attack by the Qāsimī fleet, the ally of the Wahhābī forces. Moreover, Kuwait was a walled city which could muster a defense force of between 5,000 and 7,000 armed fighters.[14]

Another reason must have been the wise political judgment of Shaikh 'Abd Allāh ibn Sabāh, who offered the Wahhābīs substantial naval aid when Bahrain and Kuwait were asked to send their fleets along with Qāsimī vessels to Masqat for a joint show of naval power. Kuwait and Bahrain agreed to do this, but not without aggravation, because the request came during the pearl fishing season.[15]

A clear indication of Kuwait's independence of the Wahhābīs can be established from the statement of Ibn Bishr, the Wahhābī chronicler. When naming the Wahhābī governors of provinces under 'Abd al-'Azīz ibn Muhammad, the only territory to be omitted was Kuwait. Had it been a province of the Wahhābī State, Ibn Bishr would not have failed to include it in his list.[16] It seems, therefore, that Kuwait maintained its independence until 1803. What happened after that is a matter to be dealt with shortly.

In retaliation for the assassination of 'Abd al-'Azīz in 1803, the new Wahhābī Amīr, his son Su'ūd, directed merciless attacks on 'Irāq. The Wahhābīs also tightened their hold on 'Umān, Hijāz and al-Hasā. Domination over Bahrain and Zubāra continued as a result of the role the 'Utūb played in putting their fleet at the disposal of the Pasha of Baghdād to convey forces and ammunition for the Ottoman expedition of 'Alī Pasha in 1798-1799. Both were adjacent to Qatar and to the coastal sea ports of Qatīf and 'Uqair in al-Hasā, the Wahhābī eastern province.[17] Zubāra served as a gathering centre for the Indian trade exported from there through al-Hasā to the towns of interior Najd. The 'Utūb of both Kuwait and Bahrain resented the Wahhābī occupation of Zubāra in 1798 since this meant a substantial commercial loss for the Āl-Sabāh in the north and the Āl-Khalīfa in the south.

Further comment must be made here concerning the question of the Zubāra and Bahrain refugees in Kuwait. Between 1800 and 1804, Zubāra and Bahrain were the Āl-Khalīfa's territories, in which both the ruler of Masqat and the Wahhābīs had control. Contemporary sources explain why those merchants deserted their homes[18] and sought refuge in Kuwait. It has been believed that those merchants were not forced out of their homes because the Āl-Khalīfa's territories were coveted for their wealth, as such a move would have been detrimental to their trade. A more valid reason for that exodus was one related to the request by the Sultan of Masqat and the Wahhābī *Amīr* for payment of a tribute by the Āl-Khalīfa. This could only be paid from duties collected in the harbours of Zubāra and Manāma (in Bahrain). If one remembers that the major reason behind Zubāra's success, and Bahrain's too, was the exemption from duties on any imports, then it becomes clear that merchants would rather go to a place where, if not completely exempted from duties, they would pay a minimal amount.

It becomes apparent from what has been said about Wahhābī relations with the Āl-Khalīfa of Zubāra and Bahrain that the former subdued those two places, but not Kuwait of the Āl-Sabāh. However, both Bahrain and Kuwait answered the call of the Wahhābīs for help against Masqat when they sent their fleets alongside the Qawāsim's fleet to that city in 1803 in a show of force.[19] The occupation of Zubāra and Bahrain did not stop Kuwait and Bahrain from offering the services of their fleets in a planned English attack on Rās al-Khayma in 1805. Kuwait intended by that offer to prove to the English that their vessels had never attacked British or British-protected ships.[20] The British, however, did not accept the offer.

This act of diplomacy on the part of Kuwait towards the Bombay Government necessitates a brief discussion of the British (Bombay Government) activities in the Arabian Gulf in 1804 and 1805. This will hopefully explain the British attitude towards Rās al-Khayma and the interference in the Qāsimī affairs.

British Policy in the Arabian Gulf (1800-1806)

The British political involvement with the Arabian Gulf countries began after the arrival of Bonaparte (later Napoleon) in Egypt with the French army in 1798. This action represented a direct threat to British routes to India. To stop the French from threatening India itself, the British tried to eliminate French piracy vessels in the Indian Ocean and Arabian Sea by attacking them vehemently. It has already been pointed out how they managed to intercept French emissaries across the Arabian Gulf and off the shores of India. To make sure that the French were kept politically isolated in the Arabian Gulf countries, the British started to sign or negotiate treaties with those countries, as will be seen shortly. The Gulf became more than a British trading zone. When force was needed, the Bombay Government of the East India Company - i.e., the

18. For the 'Umānī occupation of Bahrain, and the Wahhābī occupation of Zubāra and Bahrain later, see: Lorimer, I, i, p. 841 ff. & 1075, and *Bombay Govt. Selections, XXIV*, pp. 366 and 428-432.

19. Lorimer, I, i, p. 1007, and *Bombay Govt. Selections, XXIV:a*, pp. 367-8.

20. Lorimer, I, i, p. 1007 & p. 842.

21.   See above, p. 24-25.

22.   Tīpū Sahib (Sultān) was the King of Mysore in India from 1783-1799. His father, Haydar 'Alī, was a bitter enemy of the British. Tīpū had good relations with the French in India. The French Government made him a citizen of the French Republic in 1798. He fell in the battle field while he was defending his capital against their attack in 1799. See a brief biography of Tīpū in *Encyclopaedia of Islām*, 1st edition. The letter sent to him by Bonaparte from Egypt was the following, which was enclosed in the letter of Sultān b. Ahmad of Masqat. First, we quote the letter to Sultān. "Cairo, 5th January, 1799"

"To the Imam of Muscat, "I write to you this letter to inform you of the arrival of the French army in Egypt. As you have always been friendly you must be convinced of our desire to protect all the merchant vessels you may send to Suez. I also beg you will forward the enclosed letter to Tippoo Sahib by the first opportunity. "(Signed) Bonaparte." "Cairo, 25th January, 1799"

" Tippoo Sahib, "You have already been informed of arrival on the shores of the Red Sea, with a numerous and invincible army, animated with the desire of deliverying you from the iron yoke of England. I hasten to inform you of my desire to receive news with regard to the political position in which you find yourself placed. I even desire you will send to Suez some competent person who enjoys your confidence, and with whom I can confer. "(Signed) Bonaparte."

For text of letters, see Miles, p. 290.

23.   Danvers, *Report on the India Office Records*, p. 46. See also Miles, *Countries and Tribes:a, II*, p.290

Government of western British India - did not hesitate in dispatching forces to the Gulf to protect British interests. The first expedition was sent in 1805-1806 against Rās al-Khayma, where the Qawāsim were accused of committing acts of piracy at sea against English and English-protected vessels. Of course, this was not the first military act in which the East India Company was involved in the Gulf basin. For, as previously mentioned, the English took the side of the *Mutasallim* of Basra in fighting the Persian army while besieging the city in 1775;[21] and before that the Company's vessels fought the Banī Ka'b at al-Dawraq as well as Mīr Muhanna of Bandar Rīq at the Island of Khārij. In the latter engagements, the English were not fighting alone but as allies of the local powers.

Early Treaties

The first political agreement between the British and a Gulf Arab State was the treaty with Masqat on 12th October, 1798. Masqat was the center of rivalry between the French and British even at an earlier stage. But what made the British act in haste was the threat posed by the French after their forces had landed in Egypt earlier in July 1798. Bonaparte, in a letter dated 17th January, 1799, wrote the ruler of Masqat, Sultān bin Ahmad, informing him of his arrival in Egypt with the French army and stating that he was willing to protect Sultān's vessels which carried merchandise to Suez. He also asked him to send an accompanying letter to Tīpū Sultān[22] at Sultān's earliest convenience.

The 1798 British treaty was followed by another one signed on January 12, 1800. These two treaties with Masqat were a clear indication to the Arab chiefs of the Gulf that the British were not only satisfied by the monopoly of trade in the Gulf, which they had achieved, but were planning to assert their supremacy over its waters and shores. After the indecisive attacks on Rās al-Khayma and other Qāsimī domains in 1806, in 1809 and 1810, treaties were signed between the Qawāsim and the British. But this did not put an end to piracy in the Gulf. A major devastating attack by the British on Rās al-Khayma in 1819 resulted in the General Treaty of Peace (January 1820). References to this will be made later in the book.[23] Since British relations with the Qawāsim are not closely connected with the history of Kuwait and the 'Utūb of Zubāra and Bahrain, they will not be studied in any detail. They have been mentioned in this section because of the strong ties between the Wahhābīs and Qawāsim and because a knowledge of the extent of British involvement in the affairs of the Arabian Gulf is vital to an understanding of Kuwaitī-British relations.

Wahhābī Activities in the Gulf and Kuwait's Relations with Them (1800-1815)

The combined force of the Qawāsim and the Wahhābīs was indeed the most formidable power in the Arabian Peninsula at the time. Even Masqat with its strong sea power could not stop the joint Wahhābī-Qāsimī aggressions on its territories. No wonder then that Badr ibn Saif, ruler of Masqat, allied himself with them in 1803. While 'Irāq was being subjected to punitive attacks, Kuwait managed to escape the Wahhābī yoke, as confirmed by Ibn Bishr, the Wahhābī historian, who did not include Kuwait among the Wahhābī provinces when he wrote of the events of 1808 in his *'Unwān al-Majd*,[24] mentioning Su'ūd's pilgrimage to Makka at that time.

Indeed, that was the year when Su'ūd enlisted an army of 4,000 men and attacked the 'Utbī city of the north because Shaikh 'Abd Allāh ibn Sabāh refused to pay tribute to the Wahhābīs.[25] The latter were then (1808) preparing for an attack on Baghdād. In June 1808, the four thousand men attacked Kuwait, but failed to subdue the town or to force Shaikh 'Abd Allāh to pay the tribute Su'ūd demanded.

Later, in 1809, Su'ūd tried in vain to persuade Sultān ibn Saqr, Chief of the Qawāsim, and Sa'īd ibn Sultān, ruler of Masqat to stage a naval attack on Kuwait. They refused to execute it, preferring to disobey Su'ūd rather than lose the battle against the well-manned and equipped Kuwaitī fleet.

The Bombay Government Records for that year note that Kuwait offered the English Company assistance in an expedition against Rās al-Khayma,[26] but were regretfully turned down. It appears that there were certain motives behind this offer. In the first place, Shaikh 'Abd Allāh must have learned by then that the British were becoming involved in the politics of the Gulf and, therefore, it was a chance for cooperation that he did not want to lose. Secondly, the Qawāsim were his enemies and the allies of the Wahhābīs whom he feared most of all. He was also apprehensive of Qāsimī attacks on Kuwaitī merchant vessels and felt that the British, if helped, might reciprocate by providing protection for Kuwaitī vessels from the marauding Qāsimī pirate fleet. The Kuwaitī offer included not only warships, but the services of Kuwaitī pilots to guide the large British war vessels in the creeks of the Qāsimī coastal territories. This latter problem, Captain Wainwright thought, might be solved by the 'Umānī pilots who proved to be unskilled and ignorant of the waterways.[27] It is reported that Captain Wainwright felt sorry in the end for not having accepted the Kuwaitī offer.[28]

It might be worthwhile to investigate the rejection of the Kuwaitī offer by Captain Wainwright. Though the Bombay Government sources revealed reasons for this refusal, they can be traced to the secret orders issued by the Bombay Government to the British officers of the expedition. These instructions made quite clear that it was imperative that Captains Wainwright and Smith were not to take any action which might aggravate the Wahhābīs,[29] allies of al-Qawāsim. Indeed, they were instructed to convey to the Wahhābī *Amīr* that the expedition was limited to punishing the Qawasim for their piracy, as such, and not for their alliance to the Wahhābī *Amīr*. In other words, the British were not yet

24. Ibn Bishr, I, p. 141.

25. Corancez, *Histoire des Wahabis*, pp. 139-140. The author states that because of Shaikh 'Abd Allāh's strong resistance to the Wahhābī attacks, Sulaymān Pasha of Baghdad sent him precious gifts. See also Lorimer, I, i, p. 1007.

26. Lorimer, I, i, p. 1008.

27. *Bombay Govt. Selections*, XXIV, p. 37.

28. Colonel Smith was in charge of the troops, while Captain Wainwright was in charge of the navy.

29. Lorimer, I, i, p. 644.

30.   Lorimer, I, i, pp. 649, 789-790.

31.   For Rahma ibn Jābir, see Buckingham, *Travels in Assyria*, etc., p. 356 ff.

32.   The high fatality among the 'Utūb was caused by explosions of the gun powder on board their vessels caused by direct hits. See Ibn Bishr, I, pp. 154.

33.   Ibn Bishr, I, pp. 154-155.

34.   See Ibn Bishr, I, pp. 165 and 176, where it is stated that 'Abd Allāh Ibn Sabāh died three days after the decease of Su'ūd.

ready to fight a land battle. The Bombay Government, through its agents in the Gulf, must have known of the enmity which existed between the Wahhābīs and the Kuwaitīs at the time, and they did not want to enlist the help of a Wahhābī enemy.

For the same reason, when Mr. Hankey Smith, the British Resident in the Gulf who was stationed at Abū Shahr, asked Captain Wainwright to punish Rahma ibn Jābir, the notorious sea pirate, for his vicious attacks on various vessels sailing in the Gulf, the Captain refused to do so. The reason given was that Rahma was attacking Arab vessels,[30] not British, and that Rahma was a new ally of the Wahhābīs. This distinction between Rahma and the Qawāsim is, of course, unacceptable because piracy is the same whether committed against British or other vessels. Any sea piracy in the Gulf disturbed peace in the Sea.[31]

The question of attacking Rahma ibn Jābir must have been on the mind of Shaikh 'Abd Allāh ibn Sabāh when he sent his offer to the British. For if Shaikh 'Abd Allāh's offer had been accepted, he might have succeeded in either persuading the British to protect the Kuwaitī ships or to be helped if he decided to attack Rahma.

The expected battle between Rahma and the 'Utūb of both Kuwait and Bahrain took place later in 1810, when the Āl-Khalīfa managed to recapture Bahrain from the Wahhābī governor and after the Wahhābīs had persuaded Rahma ibn Jābir, their ally, and Abū-Husain, Chief of Huwayla in Qatar, to attack Bahrain. The Āl-Sabāh and the 'Utūb of Kuwait came to the rescue, and the resulting sea battle was one of the fiercest in the history of the wars among Arab sea powers.

Ibn Bishr,[32] a contemporary of these events, estimated the losses and casualties on the 'Utbī side to have been seven vessels and about one thousand lives. Du'aij, son of Shaikh 'Abd Allāh ibn Sabāh, was among the casualties, as were Rāshid ibn 'Abd Allāh ibn Khalīfa and numerous notables from among the 'Utūb. The Wahhābīs, on the other hand, lost seven vessels and two hundred men. Among their dead was Abū Husain, Chief of Huwayla.[33]

Soon after this battle, the Wahhābīs began to lose their grip on their territories. In 1811, Egyptian forces landed in Hijāz, and soon Madīna, Makka and the remainder of the Hijāz cities and towns fell to the invaders. In 1815, Su'ūd ibn 'Abd al-Azīz, the Wahhābī *Amīr*, died and his son, 'Abd Allāh ibn Su'ūd, succeeded him. Three days after Su'ūd's death, 'Abd Allāh ibn Sabāh, the founder of the State of Kuwait, passed away, survived by his son, Jābir.[34]

CHAPTER VI

JĀBIR IBN 'ABD ALLĀH AND SABĀH IBN JĀBIR 1815-1866

During the rule of Jābir ibn 'Abd Allāh Āl-Sabāh and his son, Sabāh, which lasted for half a century, Kuwait, in its relations with powers in the area, adhered to those same policies as had been formulated by Shaikh 'Abd Allāh with little or no change. In the first two decades of Jābir's rule (1815-1836), two major powers, the British and the Ottoman's, assumed positions of prominence in the affairs of the Gulf. Interaction with Kuwait was caused by two factors. The first was Kuwait's naval capability and the second was the amount of pressure applied by these two powers for the purpose of developing friendly relations with Kuwait.

1. Lorimer, I, i, p. 1006.

2. Especially Vol. 34 of the Company's correspondence. See also R/15/110 for the period 1820-1822.

3. See their reports in *Bombay Govt. Selections*, XXIV, pp. 302-425.

4. See Bruce's report in *Political and Secret Letters*, Vol. 34, p. 134 ff.

Kuwait, the British and the Ottomans

It is rather difficult for the student of history to follow Kuwait's relations with the British in the official records of the English East India Company during the reign of Shaikh Jābir. Lorimer, who made extensive use of these records, states that the mention of Kuwait during the forty years that followed the Company Factory's withdrawal from there in 1795 is scanty.[1] During Shaikh 'Abd Allāh's rule, relations with the British were on a cordial basis. Therefore, the question arises: could it be that Kuwait lost its independence and became a part of a larger country in the neighbourhood?

The reader of those records will notice that, between 1815 and 1836 and even earlier, the primary reports from the Gulf speak of the Qawāsim and their piracy.[2] In addition to that, they deal with the question of slave trade in the Gulf. Since Kuwait did not indulge in piracy or slave trading, it was only natural that reference to it would be a rarity. Another explanation of Lorimer's statement may be the customary reference to the 'Utūb as a combined entity.[3] The most mentioned branch of the 'Utūb in this period was the Āl-Jalāhima of al-Dammām, whose chief was the notorious Rahma ibn Jābir. He was as famous, when it comes to piracy, as the Qawāsim. The Āl-Khalīfa or the 'Utūb of Bahrain were also often mentioned owing to the fact that Bahrain became a centre for handling and dispensing whatever commodities the Qawāsim carried there for marketing.[4] The 'Utūb of Kuwait in the north were, therefore, excluded

5.   See paragraph 74 in
Malcolm's "Report on the
Trade, etc." in Saldanha,
Selections, p. 450.

6.   Philby, *Sa'udi Arabia*,
p. 149.

7.   *Ibid.*

8.   *Ibid.*

9.   Lorimer, I, i, p. 1009.

10.   See Bushire Residency
Letters of the time and also see
Lorimer, I, i, p. 1007.

from those reports because they did not indulge in the practice of piracy. It is also important to remember that until 1800, the British thought of the 'Utūb as one political unity with the Shaikh of Kuwait as the head of that confederation.[5]

Philby, in *Sa'udi Arabia*,[6] has made certain remarks concerning Kuwait and the British when discussing the Egyptian-Turkish occupation of al-Hasā in 1819. He could not understand how the British refrained in that year from occupying the whole eastern Arabian coast from 'Umān in the south to Kuwait in the north when they had a powerful force anchored off the shores of al-Qatīf, the Wahhābī harbour. However, it is very difficult to find out which force Philby was referring to in this connection. He himself states that that force was not mentioned in the Company's records or any official British document. It can only be suggested that he might have been referring to the British warships which were anchored off al-Qatīf after the signing of the 1820 General Treaty of Peace. Their objective was to maintain maritime peace as stated in the terms of that treaty. They were not there to interfere in internal Arab affairs. Philby, however, goes on to say that the British were contented after the Egyptian withdrawal from al-Hasā, with the re-establishment of the Banī Khālid rule in that district.[7]

His reference to Kuwait, which he describes as a town of little importance,[8] is perhaps due to the fact that the Wahhābīs have never been able to add it to their domains.

Lorimer seems to contradict himself when in another section of his *Gazetteer*[9] he states that Shaikh Jābir's relations with the British were always amicable for "Shaikh Jābir of Kuwait had always been regarded as a good friend of the British Government, and in his written correspondence he had never failed in courtesy". However, in the early years of Shaikh Jābir's rule when Bahrain served as a market for the sale of booty of the Qāsimī piratical raids in the Gulf, Kuwait's vessels participated in carrying much of that merchandise from Bahrain to Basra and Abū Shahr,[10] a situation that must have led to tense moments. But since Kuwait did not take part in the depredations, it did not sign the General Treaty of Peace in January 1820, as did other shaikhs whose vessels were active in that type of piracy. The British did not seem to have had any change of heart in their relations with Kuwait, for in 1821, they once again chose Kuwait as a place of refuge for their Basra Factory.

To understand the British move, one must examine the affairs of Baghdād and Basra in the few years that lapsed before the transfer of the Factory to Kuwait during the governorship of Dāwūd Pasha, the *Wālī* of Baghdād.

In 1816, the Ottoman Sultan in Istanbul issued a decree ordering Sa'īd Pasha, Governor of the Province of Baghdād, to hand over the governorship to Dāwūd Effendī (later Dāwūd Pasha) and to return to Istanbul. But because the governorship of Baghdād was considered a matter for the Mamlūk of Baghdād to decide, Sa'īd refused to obey the orders and consequently war raged between the backers of Sa'īd and Dāwūd. It was customary in these disputes for the inhabitants of the Province and its dependencies to take sides; to remain neutral was not customary.

The East India Company's representatives were, therefore, asked to clarify their position. The instructions sent to those residing in Baghdād and Basra from both the Bombay and India Governments were to retain their neutrality.[11] Thus, when Dāwūd made his triumphant entry into Baghdād, the British Resident there, Mr. J. C. Rich, had to suffer the consequences of this policy as did Captain Taylor who was in charge of the Basra Factory.

However, Captain Taylor was under instructions from the Bombay Government, if subjected to pressures from Ottoman authorities, to move the establishment from Basra to either Abū Shahr or Qishm Island where the British had built a military base after the defeat of al-Qawāsim in 1819.[12] When Mr. Rich asked Captain Taylor to leave Basra and shut down the Factory in November 1820, the latter proceeded instead to Muhammara,[13] a newly built city across the Persian border. Apparently, he wanted to stay close enough to Basra in order to observe the developments in the latter city.

Confrontation between Dāwūd Pasha and Mr. Rich led the former to order his forces to besiege the British Political Agency on the 25th of March, 1821. Mr. Rich decided to leave Baghdād and close the Agency. Dāwūd Pasha threatened at that stage to imprison Mr. Rich, who left for Basra soon after this incident and finally reached Abū Shahr on May 15, 1821. From there, he proceeded to Shīrāz where, on October 15 of the same year, he succumbed to the cholera epidemic.

Meanwhile, Captain Taylor decided to move the English Factory not to Muhammara, Abū Shahr or Qishm, but instead to an island near Kuwait. Though the name of that island was not specified, it is believed to have been the Island of Failaka, the largest of Kuwait's islands, and known to vessels of the East India Company since the last quarter of the eighteenth century.

The removal of the Factory to Kuwaitī territory tells much about its position in Gulf politics. A brief account of how the problems between Dāwūd Pasha and the British were solved is essential here because it is pertinent to the history of Kuwait.

First, Elphinstone, Governor of Bombay, asked Strangford, the British Ambassador in Istanbul, to intervene on behalf of Mr. Rich and call the attention of the Ottoman authorities to the injustices done to him and the British. But the problem was not resolved until the Bombay Government addressed a letter directly to Dāwūd Pasha who took immediate action to restore friendly relations with the British. He had ascertained from the letter that not only Baghdād but also Basra would suffer great economic hardships if the English Company diverted its trade with the Gulf to other ports. The letter which contained twelve items[14] called for the respect of previous pledges and agreements relating to trade

11. Lorimer, I, i, p. 1324.

12. Lorimer is inclined to think that the Najdī tribal attacks were carried out at the instigation of the Najdī merchants residing at Basra. See Gazetteer, I, i, p. 1324.

13. Al-Muhammara was founded in 1812. See *Four Centuries of Modern Iraq*, p. 248.

14. Lorimer, I, i, pp. 1329-1330.

15.   *Gazetteer*, I, i, p. 1329.

16.   No mention of this event occurs in Wilson's *The Persian Gulf*, though he talks about the Factory's movement to Kuwait in 1793. Lorimer was also puzzled for he did not know the exact location in Kuwait. Lorimer, I, i, p. 1008.

with the British. Dāwūd's reaction was positive and he instructed his *Mutasallim* at Basra to receive Captain Taylor with due honours on his return.

Captain Taylor left the Kuwaitī territory on the 19th of April, 1822 arriving in Basra on May 1 of the same year after he had accepted Dāwūd Pasha's formal letter of apology. This was the one condition of the twelve items to which Dāwūd Pasha had previously been unwilling to concede. Thus, relations between Baghdād and Bombay were restored, but it was not until 1823 that the official letter reached Bombay. Captain Taylor, on his arrival in Basra, was received with cordiality by the *Mutasallim* and presented with a fully fitted Arabian stallion sent to him especially for the occasion by Dāwūd Pasha.[15]

A few reflections on the position of Kuwait should be considered at this point. Three distinctive matters draw the attention of this historian when attempting to analyze this episode. First are the friendly relations between the British and Shaikh 'Abd Allāh which continued to flourish under his son, Jābir. Second is the choice of Kuwait once more as a safe retreat from which the British Factory could continue its commercial activities. One can, therefore, argue that Kuwait could not have been, in any direct or indirect manner, controlled by Ottoman 'Irāq or other local Gulf powers such as the Wahhābīs. Kuwait could not have maintained its independence without having the economic stamina and military power to defend itself against aggression. The backbone of that defence was its well-equipped fleet, which was put into action ten years later in a similar crisis at Basra. Third is a question as yet unanswered: where was the exact location of the Basra Factory in Kuwait's territory?[16] Failaka Island has been mentioned as a likely site, but it could also have been Kuwait town or another island. Research in the British records did not help in pinpointing that site. Perhaps future investigation will provide a more definitive answer.

The choice of Kuwait by the British as their trading station in the Gulf during this period must indicate how stable and prosperous she was in the political and economic spheres of the region. That Kuwait was not involved in piracy is indicated by the fact that the Basra Factory affair happened in 1820 at the same time the General Treaty of Peace was signed by other shaikhs in the region and not by the Shaikh of Kuwait.

British relations with Kuwait continued to be cordial for quite some time after the return of the Factory to Basra. The only disturbing incident took place in 1839 between Shaikh Jābir and a Lieutenant Edmunds. This matter will be discussed later in connection with the undeclared British war on the Egyptian-Turkish presence in the Arabian Peninsula, after the Egyptians had reached the Gulf shores in 1839. The British were then trying to find out the Egyptian and Ottoman plans for Eastern Arabia and 'Irāq, plans that Kuwait was also anxious to know.

Kuwait and Eastern Arabian Affairs (1835-1840)

Students of the history of Eastern Arabia in the first four decades of the nineteenth century will discover that the British became more active in the region's politics and trade than they had been in the second half of the previous century. Reasons for the change in British attitude can easily be traced to the attitudes of other rival powers. The French, for instance, by their invasion of Egypt in 1798, which lasted until 1801, and by escalation of their attacks on British vessels in the Indian Ocean, were a great source of aggravation to British trade. Egyptian invasion and occupation of Wahhābī territories in the west and east of the Arabian Peninsula, from 1811 to 1840, jeopardized British dominance in the Arabian Gulf on the one hand, and represented a threat to their interests in the Red Sea route to Europe on the other. Thus two arteries of overland trade between India and Europe were threatened. The sea route via Capetown in South Africa was a much longer distance. The Egyptians, under Muhammad 'Alī, conquered not only Arabia, but also Syria which they captured during the third decade of the century. The forces of Ibrāhīm Pasha, son of Muhammad Alī, stopped short of conquering Istanbul, the capital of the Ottoman Empire. The British viewed Muhammad 'Alī's presence in Arabia and Syria as a great threat to their growing political power in India and the Gulf region. This is not to say that Muhammad 'Alī was planning an attack on India under any circumstances, but the presence of his powerful army on the shores of the Red Sea and Arabian Gulf were not to be lightly dismissed.

It is not the purpose of this book to study the rivalry between the British and other powers *per se*, but its effect on Kuwait must be considered. This can only be achieved by briefly discussing British interests on the eastern shores of the Arabian Peninsula; a matter that is linked to British interests in India and the safeguarding of the routes that connect India and Great Britain. Although it is necessary to compare the value of using either route - Red Sea or Gulf - it must be pointed out that both routes proved to be of equal importance at various periods of history and consequently were used by the British as well as by others.

The Egyptian occupation of Arabia and Syria also had its effects on the prosperity of Kuwait. Indeed, the fact of a power struggle in the Gulf between the British and Ottomans, which resulted from the Egyptian-Turkish invasion of 1811, was bound to interfere in the growth of the shaikhdoms of Eastern Arabia for a lengthy period following the withdrawal of the Egyptian forces in 1839-1840. The earlier intervention of the Egyptian General Ibrāhīm Pasha into the affairs of Eastern Arabia was of a temporary nature for, after the destruction of al-Dir'iyya in 1818, he returned to Hijāz early the following year. On the other hand, when Muhammad Khurshid Pasha attacked Najd in 1838, he did not stop his advance at Riyād, the new Wahhābī capital, but marched on to al-Hasā until he reached the western shores of the Gulf and beyond. Bahrain was added to the new administration and rumours were that the

Egyptians were intending to march northward to 'Irāq in order to tighten their grip on the entire eastern Arabian coast of the Gulf. It is in this context that Kuwait's relations with the Egyptians should be studied.

Kuwait and the Second Egyptian Expedition in Eastern Arabia (1836-1839)

A study of Kuwait's place in the Egyptian strategy between 1836 and 1839 will be better served by referring the reader to materials kept at the Egyptian National Archives (formerly 'Ābidīn Palace Archives), since these contain the original letters exchanged between Muhammad 'Alī and his generals and administrators in Arabia. A study of this kind has not, to this author's knowledge, been attempted by other writers. Contemporary British documents present the British point of view as do reliable British sources dependent on British archives.

In order to appreciate and understand the role that Kuwait played in the history of the Gulf region during this period, Khurshid Pasha's objectives will be discussed first. When he proceeded eastward from Madīna in Hijāz at the head of a well equipped army, and brought the towns of al-Qasīm and other districts of Najd under their control, it became quite apparent that the Egyptian army had come this time to Eastern Arabia to implement a new policy and execute new ambitious plans. The plan for reoccupation of Najd and al-Hasā was going to be followed by an even more zealous scheme. Muhammad 'Alī must have decided to include Ottoman 'Irāq in his territories in order to join his forces in Arabia and Syria by land. Though this was not the declared intention of Khurshid Pasha, his deeds testified to it. But to march on Basra and Baghdād[17] from al-Hasā would be to use a strategy in opposition to that of the previous Ottoman expeditions in al-Hasā, such as Thuwaynī's expedition of 1789 and 'Alī Pasha's of 1798. This would require an army marching by land and naval power to transport soldiers, ammunition and food. In this connection, the shaikhship of Kuwait was to be taken into consideration, for, as pointed out earlier in this book, Kuwait, by virtue of its location, wealth and fleet, had been indispensable to previous Ottoman expeditions sent to al-Hasā. The British presence in Gulf waters must also have been taken into account, but this question belongs to Ottoman and British imperial history.

Khurshid Pasha and Shaikh Jābir

A look at contemporary Turkish and Arabic documents and in a reading of Khurshid's letters to Muhammad 'Alī in Egypt in the 'Abadīn archives verifies what has been said of the Kuwaitī position and its future importance in Khurshid's plans.[18] He had learned that Kuwait was ideally situated between the occupied territories of Najd, al-Hasā and 'Irāq and could assume a major role in supplying his army with the information essential to the conquest of 'Irāq. Furthermore, because of the Najdī origin of its people and relation to other Najdīs living at Basra and neighbouring Zubair, Kuwait would be able to supply his army with the intelligence required in preparation for and following the invasion of 'Irāq. If we remember that "the Egyptians, on reaching the coast of the Arabian Gulf in al-Hasā in 1838, sent an agent to reside at Kuwait, nominally to purchase supplies",[19] but who was actually a news writer, then we can understand how intelligence from Kuwait could be channelled. Through that agent, Khurshid must have learned much about the Kuwaitī fleet and its potential.

'Abd Allāh al-Faddāgh

An examination of some of the Egyptian documents may, therefore, illustrate Kuwait's role in the history of Eastern Arabia at the time of the second Egyptian occupation. One of the first documents to draw our attention was a letter of 'Abd Allāh al-Faddāgh of Kuwait to Faisal ibn Turkī, the Wahhābī *Amīr*. This letter was forwarded to Cairo as an enclosure in a letter from Khurshid Pasha to Muhammad 'Alī Pasha in July 1838. This enclosure,[20] though important in itself, becomes more important from comments made in it by Khurshid Pasha.

'Abd Allāh al-Faddāgh wrote to "Faisal Āl-Su'ūd" telling him of the movements of 'Alī Pasha, *Wālī Wālī* of Baghdād near Muhammara and Basra, and relating that the *Wālī* had sent a messenger to him (Faisal) via Kuwait. He hoped that Faisal would answer 'Alī Pasha who would then forward certain "Firmāns" [declarations] attacking Muhammad 'Alī's administration in Arabia, which should be read to the people of Najd and other parts of Arabia under Egyptian occupation. The letter also contained tribal news of al-Muntafiq and 'Anaza, and mentioned gifts of clothes on their way from Baghdād to Faisal.

Khurshid Pasha's comments reveal that he had employed certain informants to keep track of Faisal's connections with Baghdād and Istanbul. It was one of those persons who intercepted al-Faddāgh's letter. It was through those informants also, that Khurshid found out that al-Faddāgh was a well-to-do Kuwaitī merchant who had access to the Pasha of Baghdād's court.[21]

New Rush of Espionage Activities

It seems both from what al-Faddāgh wrote in his letter to Faisal, and from other letters kept in the Egyptian National Archives and similar letters in the India Office Records, that Kuwait and parts of Eastern Arabia were used extensively by Egyptian, 'Irāqī and British intelligence agencies. This is reminiscent of the French emissaries sent to that same area before the end of the eighteenth century.

Although none of these letters hint at the involvement of Kuwaitī authorities on behalf of any other powers, they serve to provide more

19. See Lorimer, I, i, p. 1009.

20. See a letter from 'Abd Allāh al-Faddāgh to Faisal Āl-Su'ūd, enclosure to the Turkish document No. 66, Case 264. The letter is dated 17th March, 1837.

21. Address sent from 'Unay'za in Najd and dated July 2nd, 1838, No. 66, Case 264.

22.   Enclosure to letter No. 76
from Hennell to Willoughby
dated 12th July in *L/P & S, Vol.
14. See also letters dated 29th
April and 7th May, 1839, Nos.
37 and 41 for Hennell's letter to
Khurshid, dated 29th April,
1839.*

information about Kuwaitī history. If it is remembered that knowledge of Kuwait in the first half of the nineteenth century was scanty, the materials in those letters become immensely valuable.

Khurshid's letter, for instance, points out Kuwait's importance as a centre for gathering information from both 'Irāq and Najd. This was because of its location on the routes which led to 'Irāq in the north, Najd in the east and al-Hasā in the south. It is, most probably, because of this geographical position that an Egyptian news writer was appointed by Khurshid and stationed there to purchase food and ammunition for the Egyptian soldiers as well as fodder for their camels and horses. It is written in the British sources that an Egyptian, when attending the Shaikh's *majlis* (audience), was placed on the right of the ruler, a sign of honour and respect. The Ottoman Pasha of 'Irāq must have assigned his own spies and informants in Kuwait to collect intelligence on the Egyptian army in Eastern Arabia. It seems too that Shaikh Jābir managed to play his cards very well with rival powers in the area.

Hennell and Shaikh Jābir

Captain Hennell, British Resident in Abū Shahr, sent a letter to Khurshid Pasha through Shaikh Jābir warning him not to extend Egyptian occupation in Eastern Arabia beyond the borders of al-Hasā.[22] The historian can read much in Hennell's letter, but we shall limit the analysis to the scope of this book, i.e. how it affected the history of Kuwait. This becomes clearer when it is seen how Shaikh Jābir handled the situation.

In May, 1839, Hennell sent two consecutive missions to Kuwait whose main objective was to check out rumors that Khurshid was planning to extend his territories in Eastern Arabia to 'Irāq in the north and beyond al-Hasā borders in the south.

Dr. MacKenzie, physician of the Abū Shahr Residency, sailed on board the "Emily" on a fact-finding mission to Kuwait, Basra and Muhammara on May 5, 1839. He was followed two days later by the "Clive" whose Captain carried a letter addressed to Khurshid Pasha, which was to be handed over to Shaikh Jābir whom Captain Hennell asked to deliver it personally to Khurshid. Hennell believed that Shaikh Jābir, acting as an intermediary, would have the prudence to warn Khurshid of the dangerous situation which would develop if the latter contemplated extending the Egyptian sphere of influence beyond the borders of al-Hasā. This letter to Khurshid was a copy of one Hennell had previously sent to him via al-Qatīf on April 29, 1839. Shortly thereafter, Hennell heard that Shaikh 'Abd Allāh Āl-Khalīfa had signed an agreement with Khurshid's envoy (Muhammad Rif'at) to Bahrain on the 7th of May of the same year. Bahrain was, of course, beyond the boundaries of al-Hasā, not to the north or south but to the east. The British were indignant at 'Abd Allāh's attitude. His signature finally cost him the loss of his title when he was removed from the shaikhship of Bahrain.

In the second week of May 1839, Shaikh Jābir, in a friendly gesture to Hennell, informed the latter that Khurshid was in Riyād and that his Egyptian agents at Kuwait were busy buying supplies for their forces in al-Hasā. The Shaikh did not mention in this letter anything concerning Khurshid's intentions to attack Basra.[23] The reader of the India Office documents and National Egyptian Archives will soon discern that Hennell continued a steady flow of correspondence with Khurshid and at the same time kept his agents at al-Hasā busy monitoring the Egyptian army's movements.[24] This however, concerns British-Egyptian relations more than it does those between Kuwait and Egypt.

Kuwait, Supplier of Food and Ammunition

Kuwait was seldom excluded in any of Khurshid Pasha's dispatches from Najd or al-Hasā. It was always mentioned in connection with supplies, whether these were food for soldiers, fodder for animals or ammunition for the army.

Khurshid's need for those supplies always seemed to have been very pressing. This was perhaps due to the fact that his army was so far away from Madīna in Hijāz that it was impossible to receive supplies from there. For this reason, he decided first to depend on al-Hasā after its conquest, and later on Kuwait, Basra and Abū Shahr. This led him to send Muhammad Effendī to Kuwait to ensure that necessary supplies bought there would be forwarded to al-Hasā. Muhammad Effendī was sent, not only as a news agent as some British sources indicate,[25] but also as food purchaser and forwarder stationed at Kuwait.

As a matter of fact, Khurshid tried to solve the problem of supplies before reaching al-Hasā and before the defeat of Faisal ibn Turkī.[26] This predicament was aggravated by the problem of how to finance his purchases since the necessary cash was not available. The shortage in ammunition[27] was felt when the towns of Dilam and Zumayqa[28] were attacked. There was growing concern that his army might not be able to accomplish its goal because expectations of enough food for at least another year were not being met. It was during the siege of those two towns that Khurshid Pasha decided to send a representative to Kuwait and Basra to borrow money for the purchase of those commodities. He was hoping that British[29] trading vessels in those ports might then sell his representative the badly needed food supplies.

On the 18th of January, 1839, Khurshid wrote to Muhammad Alī requesting that two Egyptian vessels be sent from Jidda to al-Qatīf to assist in conveying food supplies from Basra and Kuwait.[30] Khurshid must have been optimistic at that time because, in another letter dated January 20, 1839, immediately after the fall of Dilam, he wrote expressing great doubt about the possibility of obtaining any supplies

23. See *L/P& S/14* for letter No. 87, dated 16th July, 1839 from Hennell to Willoughby. See also enclosure of letter No. 53, dated 10th May, 1839 for Shaikh 'Abd Allāh's letter to Hennell.

24. See appendices to L/P & S/12. In Appendix 41, see a letter dated 9 February, 1839 from Khurshid to Hennell enclosed in Hennell's letter to Willoughby dated March 2, 1839.

25. This was Lorimer's opinion of Muhammad Effendi, *(Gazetteer, I, i, p. 1009)*, *who was followed by Bayly Winder*, *(Sa'udi Arabia*, p. 128). Had those two authors read the correspondence between Khurshid Pasha and Muhammad 'Alī Pasha concerning the grave food and fodder situation in the Egyptian army, Lorimer and Winder could have changed their thinking about the nature of Muhammad Effendi's job.

26. Muhammad Khurshid to Muhammad 'Alī, Dilam (in Najd), 16th September, 1838, No. 143, Case 264.

27. What is meant is the shortage of ammunition necessary for the rifles and the guns, which came as a result of the stubborn resistence of Dilam and Zumayqa.

28. The letter was sent to Muhammad 'Alī before the capture of Dilam. See Khurshid to Muhammad 'Alī, 16 September, 1838, translation of the Turkish letter No. 143, Case, 264.

29. What is meant were, perhaps the vessels that carried the British flag, but were owned by Indians and others.

30. Turkish document No. 58, Case 264.

31.   Dilam, 20th January, 1839, No. 64, Case 264.

32.   This letter was sent from Riyād on April 2nd, 1839. But Muhammad Effendī was sent earlier on 27th of January, 1838. See Muhammad Khurshid to Husain Pasha, document No. 1, Case 267.

33.   Khurshid to Husain Pasha, Tharmada (Najd), May 16th, 1839, No. 156, Case 266.

34.   Khurshid to Husain Pasha, 26th February, 1839, No. 110, Case 267. See also footnote 36.

35.   *Ibid.*

36.   Enclosure in Khurshid to Muhammad 'Alī Pasha, 16th June, 1839, No. 7, Case 267.

through Basra and Kuwait. It seems the governments of those two towns had instructed their merchants not to cooperate with the Egyptian emissary. In another attempt, Khurshid sent his chief medical officer, who was an old friend of the French Consul in Basra, on a special mission to that place to borrow two thousand sacks (money bags) from him and then buy and ship the supplies to al-Qatīf, but Khurshid Pasha was not sure of the mission's success.[31]

Other dispatches[32] from Khurshid Pasha give the details of certain items that were sought. Heading the list were rice for the soldiers and barley for the horses which were exported from Persia. Apparently the Persians often refused to sell, but even if they did sell, they refused to ship what was bought to al-Hasā.[33]

This entire dilemma was finally resolved when Kuwait, bought and transported these commodities to al-Hasā.[34] Khurshid Pasha, in one of his messages, pointed out quite clearly how both Basra and Baghdād were angered by the Kuwaitī participation in solving those problems for the Egyptian army, by supplying them not only with food for the soldiers and fodder for their horses, but also carrying those commodities on board their vessels to the ports of al-Hasā.[35] In May 1839, a battalion from the Ottoman garrison at Basra defected to Kuwait explaining to the ruler that they wished to join Khurshid Pasha. Led by Captain Mahmūd Aghā al-Mōradī, they originally numbered five hundred soldiers but only seventy reached Kuwait due to the lack of transportation.

Al-Mōradī wrote a letter to Muhammad 'Alī Pasha which was enclosed in a dispatch from Khurshid Pasha to Muhammad 'Alī Pasha, both dated June 16, 1839. In his letter, al-Mōradī says, "...we forced a few boats [at Basra] to convey us to Kuwait, and I went to see Muhammad Effendī, who is in charge of the purchase of food on behalf of Khurshid Pasha. And while Muhammad Effendī was planning for us to stay a few days at Kuwait, a special messenger arrived from Basra carrying a letter to ibn Sabāh [Jābir ibn 'Abd Allāh ibn Sabāh], the *Amīr* of Kuwait, asking him to imprison us and send us back to Basra. But he did not pay any attention to that letter, and said that he could not lay his hands on us, and then the mentioned *Amīr* put me, Muhammad Effendī and the soldiers who were with us, on board a vessel ... and when our vessel was about three hours or four away from Basra, news reached us from the other soldiers, who agreed [previously] to join us, asking whether they could be accepted to join the Egyptian military service ..."[36] Al-Mōradī attached, to his letter, a list of the names of those soldiers.

This document shows how Kuwait offered every possible and feasible assistance to Khurshid's army. Its political significance will be discussed in the following section.

Political Implications and Difficulties at Kuwait

The Egyptian occupation of al-Hasā and the Egyptian agreement of May 7, 1839 with the ruler of Bahrain put the British in the Gulf in a tense mood. If the Egyptians, who so far had had good relations with Shaikh Jābir, managed to persuade him to sign a treaty along similar lines as those of his cousins, the 'Utūb of Bahrain, all of the eastern coast of Arabia, from al-Hasā in the south to Kuwait in the north, would be lost to British influence. Such agreement could jeopardize their position in the southern region of the Gulf because the Egyptians were in communication with the ruler of Masqat and might claim authority over al-Qawāsim, who were subjects of the Wahhābīs and recognized their authority until the destruction of al-Dir'iyya in 1818.

Lieutenant Edmunds in Kuwait (October 1839)

The British had always regarded Shaikh Jābir as a "good friend" but in October 1839, an event took place at Kuwait which could have weakened those good relations. On October 30, Lieutenant Edmunds, the Assistant Resident at Abū Shahr, arrived at Kuwait on a special mission from the Resident, Captain Hennell. His mission was to find out if Kuwait was willing to welcome the establishment of a British line of post across the desert from Kuwait to the Mediterranean. The British war vessel fired the usual salute in honour of the Shaikh after it had anchored in the waters of Kuwait Bay. The salute was not acknowledged and Edmunds waited in the vessel for three days before he was able to communicate with the Shaikh.

After Edmunds' return to Abū Shahr, both he and Captain Hennell explained this unusual behaviour of the Shaikh, to have been due not to ill-will, but principally to a desire to mislead the Egyptian agent at Kuwait as to the nature of his relations with the British. Therefore, they considered that Jābir's conduct did not indicate any change in his friendly policies towards the British.

Political Asylum in Kuwait

If the British tolerated the attitude of Jābir towards Edmunds, so also did the Egyptians. Earlier in the same year, some of the most wanted men in the Wahhābī camp, such as 'Umar ibn 'Ufaisān, the Wahhābī general in al-Hasā, and Wahhābī tribes like al-Duwaish, sought refuge in Kuwait. Protection of refugees seeking political asylum in his country was a policy that had been adopted earlier by Shaikh 'Abd Allāh ibn Sabāh. This can, therefore, be looked upon as an indication of self-confidence, an outcome of Kuwait's independence from foreign powers. It corroborates the fact that Kuwait, if necessary, was prepared to defend itself against more powerful neighbours.

Merchant Fleet

This defence depended not only on the walls of the city, but also on bedouin tribes in its neighbourhood and a merchant fleet equipped with the necessary guns comparable to other Arab fleets of the time.

As to Kuwait's position between 1815 and 1839, one can safely state that it managed to maintain a neutral policy with regard to the struggling Wahhābīs and Egyptians. Relations with the British and even with the Pasha of Baghdād continued on good terms. How Kuwait fared during the remaining years of Jābir's rule and Sabāh's after him will be the subject of the following chapter.

CHAPTER VII

INTERNAL DEVELOPMENT AND EXTERNAL AFFAIRS OF KUWAIT 1815-1866

Reference has already been made in the previous chapter to Kuwait's relations with the various powers in the Gulf region, especially the Wahhābīs, the British and the Ottoman Provinces of Irāq and Egypt, between 1815 and 1840. These references were in certain cases brief. Jābir was the Shaikh of Kuwait during those years, and he continued to rule until his death in 1859. However, towards his later years, his son, Sabāh, shared with him that responsibility, not as joint ruler, but as his father's delegate on certain occasions. Though Chapter VI examined many external problems which Jābir was forced to solve, it did not deal with other aspects of life, such as the structure of society, commercial growth and relations with certain areas in the neighbouring Arab countries. The period between 1840 and 1859, the remaining years of Jābir's rule, is still to be taken up as are the years of Sabāh's rule between 1859 and 1866.

It should be pointed out here that the two regimes of Jābir and Sabāh will be treated as one, because Sabāh participated in the administration of the country before actually becoming ruler in 1859. One must add that the historian of this period will not gain as much from what is written in local traditional sources, or in Arabic materials in general, as he will from European sources, documents and travellers' reports.

Travellers' accounts are usually of special importance to historical works. Jābir's and Sabāh's reigns are very well documented in the works of three of these travellers: the first, Buckingham (1818) was in the environs of Kuwait when Jābir first took office[1]; the second was Stocqueler (1831)[2] and the third, Pelly (1863)[3] came before the end of Sabāh's rule.

To form a clear idea and picture of the town and its people one must study the information concerning Kuwait as reported by each of these travellers, and compare it with other information available in Arabic and foreign sources.

Buckingham speaks of Kuwait as a great seaport in the north-western corner of the Gulf with a sizable population.[4] The city was walled, as it had been before, with the sands creeping upon it from the neighbouring desert. The people of Kuwait, he reports, are in the main merchants who are brave and freedom loving, for Kuwait, unlike other cities and countries in the region, has always kept its independence. Buckingham was writing about Kuwait while in the vicinity of Basra. The second traveller, Stocqueler, not only stayed in Kuwait for a few days

1. J. S. Buckingham (1786-1855), travelled between England and India and published a number of extremely useful books on travel and other subjects. The book quoted in this history is his *Travels in Assyria, Media and Persia* etc., London, 1829. See his biography in *The Dictionary of National Biography*, vol. XV, pp. 202-203.

2. J. H. Stocqueler (1800-1885) spent twenty years in India. He did much journalistic work. He also compiled several works including *Fifteen Months' Pilgrimage through Khuzistan and Persia*, (2 vols., London 1832). For a fuller biography see *The Dictionary of National Biography*, Vol. XVIII, pp. 1282-1283.

3. Lewis Pelly (1825-1892) was born in England, 14th November 1825. In 1841 he was appointed to the Bombay army of the East India Company as ensign. He became captain in 1856, major in 1861, Lieutenant-Colonel in 1863, Colonel in 1871 and finally Lieutenant-General in 1863. In 1862 he became the Political Resident in the Persian Gulf. His journey in 1865 to Riyad, the Wahhābī capital of Najd, was one of his most notable exploits. See a fuller biography of Pelly in *The Dictionary of National Biography*, Vol. XV, pp. 720-723.

4. Mr. J. H. Stocqueler made the journey from Bombay to Kuwait in 1831 in a Kuwaitī *baghla*. He gives the following interesting and informtive report

of the vessel itself and the Kuwaiti seafaring character: Buggales are large boats averaging from one to two hundred tons burthen; they have high sterns and pointed prows, one large cabin on a somewhat inclined plane, galleries and stern windows; they usually carry two large latteen sails, and occasionally a jib; are generally built at Cochin and other places on the Malabar coast, and are employed by the Arab and Hindoo merchants on the trade between Arabia, Persia, and the Indian coast. The Nasserie, on which I engaged a passage for the sum of one hundred and fifty rupees, was manned by about forty or fifty natives of Grane, or Koete, on the western side of the Persian Gulph, and commanded by a handsome Nacquodah in the prime of manhood. The sailors acknowledged a kind of paternal authority on the part of this commander, and mixed with their ready obedience to his mandates a familiarity quite foreign to English notions of respect, and the due maintenance of subordination. The Nacquodah took no share in the navigation of the vessel while it was crossing to Muscut, this duty being entrusted to an old Arab who understood the use of the sextant, and who was so correct in his observations that we made Ras-el-Lad within an hour of the time he had predicted we should. Stocqueler, *Fifteen Months Pilgrimage, Vol. I*, pp. 1-3. The *baghla*, according to Low, was a vessel of great size, sometimes of 200 or 300 tons burden, and carrying several guns. *Baghlas* were long-lived; one of them which had been built in 1750 was still sailing in 1837. See Low, *History of the Indian Navy*, I, p. 169. "The Arab dhow is a vessel of about 150 to 250 tons burthen by measurement, and sometimes larger...Dhows may be distinguished from baghalahs by a long gallery projecting from the stern, which is their peculiar characteristic." See *Ibid.* About 1876 the dhows disappeared from the Gulf. *Ibid.*

5. Stocqueler, *Fifteen Months Pilgrimage*, I, p. 18.

6. *Idem.*

in 1831, but also travelled on one of its ships from Bombay in a journey that started on the 18th of February, 1831 and ended at Kuwait on April 4. Stocqueler was on his way to Basra in continuation of his journey to England, but because no boat going directly to Basra was available, he spent four days in Kuwait, thus allowing him enough time to observe the town and its people.

Stocqueler's Description of Kuwait

Stocqueler's Kuwaitī vessel[5] was too large to sail up the Shatt al- Arab to Basra. He was told by the Kuwaitī captain (*nōkhadha*) that a smaller boat would take him to Basra, and hence came the fortunate delay at Kuwait. Stockqueler writes,

> ...it was the wish of the owner of the buggala (*baghla*) that we should go on shore and stay a few days, until a vessel could be got ready for Bussourah (Basra)...... After breakfast I went on shore, and was conducted to the owner's house. Passing two or three courtyards, I reached an apartment arched in the centre, where the owner and his two brothers were seated smoking ...... After taking coffee, milk, bread and hulwah, I left Abdul Assan's (al-Hasan) (the owner's) house to take a stroll about the town.

> Koete, or Grane as it is called in the maps, is in extent about a mile long, and a quarter of a mile broad. It consists of houses built of mud and stone, occasionally faced with coarse chunam, and may contain about four thousand inhabitants. The houses being for the most part square in form, with a courtyard in the centre, (having the windows looking into the yard), present but a very bare and uniform exterior, like, indeed, all the houses in the Persian Gulph...The streets of Kuwait are wider than those of Muscat or Bushire, with a gutter running down the centre.

The wall that surrounded the town "on the desert face" was more for show than protection, "as it is not a foot thick". That wall had three gates "and two honeycombed pieces of ordinance" protecting each of the three gates. There were no plantations within or outside the wall, and the water was far from sweet.[6]

Stocqueler added that Kuwait was governed by a shaikh who possessed no armed force and who levied a duty of two percent upon all imports.

"The circumstance which struck me as most singular in Koete (Kuwait)", said Stocqueler, "was the exact uniformity of costume among all ranks and ages, and the fact of there being no natives of any other country resident in the place."[7]

It is clear from Stocqueler's observations that he was fascinated by the town and its people and that he did not encounter any difficulties which might have caused him displeasure. However, comments on what he wrote will be made after looking at the third traveller's remarks.

Colonel Pelly in Kuwait

Pelly paid his first visit to Kuwait in 1863 when Shaikh Sabāh ibn Jābir was its ruler. Since Colonel Pelly was the British Resident in the

Gulf, his remarks carry more weight than Buckingham's and Stocqueler's. He was also more familiar with other ports in the Gulf. These remarks can be traced in three reports which Pelly wrote in 1863 and 1865.[8]

When Pelly visited Kuwait for the first time on March 3, 1863, he was met at Jahra by Shaikh Mubārak, the second son of the ruler, Shaikh Sabāh. Just before he reached Kuwait town on March 4, he was met by Shaikh Abd Allāh, the eldest son and heir apparent, who accompanied him to the town gate on their way to "a very good home", which had been prepared for Pelly and his companions. "Scarcely had we entered it", says Pelly, "when Shaikh Subbah himself came." This description of Pelly's reception indicates that to a certain degree it was run according to protocol. Pelly then proceeds to give a brief description of Shaikh Sabāh which is not found in Buckingham or Stocqueler. "He is," says Pelly, "a fine, stout, hale, old man, upwards of 80 years of age, rough in appearance and manner, but kind at heart." Pelly remarked that the town was "compact of about 15,000 inhabitants, built on a promontory of loose sandstone covered with sand." For the most part, healthful conditions existed in the town for "there is little or no opthalmia at any time, and very little intermittent fever. There has been no small pox for long." However, there were some sicknesses for Pelly continues to say, "The chief diseases seem to be the syphillis and gonnorrhoea brought from Bombay, and the consequent secondary syphilis and stricture."[9]

The governmental system of Kuwait and administration of justice were the subject of comments made by Pelly.[11] "The Government is patriarchal," says Pelly, "the Sheik managing the political, and the Cazee [*Qādī*] the judicial departments. The Sheik himself would submit to the Cazee's decision." Punishment was rarely inflicted. "Indeed, there seems little government interference anywhere, and little need of an army." Pelly, in admiration of how the Shaikh ran the affairs of the country, retold the following remark which the Shaikh had made to him:

> When my father was nearly 120 years old, he called me and said, "I shall soon die. I have made no fortune, and can leave you no money; but I have made many and true friends, grapple them. While other states around the Gulf have fallen off from injustice or ill-government, mine has gone on increasing. Hold to my policy, and though you are surrounded by a desert, and pressed by a once hostile and still wandering set of tribes, you will flourish."

It was, indeed, because of this policy followed by successive rulers in the Sabāh family that their country continued to prosper; this policy that had been fostered by Abd Allāh I ibn Sabāh, grandfather of Sabāh ibn Jābir about whom Pelly was writing.

The traditional hospitality of the Arabs was reflected in another comment made by Pelly when he noticed that Shaikh Sabāh left the main gates in the wall of the city open after sunset to allow the bedouins to enter and have an evening meal inside. The only condition enforced upon them when entering the gates was to lay their arms outside to insure the town's safety. The huge, rich banquet which was offered these guests was

7. *Ibid.*, p. 20.

8. These reports are:
a) "Recent tour around the northern portions of the Persian Gulf,77 in *Transactions of the Bombay Geographical Society*, XVII, (1863-1864), pp. 111-140.
b) "Remarks on the Tribes, Trade and Resources around the shore line of the Persian Gulf," *Transactions of the Bombay Geographical Society*, XVII, (1863-64), pp. 32-112.
c) "A visit to the Wahhābī Capital, Central Arabia", in *Journal of the Royal Geographical Society*, XXXV, (1864-1865), pp. 169-191.

9. See Pelly, "Recent Tour, etc.", pp. 118-121.

10. Pelly, "Remarks on the Tribes, etc.", p. 74.

11. Cf. Qinā'ī, *Safahāt*, p. 14,
     and al-Rashīd, *History of
     Kuwait*, II, pp. 9-10.

12. See al-Rashīd, II,
     pp. 18-19.

also shared by the poor inhabitants of the city. Pelly was told by the Shaikh that this was a tradition kept up by the ruling family.

Shaikh Jābir was not mentioned by Pelly since his death occurred before Pelly's visit. However, the practice of administering justice by a *Qādī* and the act of hospitality mentioned by Pelly were old institutions in Kuwait and are referred to as such in the works of local historians. In fact, both al-Rashīd, in his *History of Kuwait*, and al-Qinā'ī, in his *Safahāt min Tārīkh al-Kuwait*, deal more extensively with the hospitality of Jābir than with Sabāh. Tradition in Kuwait, even today, has it that Jābir was their most generous ruler.[11] The reader of these works will be surprised by the minimal amount of information they offer on Sabāh's rule, probably because it lasted for just seven years, in contrast to his father's reign of forty-five years.

To sum up, therefore, what local and foreign authors wrote about the internal state of affairs in Kuwait, one can surmise that prosperity here can be attributed to the preservation of peace within the community. This was achieved by the mutual respect between Jābir and Sabāh, the rulers, and the ruled. This respect, according to al-Rashīd, was rooted in the shrewdness manifested by rulers in acting to protect the rights of the prominent merchant community against the greed of foreigners.[12] Al-Rashīd cites a case where long overdue debts were owed to a member of Āl-Badr, the Kuwaitī business family by some of the Muntafiq tribe of Irāq. Upon intervention by Shaikh Jābir ibn Abd Allāh, these debts were settled immediately.

Justice and peace at home should indicate that neither Jābir nor Sabāh met with great difficulties in trying to solve problems with their neighbours. They managed to handle disagreements that resulted from the Egyptian occupation of Najd and al-Hasā and to maintain a friendly association with the British. Our concern in the remainder of this chapter will be some minor, though sensitive problems with Ottoman Irāq which arose from time to time.

Kuwait's Policy Towards Irāqī Ottoman Subjects

Kuwait's relations with Irāqī Ottoman subjects can be examined under three headings. The first deals with Kuwait's attitude towards the neighbouring town of al-Zubair, the second with large confederate tribes such as al-Muntafiq and the third with the *Wālī* [Governor] of Baghdād in those instances when he sent his forces or some Irāqī tribes on missions against Persian territories.

Kuwait and al-Zubair

Many families living in Kuwait had relatives in al-Zubair. Enmity between these towns was caused by jealousy which jeopardized their relations. Misfortune and adverse circumstances in one area often meant prosperity for another area.

At al-Zubair, like Kuwait, the majority of the population were of Najdī stock. Also like Kuwait, al-Zubair prospered during the second half of the eighteenth century and first half of the nineteenth when desert caravans, in their journeys between the Gulf and Syria, in order to avoid payment of duties at Basra,[13] and travelled via Kuwait or Zubair. The prosperity of Zubair caused consternation at Basra whose *mutasallim* was waiting impatiently for an opportunity to intervene in the former's affairs.

The occasion arose when enmity between two influential families over leadership of the town reached a critical point necessitating interference by the *mutasallim*. Al-Zubair lacked the political leadership which could keep peace among all its families who originally came from Najd. The affairs of al-Zubair have been included in this history since Kuwait had become entangled in that internal strife.

The two houses competing for leadership in Āl-Zubair were Āl-Thāqib and Āl-Zuhair. When rivalries such as these existed, other houses in the town and outside tribes assisted in the fight that usually accompanied the resultant dissension. Since the Āl-Zuhair were at that time in the seat of leadership, the large and influential tribe of al-Muntafiq involved in a blood feud with the Āl-Zubair, joined the side of the Āl-Thāqib. However, the real reason behind al-Muntafiq's participation in this case was the *mutasallim* of Basra, whose city environs were attacked repeatedly by the Zubair people. In fact, certain authors claim that they besieged Basra at an earlier date and forced its *mutasallim* to flee.[14]

Apparently, the enmity between Āl-Zuhair and Āl-Thāqib was one of long standing, and whenever either lost to the other, the loser sought refuge at Kuwait. Ibn Bishr, the reliable Wahhābī historian, tells in his history of Najd[15] how the Āl-Zuhair conspired with the *mutasallim* of Basra to rob the Āl-Thāqib of their leadership of Āl-Zubair in 1827. After the success of that plot, Alī ibn Yūsuf Āl-Zuhair became the head of the town, while the defeated house of Āl-Thāqib sought refuge at Kuwait.[16] The Āl-Zuhair remained in power until the deterioration of its relationship with the al-Muntafiq. Hence the new plot which ended the supremacy of Āl-Zuhair. In this last battle Kuwait's role was a significant one in that it took the side of Āl-Thāqib and their allies, the Muntafiq.

Ibn Bishr, when chronicling the events of 1833, says: "The Muntafiq Chief Īsā ibn Muhammad ibn Thāmir and ... the Āl-Thāqib attacked the town of Zubair and after its encirclement laid siege to it ...The siege lasted a long time, and they were helped [in the siege] by the Chief of Kuwait, Jābir ibn Abd Allāh ibn Sabāh, and this siege lasted for seven months." After those months, the town surrendered because it was hard pressed for food, gun powder and bullets.[17] Ibn Bishr adds that all of the Āl-Zuhair were killed, including their Chief and his brothers.

According to what ibn Bishr has said, Kuwait took a crucial step when her fleet blockaded the waterways to Zubair thus preventing the inhabitants from obtaining fresh supplies of food and ammunition.

It is told that a survivor of the Āl-Zuhair family sought refuge at

13. See Chapter 9 below, pp. 193-197.

14. See in a footnote in Lorimer, I, i, p. 1312 where he quotes a comment made by Arnold Wilson that the people of al-Zubair together with some Najdī tribes attacked al-Basra and forced its *mutasallim* to seek refuge with the Banī Ka'b Arabs at Muhammara.

15. See Ibn Bishr, II, pp. 23-35.

16. See *Ibid*.

17. *Ibid*. p. 49.

18.   Lorimer, I, i, p. 1008.

19.   Al-Rashīd, II, p. 15.
Al-Sūfiyya estate is described by
the author as a very large piece
of date plantation.

20.   Lorimer, I, i, p. 1008.

21.   Nāmiq Pasha in his second
term in office. His first term was
for one year, 1852-1853, and the
second lasted from 1861-1868.

22.   Lorimer, I, i, p. 1013.

Kuwait, after Āl-Thāqib had become the new ruling house. The main sources dealing with this incident disagree as to his name. Lorimer,[18] an authority on the region's history, calls him Ya'qūb Āl-Zuhair, while al-Rashīd,[19] the Kuwaitī historian, refers to him as a member of Āl-Zuhair. In any event, the important result of his stay at Kuwait was the question of al-Sūfiyya, a parcel of land that he had sold to Shaikh Jābir of Kuwait but which was later claimed by others from among the Āl-Zuhair who apparently had escaped the massacre of 1833. Arabic sources, however, state that Sūfiyya, in the Ma'āmir district of Shatt al-Arab, was presented as a gift to the Shaikh of Kuwait in appreciation of his kind reception of this refuge. Lorimer does not agree with these sources and clearly states that the land was bought by the Shaikh - "a circumstance which was to give rise to many troubles in the future."[20]

The Sūfiyya Dispute

In 1866, trouble developed over the possession by Shaikh Sabāh of that estate which was bought by his father, Shaikh Jābir, in 1836. This property was sequestered by a Turkish *Qā'immaqām* [representative] on the basis of a claim by the Āl-Zuhair that the vendor had been the owner of a share and not of the n 100e Sūfiyya. At the same time, Shaikh Sabāh was required to expel from other lands owned by him at the Island of Fāo some cultivators who had immigrated from Persian territory. It should be recalled that the Turkish officials from the start showed strong prejudice in favour of the Zuhair claimants. Abd Allāh ibn Sabāh, the eldest son of the ruler of Kuwait who went to Basra as his father's agent in the case, narrowly escaped being thrown into jail upon his refusal to make a payment amounting to the value of seven years produce which the Ottoman authorities deemed the plaintiffs were entitled to receive.

Eventually, the dispute was settled by the *Wālī* [Governor] of Baghdād in favour of the Shaikh of Kuwait.[21] The decision of the Governor of Basra in favour of the Shaikh was apparently made for various reasons. Some writers think that the Governor wanted to win Abd Allāh over to the Turkish side, and suggest that the Governor, Nāmiq Pasha, even offered him the title of *Qā'immaqām*, which he declined. Nevertheless, the proceedings of the Turks in this case were regarded by the inhabitants of Kuwait as attempts to cause a confrontation with Zubair. It seems that they had anticipated a conflict and according to reports by the British Agent at Basra, the people of Kuwait were prepared to a man to abandon their town rather than submit to Turkish rule. Lorimer suggests that the final order of Nāmiq Pasha, upholding the Kuwait Shaikh's title to Sūfiyya, was perhaps due to a report that Shaikh Sabāh, "with the object of attacking Zubair if the decision should go against him, had obtained a promise of countenance and armed support from the Wahhābī *Amīr*."[22]

In addition to this legal matter with Zubair, Kuwait had had other problems with Basra whose courts tried to jail Abd Allāh ibn Sabāh, as explained above. However, Kuwait's relations with the Ottoman mutasallims of Basra had at times been amicable and in several instances, those mutasallims even sought refuge at Kuwait when pressured by the Pashas of Baghdād who exercised control over them.

23. See *Ibid.*, pp. 1006 and 1313.

24. See Longrigg, *Four Centuries of Modern Iraq*, p. 271.

The Siege of Basra (1831)

The question of offering asylum in Kuwait to political personalities drew the Shaikh into the arena of inter-tribal politics, not only within Kuwait, but also as far as the neighbourhood of Zubair and Basra. In and around Basra, tribal- *Mutasallim* relations were for the most part unstable. The *Mutasallim* was the representative of a central government, and the tribal Shaikhs were heads of nomadic tribes whose allegiance shifted between *Mutasallim* and Pasha, or even from one state to another. A classic example of this was the Banī Ka'b tribe whose loyalty had always vacillated between Ottoman and Persian authorities, dependent on which was the stronger power in the region.

This practice was apparently discontinued in support of the deposed Dāwūd Pasha, Governor of Baghdād, a matter in which Kuwait became involved. On the 21st of February, 1831, it was learned in Baghdād that the Ottoman Sultan had declared Dāwūd Pasha a rebel and outlaw, and named Alī Ridā Pasha the new Governor. Since Dāwūd Pasha was on good terms with the Arab tribes of Banī Ka'b and al-Muntafiq residing near Basra, they decided to show their support for him by staging an attack on that place. Shaikh Thāmir of the Banī Ka'b approached Shaikh Jābir of Kuwait and requested him to join them in the siege.[23] It is interesting to note that even Azīz Aghā, the *Mutasallim* of Basra under Dāwūd Pasha, sought refuge with the Shaikh of the Banī Ka'b also, when Alī Ridā's new appointee for the post of *Mutasallim* arrived. While the first stages of the siege of Basra were begun in support of Dāwūd Pasha and against its Ottoman representative, in this case, Azīz Aghā, it continued after that on behalf of Azīz and against the new appointee. This may seem paradoxical, but such were tribal politics at that time. When Azīz Aghā found out that Alī Ridā was going to win the battle for Baghdād's governorship, he shifted his allegiance to Alī Ridā's side and the chiefs whose forces were besieging Basra sent messages to him expressing their faith in Azīz Aghā as a good *Mutasallim*.

The siege of Basra lasted for several weeks[24] but apparently ended favourably because Azīz Aghā was reinstalled in his former position. Local Kuwaitī historians refer to this event as the instance in which Shaikh Jābir intervened to restore a *mutasallim* to his previous office. It could not have been possible, however, in the author's view, for Shaikh Jābir to have restored Azīz Aghā had not Alī Ridā, the new Pasha of Baghdād, been willing to do so.

25. Lorimer, I, i, p. 1313.

26. *Ibid.* p. 1006.

Invasion of Muhammara (1837)

It seems, however, that Shaikh Jābir ibn Abd Allāh and Alī Ridā Pasha solidified the relationship between Kuwait and Baghdād, and when Alī Ridā prepared for an attack on Muhammara, the stage was set for cooperation between the two men.

It had become clear after Shaikh Thāmir of the Banī Ka'b had encouraged Dāwūd Pasha in his attempt to continue as Governor of Baghdād in 1831 that Alī Ridā Pasha would punish Thāmir sooner or later. However, some historians are inclined to believe that Alī Ridā's attack on Muhammara could be attributed to other reasons. Muhammara was a rather new town compared to Basra, but in 1812, after eighteen years of existence, it became a great rival to Basra. Much of the merchandise that formerly went to Basra was directed to Muhammara and Kuwait as the result of an outbreak of cholera in 1821[25] and the loss of trade caused by the struggle between Alī Ridā Pasha and Dāwūd Pasha in 1831.[26]

In all probability, the only way to restore Basra to its commercial prominence in the Shatt al-Arab, in Alī Ridā Pasha's view, was the destruction of its rival, Muhammara. In order to achieve this objective in the most efficient manner, Alī Ridā decided that Muhammara should be cut off from Shatt al-Arab by a sea blockade. Otherwise, the besieged town might receive supplies which would help it to resist the invasion successfully. Hence, the Kuwaitī fleet became crucial for Alī Ridā's plans. Shaikh Jābir honoured the request for help. Thus Muhammara was invaded by Alī Ridā's forces and capitulated to the attackers who were merciless, not only capturing the town, but also destroying it completely. When Shaikh Thāmir saw the destruction, he fled the area and sought refuge with the Shaikh of Kuwait. Though Shaikh Jābir was fighting on the Ottoman side this time, he offered Shaikh Thāmir asylum. Eventually, Shaikh Thāmir went back to Fallāhiyya, his capital town, after offering to pay homage to the Ottomans rather than the Persians. It is noteworthy to mention that the destruction of Muhammara by the Ottomans left Kuwait unrivalled in sharing with Basra the commercial prosperity of the northern region of the Arabian Gulf and in winning the support of a major power in the Gulf area, the Ottomans.

Kuwaitī-Wahhābī Relations (1815-1866)

Now that we have discussed the relations between Kuwait and its neighbours in the north - Zubair, Basra and Muhammara - it is time to examine her relations with the Wahhābīs of Najd and al-Hasā.

It might be useful to recall that relations with the first Wahhābī state which came to an end in 1818 with the destruction of Dir'iyya, its capital, were undoubtedly not friendly. Wahhābī raids were carried out on Kuwait and its surrounding area quite frequently in the last decade of the 18th century and even later. But the reigns of Shaikh Jābir ibn Abd

Allāh and his son, Sabāh (1815-1866), witnessed a lull in the history of the Wahhābī state because of the impact of Egyptian-Turkish rule in Arabia between 1810 and 1841, and the length of time it took the Wahhābīs to recover after Egyptian withdrawal in 1840.

The threat of Wahhābī intervention looming over Kuwait at the beginning of the 19th century was temporarily allayed, first because the Wahhābīs were occupied with the invading Egyptians in their western province of Hijāz and secondly, because with the destruction of Dirʿiyya in 1818 their government was in abeyance from that date until 1824. The resurgence of the Wahhābīs between 1824 and 1838 was of brief duration, for soon the Egyptians, under Khurshid Pasha, captured their cities in Najd and al-Hasā and the Wahhābī *Amīr* Faisal ibn Turkī was forced to surrender to them.

Kuwait's attitude towards the Wahhābī *Amīrs* and generals who fled to its territories was characterized by utmost hospitality and generosity. Umar ibn Ufaysān, Faisal's general in al-Hasā, fled to Bahrain when the Egyptians defeated the Wahhābī armies under his leadership. From there he sought refuge in Kuwait with Shaikh Jābir in 1839.[27] In 1841, after Egyptian withdrawal from al-Hasā and their appointment of Khālid ibn Suʿūd as Governor, a war ensued between Khālid and Abd Allāh ibn Thunayyān Āl-Suʿūd, in which the latter was defeated and sought refuge in Kuwait.[28] However, a year later, Ibn Thunayyān fought and subdued Khālid ibn Suʿūd, who, thereupon, fled to Kuwait where he was offered asylum by Shaikh Jābir.

Jābir and his son, Sabāh, after him, observed strict neutrality in the Suʿūdī family strife yet Kuwait was prepared to receive any member of that family with all due respect. It was pointed out in the previous chapter that Khurshid Pasha, the Egyptian Commander in al-Hasā, had placed an Egyptian Agent in Kuwait and, apparently on similar lines, the Wahhābī *Amīr*, Faisal ibn Turkī, on his return to power, had appointed a Wahhābī Agent in Kuwait in 1851.[29] This move indicates that Kuwaitī-Wahhābī relations continued to be harmonious. Though the nature of the work carried out by this new Egyptian Agent was specified as news writer and as supervisor of buying and shipping supplies to the Egyptian armies in al-Hasā, nothing is known of the actual nature of the work of the Wahhābī Agent. The hospitable reception of the Wahhābī *Amīrs* at Kuwait continued until the termination of Sabāh's rule in 1866. Abd Allāh ibn Faisal (1865-1871), who ruled after his father Faisal ibn Turkī, appointed an Agent in Kuwait[30] just as his father had before him. When Pelly visited Kuwait in 1863 and 1865, he noted that Kuwaitī-Wahhābī relations were cordial.[31]

These observations are a general evaluation of the fifty-year reign of Jābir ibn Abd Allāh and his son, Sabāh, insofar as peaceful relations with the Wahhābīs were maintained. In that half century, Kuwaitī rulers followed in the footsteps of Abd Allāh I ibn Sabāh who combined leniency with force in achieving his ends. Thus, Jābir and Sabāh gave Kuwait and its population peace which produced prosperity which is in

27. Ibn Bishr, the Wahhābī chronicler, remarked that while the people of al-Hasā proceeded, after the surrender of Faisal to Khorshid Pasha, to pay their homage to the Egyptian commander, ʾUmar ibn ʾUfaysān refused to do so and proceeded to Bahrain instead. See *ʾUnwān al-Majd*, II, p. 41, and also, Philby, *Saʾudi Arabia*, pp. 181 and 184.

28. See Lorimer, I, i, pp. 1005 and 1011.

29. *Ibid.*, p. 1111.

30. *Ibid.*, p. 1011.

31. See Pelly, "Remarks etc.", p. 74.

32.   See Lorimer, I, i, p. 1013.
      See also Landen pp. 79-80.

itself power and strength. All of her people were assured equality of justice. Kuwait's independence in this period was secure because it was prepared to defend it and the tribes were ready to stand behind Jābir and his son whenever called upon for help by one of its friendly neighbours. Examples of this are numerous. Satisfactory and open relations between the rulers and their subjects served as a basis for planning similar strategies with neighbouring tribes and powers. The years after 1840 witnessed a more flourishing trade due to the introduction of the steamship which facilitated communications, postal services and sea freight.[32]

Kuwait after this half century was prepared for further advancement in the aforementioned fields. These matters and others will be discussed in the following chapter which will cover the rule of Shaikh Abd Allāh II ibn Sabāh ibn Jābir and his brother, Muhammad, who ruled between 1866 and 1896.

CHAPTER VIII

ABD ALLĀH IBN SABĀH IBN JĀBIR, 1866-1892
MUHAMMAD IBN SABĀH IBN JĀBIR, 1892-1896

Abd Allāh ibn Sabāh ibn Jābir, referred to as Abd Allāh the Second, assumed command upon the death of his father, Sabāh. He was then fifty years of age and mature enough to lead a country at a time when the region was not politically stable. The Suʿūdī family, which governed the mainland of the Arabian Peninsula, was left divided among itself after the Egyptian withdrawal in 1840, and continued so for some time to come. By the time Abd Allāh II came to power in 1866, the rivalry between Abd Allāh ibn Faisal and his brother Suʿūd had reached the point that led in 1871 to the return of Ottoman rule in Najd and al-Hasā. The Ottomans had been waiting for this opportunity. The British on the other hand were not in favour of interfering in the internal affairs of Arab Shaikhs on the mainland; they viewed the Ottoman attempt to make a comeback with a watchful eye, to say the least, since their own policy in that part of Arabia was to maintain the *status quo*, for as long as possible.

Before getting involved in the political aspect of Abd Allāh's era, it might be helpful to assess his qualities and characteristics. These qualities, rarely mentioned in contemporary European documents dealing with his attitude towards the Ottoman expedition to al-Hasā in 1871, can be deduced from the writings of the two Kuwaitī historians, al-Qināʿī and al-Rashīd, who lived during and after Abd Allāh's rule. Both of them speak about his personality and al-Qināʿī gives the impression that Abd Allāh's quiet nature was characterized by decency and fairness. He was not a haughty or arrogant man, and one would never think, while in his presence, that he was the *Amir* of the country. Al-Qināʿī adds that Abd Allāh was loved by all his subjects.[1]

Al-Rashīd described Abd Allāh as a person who did not give his audience an impression of how intelligent he actually was, and whenever faced by a crisis, he always found a clever way out.[2]

These few words about Abd Allāh's personality do not illustrate these rare qualities which will be evident from the way he handled the affairs of the Ottoman expedition to al-Hasā, passing through Kuwait.

The Ottoman Expedition to al-Hasā (1871-1873)

Previous chapters of this book recount how the Ottomans added al-Hasā to their empire in 1555 after acquiring Syria in 1516 and Irāq in 1534. They also explain how the Banī Khālid had replaced the Ottomans

1. See *Safahāt*, p. 2.

2. Al-Rashīd, II.

3. See above, pp. 46-47.

as governors of al-Ḥasā in the 17th and 18th centuries. After the establishment of the Banī Khālid, the Ottomans ruled eastern Arabia in name only. It seems that Midhat Pasha, who was appointed Governor of the Province of Baghdād in 1869, anticipated the reassertion of Ottoman rule in al-Ḥasā. However, because of an inadequate transport system on both land and sea and the lack of local popular backing for the Ottomans, this desire for a return to power proved to be almost impossible.

The opportunity presented itself when the ruling house of the Āl-Suʿūd, soon after the death of Faisal ibn Turkī, divided into two opposing camps; one camp supported Abd Allāh ibn Faisal and the other, Suʿūd ibn Faisal.

Struggle between Suʿūd and Abd Allāh

Although this struggle between the two brothers pertains more to Najd than to Kuwaitī history, it cannot be considered unrelated to the history of Kuwait. Kuwait was on the borders of Najd and al-Ḥasā, both Suʿūdī territories, and has always been within the reach of the Āl-Suʿūd, whether they came as raiders, as in the 1790's[3], or as refugees whenever forced out of their capital, Riyāḍ. An example of the latter situation occurred when the Āl-Suʿūd were routed from Najd by the invading Egyptian forces in the first half of the 19th century

Kuwait, interjacent between Ottoman Irāq in the north and the Suʿūdī territories to the east and south, was bound to be affected by the change in relations between those two powers. Such a change came as a result of the internal strife which took place between Abd Allāh ibn Faisal and his brother Suʿūd soon after the former succeeded their father upon his death in 1865.

Suʿūd assembled the bedouins of Najd around him, while the settled section of the Najdīs remained loyal to Abd Allāh ibn Faisal. When the bedouins, under the leadership of Suʿūd defeated Abd Allāh's forces, the latter sought refuge at Ḥāʾil, in northern Najd, with Ibn Rashīd who, at this time, was contemplating extending his authority over Najd. Upon his accession, the Ottomans bestowed Abd Allāh the title *Qāʾimmaqām* of Najd, which meant that he was ruling Najd and al-Ḥasā in their name. Obviously, the Ottomans continued to consider al-Ḥasā as one of their provinces.

Thus when Abd Allāh wrote to Istanbul seeking assistance from the Sultan in regaining his position in Riyāḍ, the Ottomans did not want to lose this golden opportunity which would re-establish them in al-Ḥasā, and possibly in Najd as well.

By 1869, Midhat Pasha, one of the most capable administrators of the time, was appointed Governor of Baghdād, and was himself anxious to recapture al-Ḥasā from the Āl-Suʿūd; this manoeuvre would extend the Ottoman territories eastward following their loss of territory in the Balkans and on the Russian borders. Instructions were sent from Istanbul to Baghdād asking Midhat Pasha to prepare his forces for an expedition to al-Ḥasā to help Abd Allāh regain the territory for which he had been appointed a *Qāʾimmaqām* by the Sultan in 1865.

The British and the al-Hasā Expedition

Midhat's preparations, however, aroused the fears of the British in London and India who were intent on maintaining peace in the area. Convinced that he was about to convey men and arms in war vessels, they became very apprehensive and concerned about the "peace" in the waters of the Gulf, for which they had been working and often fighting, since the early 1800's. The General Treaty of Peace signed in 1820 by the Shaikhs of the Pirate (Trucial) Coast was followed by other Maritime Treaties, the last one of which was signed in 1861 by the Shaikhs of the Trucial Coast, and in turn by Bahrain and Musqat.

The British were also afraid that the Trucial Shaikhs and Bahrain might join Su'ūd, especially when they learned that Shaikh Abd Allāh ibn Sabāh, Shaikh of Kuwait, supported Abd Allāh ibn Faisal. What the British feared most was that this expedition of Midhat Pasha might be looked upon by the Shaikhs of the Gulf as a challenge to British supremacy over the waters of the Arabian Gulf, which they had worked very hard to establish. These fears were revealed in British representatives' correspondence from Istanbul and Baghdad.[4] It may be interesting to note that Kuwait was not a signatory to the 1861 Maritime Treaty along with other shaikhdoms; Kuwait had not signed that treaty or any other until the 1899 Exclusive Agreement between Mubārak Āl-Sabāh and the British. However, Shaikh Sabāh ibn Jābir ibn Abd Allāh signed, on behalf of his father, an earlier maritime truce in 1841. The reason for not signing the 1861 Maritime Treaty is not clear, but it could possibly be that by not doing so Kuwait avoided any misunderstanding of her position by the Ottomans whose territory in Irāq was nearer to Kuwait than to other Arab Shaikhdoms of the Gulf. This question, together with Kuwait's participation in Midhat's expedition, will be discussed following consideration of the expedition routes.

The Expedition Route

The meeting point for the forces, composed of three thousand Turkish soldiers and one thousand five hundred horsemen from the Muntafiq Arab tribe of southern Irāq, was Basra, in southern Irāq. From there, the expedition planned to proceed by sea and land where all forces would meet at Kuwait. Those horsemen who marched by land carried with them nine cannons. At Kuwait, the Kuwaitī fleet was prepared to carry Turkish soldiers while more Kuwaitī horsemen joined the military cavalry and marched with them to the next meeting point for both sea and land forces which was Rās Tannūra in al-Hasā. The first Ottoman forces left Basra on April 20, 1871 on a warship which had on board from 400 to 500 soldiers. Another group followed on April 23. Arriving at Rās Tannūra on May 26, both marine and land forces proceeded to their first target, the fortified town of al-Qatīf. When this town refused to surrender, it was subjected to a dual attack - the Kuwaitī

4. See the correspondence sent from both cities to London and to the Government of India.

fleet by sea, and the cavalry by land. In a battle that lasted for three hours with the Kuwaitī fleet showering it with bomb shells, the town surrendered to the attacking armies on June 3 of the same year. A declaration, whose text will be discussed later in this chapter, was read to the inhabitants by Nāfiz Pasha, officer in charge.

The expedition continued its march southward to attack al-Dammām which on June 5 surrendered without offering any resistance.

Early in July, the expedition resumed its march southward to al-Hasā oasis (Hufūf) which was reached in two weeks. The Ottomans lost four hundred soldiers because of the hardships the army met on its way to that desert town. Another thousand of those soldiers fell victim to disease as well as others who were left behind to guard al-Qatīf and al- Uqair. At that stage the expedition's march towards al-Riyād became an impossible task; but the war raging around Riyād between the forces of Abd Allāh and his brother Su'ūd continued until the defeat of the former, who then sought refuge at al-Hasā oasis with the Ottoman forces.

At this desperate stage of the battle against the Su'ūdī forces, Shaikh Abd Allāh ibn Sabāh proceeded to Dōha in Qatar hoping to persuade Muhammad ibn Thānī to join ranks with the Ottoman expedition. His efforts were not successful. Muhammad refused to declare himself an ally of the Ottomans, but his son Jāsim ibn Muhammad ordered the Ottoman flag to fly on its mast at Dōha during the visit despite his father's protests. Jāsim, by doing so, was most probably hoping to call upon the Ottomans in a final showdown with the Āl-Khalīfa in Bahrain in order to legitimize the seizure of their territories on the Qatar Peninsula.

Midhat Pasha in al-Hasā

Towards the end of 1871, Midhat Pasha decided to travel to al-Hasā to inspect his forces stationed at al-Qatīf, al-Dammām, al- Uqair and al-Hasā oasis. A few days before his arrival, and in continuation of the internal struggle among members of the Su'ūdī family, Abd Allāh ibn Turkī, the uncle of Su'ūd ibn Faisal, had forced Su'ūd out of Riyād. The latter sought refuge among the bedouins who were encamped between Qatīf and Hufūf, and started raiding the caravans which were carrying food and ammunition to the Ottoman army. Soon after he was thrown out of that area and left for Qatar where he sought refuge among its bedouins.

When Midhat reached al-Hasā and landed at al-Qatīf, he found that both Su'ūd and his brother Abd Allāh were powerless. He therefore declared to the people of al-Hasā and Najd in al-Qatīf that the rule of the Su'ūdī dynasty was over and that he had appointed Nāfiz Governor *mutasarrif (Sanjaq)* of the district *(Sanjaq)* of al-Hasā and Najd.

On hearing Midhat's declaration, Abd Allāh ibn Faisal, who was at Hufūf in al-Hasā, fled to Riyād and from there sent messages to the Sultan in Istanbul stating that he was still ready to be a loyal subject of the Ottoman empire, if he (the Sultan) would recognize him as a ruler of

Najd and al-Hasā.

Midhat Pasha, meanwhile, returned to Baghdād on December 18, 1871, and the Ottoman rule in al-Hasā continued until March 1874, when Farīq Pasha, the Ottoman *Mutasarrif*, handed over his powers to the most influential Shaikh of the Banī Khālid, Barrāk ibn Uray'ir, to govern in his stead. Barrāk was chosen because he belonged to the famous tribe of Banī Khālid of al-Hasā[5] and because his brother-in-law, Nāsir Pasha Āl-Sa'dūn, Chief of the Muntafiq Irāqī tribe, guaranteed his loyalty to the Ottomans. Farīq Pasha left behind a small police detachment to keep law and order on the borders between Najd and al-Hasā.

This ended the expedition of 1871 by which Midhat Pasha hoped to reinstate Ottoman rule in the Arabian peninsula. Kuwait participated fully and in good faith, and her position in this situation will be examined in the next section.

Kuwaitī's role in the Ottoman Expedition, 1871-1873

The role of Kuwait in the 1871 expedition to eastern Arabia can be studied under two major divisions: first, her part in the success of the expedition (namely its role within the march to al-Hasā) and second, the reasons behind her participation in light of the fact that Kuwait was the only shaikhdom in eastern Arabia to fully participate on the side of the Ottomans. A note of interest here is the fact that on two previous occasions the Ottomans had led expeditions through Kuwait - Thuwaynī in 1787 and Kaya Alī Pasha in 1798.[6]

As far as the first, it was clear from the routes the expedition followed that Kuwait was the starting point for sea and land forces which proceeded from Basra on their march southward to al-Hasā. This brings up the questions: why did the Ottoman ships stop at Kuwait before continuing on to Rās Tannūra? When would the al-Muntafiq cavalry join the horsemen of the Kuwaitī tribes? It could be that those ships were not carrying enough ammunition and also that they wanted to make certain the cavalry of the Muntafiq tribes and other foot soldiers were not left far behind, since most of them planned to make their journey on board the three hundred Kuwaitī vessels that the ruler put at the disposal of the expedition.[7]

What made it possible for the Ottomans to use the facilities at the harbour of Kuwait was the fact that Shaikh Abd Allāh ibn Sabāh wholeheartedly endorsed this operation, and because it was almost impossible to use other ports under the control of Shaikhs having treaty relations with Britain. Kuwait was free of any such obligation towards the British who could not interfere in its internal or external affairs. Hence Shaikh Abd Allāh sent his brother Mubārak as the head of the Kuwaitī cavalry force. The British, as a matter of fact, were apprehensive that some of the Shaikhs, like those of Trucial Umān or of Bahrain might join Su'ūd's side against the Ottomans. For this reason, the British Resident in the Gulf hastened to remind those Shaikhs of the 1861 agreement which forbid them from becoming involved in sea or land warfare, even if

5. It is interesting to see that the Ottomans returned the Shaikhs of the Banī Khālid to power, like the Egyptians had do.￼ before when they captured al-Dir'iyya in 1818. This has been done despite the fact that the Banī Khālid had forced the Ottoman rulers out of al-Hasā early in the seventeenth century.

6. Al-Rashīd in his work *Tārikh al-Kuwait*, discussed Kuwaitī participation in the 1871 expedition at length. See Al-Rashīd, II, pp. 29-30.

7. See above, p. 85.

8.   See Appendix No. V for
1861 treaty between Bahrain and
the British Government.

9.   Al-Qatīf was one of the two
major ports in al-Hasā, the other
being al-'Uqair. Al-Qatīf was
fortified against sea attacks by
pirates and land attacks by
bedouin raids.

10.   See in *Letters from the
Persian Gulf*, Vol. 21, a letter
dated 20 July 1872, pp. 141-147.

11.   See *Ibid.*, vol. 20, a letter
dated Bahrain, 13th February,
1872, p. 543.

attacked by foreign armies, because the responsibility of their defence was entrusted to the British forces in the Gulf region. [8]

Abd Allāh's Direct Role in the War

Abd Allāh's role in the fighting was not a minor one. He joined the expedition as a commander of the large Kuwaitī fleet and was the first to use its guns against the besieged town of al-Qatīf.[9] Had it not been for this bombardment by the Kuwaitī fleet, al-Qatīf obviously would not have surrendered in a mere three hours.

In relation to this, a question arises as to why the Ottoman warships refrained from participating in the bombardment. The answer lies in reports relating to the political movements that preceded accounts of the progress of the expedition. Because the Ottomans were unwilling to jeopardize the maritime peace imposed by Britain in the area, the Sultan and the Pasha promised their warships would not be used in the war against Su'ūd or any shaikh in the war zone. Kuwait, which was not a party to the above-mentioned treaty of 1861, was under no such obligation especially since the expedition was not directed against those who had signed it.

When Su'ūd's resistance broke down in Riyād, and, as already mentioned, he sought refuge among the bedouins of al-Hasā, launching raids on the Ottoman communication lines between al-Qatīf and al-Hufūf, Nāfiz Pasha sent Abd Allāh ibn Sabāh on a mission to Dōhā to seek the agreement of its ruler in stopping those raids. Although Muhammad ibn Thānī did not give a positive response, the idea of asking 'Abd Allāh to talk to Ibn Thānī was in a way a reminder to the latter that his enemies, the Āl-Khalīfa of Bahrain, were the cousins of the Āl-Sabāh of Kuwait, and that Bahrain, which was ruled by the Āl-Khalīfa, was still considered by the Ottomans a part of their Empire. This reminds one of how Khurshid Pasha claimed Bahrain as Ottoman territory in 1838 because it was a part of the Wahhābī lands that were conquered by Khurshid on the instructions of Istanbul.

Naturally, the Ottomans' position in the second half of the 19th century in Arabia was not as strong in the first half *vis-a-vis* the British who had signed the 1861 treaty with Bahrain, the terms of which guaranteed the defense of Bahrain against foreign attacks.

Another issue pertinent to the 1871 Ottoman expedition is whether Abd Allāh was expecting to be paid for his assistance in the war. Some sources suggest that Abd Allāh must have put a price on his participation.[10] Kuwait was expected to be paid, at least, for the expenses which by all indications were enormous. The role of the Kuwaitī fleet must have been crucial, not only to winning the war in its first stages, but also in continuing services to the Ottoman forces left as garrisons in the occupied seaports of al-Hasā. This fleet not only conveyed subsistence for those garrisons, but also transported troop reinforcements.[11]

Whether Abd Allāh did receive any financial reward or

reimbursement for his expenditure, though it seems probable, cannot be confirmed. But what can be verified is that the three brothers, Abd Allāh, Mubārak, and Muhammad participated personally in the expedition. This may be taken as a sign of the heavy Kuwaitī commitment in the war effort. While Abd Allāh was commanding the Kuwaitī fleet (April, 1871), a fighting squadron led by Mubārak, on instructions from Abd Allāh, proceeded alongside the Muntafiq cavalry to al-Qatīf. At a later stage, towards the end of 1872, Muhammad left Kuwait for al-Qatīf and al-Hufūf. The *modus operandi* of the three brothers in this war required a great deal of thought on the part of Shaikh Abd Allāh as to the future of Kuwait as an independent entity. But before this problem is considered, a return to Nāfiz Pasha's declaration at al-Qatīf is necessary.

Nāfiz Pasha's Declaration at Qatīf

In Nāfiz Pasha's address to the people of al-Qatīf, he stated that Najd and its dependencies were an integral part of the Ottoman Empire. He added that Su'ūd had overthrown the legitimate ruler, Abd Allāh, the *Qā'immaqām* of Najd, and that the purpose of the expedition was to reinstate Abd Allāh to his former position. Su'ūd, according to Nāfiz Pasha, would be pardoned if he gave himself up and offered apologies for his misdeeds to Istanbul; otherwise, he, and all those who helped him, would be pursued and killed.

This is the essence of Nāfiz Pasha's address to the people of al-Qatīf upon its capture. However, Midhat Pasha, when he arrived for his inspection tour at al-Hasā, said something totally different. He stated that the rule of the Āl Su'ūd had terminated and that Nāfiz Pasha had been appointed to the Governorship of al-Hasā and Najd which were designated as one *sanjaq*.

It seems apparent, therefore, that the purpose of the expedition was not to reinstate the legal heir who had been overthrown by his brother, but rather to banish both brothers and place Najd and al-Hasā under the control of Istanbul. Could Abd Allāh ibn Sabāh have been aware of this Ottoman strategy on the eve of the preparation for Midhat's expedition in 1871 or even earlier? Conversely, did this have any direct effect on Abd Allāh's attitude towards the Ottoman designs which might have affected Kuwait had it not shared in the expedition wholeheartedly?

The Effects of al-Hasā Expedition on Kuwait

In all likelihood, the attitude of the two strong powers, the Ottomans and the British, towards the Shaikhdoms in the Gulf region forced Abd Allāh to take the line of action that we have already seen. The British, who were not pleased with Kuwait's participation in the Ottoman expedition, had been asked by the Trucial chiefs to enlist Kuwait's assistance in the war. However, the Ottomans were not in a position to exert any pressure on Kuwait because, unlike the Trucial chiefs, their

12.   This kind of friendship
recalls Mr. Manesty's letters to
Shaikh 'Abd Allāh ibn Sabāh in
1787 and 'Abd Allāh's answer.
See Appendix No. I.

13.   See in *Letters from the
Persian Gulf*, vol. 20, a letter
from Ghulām Husain in Bahrain
to Pelly dated 13th February
1872, pp. 546-547.

ally, the ruler of Kuwait, was not bound by treaties with the British which would enable them to interfere in his country's affairs.

In dealing with the Ottomans, Kuwait had always had good friends at the courts of the Governors of Basra and Baghdād who kept the rulers well informed of the intentions and plans of the Ottoman Governors [Pashas].[12] Though it is impossible to confirm that Abd Allāh ibn Sabāh had any advance knowledge of Midhat Pasha's plans concerning the entire coast of eastern Arabia, from Kuwait in the north to Qatar in the south, it could be conceived, judging by Kuwait's support of the expedition, that Abd Allāh knew what to expect had he refused to aid the Ottoman expedition. Remarks made at first by Nāfiz Pasha in al-Qatīf, and later by Midhat Pasha during his tour of inspection in 1871 prove that from the onset of the expedition, it was Ottoman intention to restore complete control over that eastern coast of Arabia.

Thanks to Abd Allāh's foresight, Kuwait's fate was not the same as that of Najd and al-Hasā, for Kuwait managed to remain independent not only of the Ottomans but of the British as well.

While Abd Allāh ibn Faisal was granted the title of *Qā'immaqām* by the Ottomans on his succession to the office of *Amīr* of Najd, Abd Allāh ibn Sabāh was not granted that same honour until later in November 1871 when Midhat Pasha, on his tour of inspection to al-Hasā, stopped at Kuwait. Abd Allāh was then rewarded with that title of honour for his services during the 1871 expedition. The title of *Qā'immaqām* in this case should be viewed as an honour conferred on a friend for special services and not as an administrative title.

Relations between Baghdād and Kuwait during the first ten years of Abd Allāh's rule were not always cordial. In February 1872, Abd Allāh ibn Sabāh was warned of rumours circulating in Baghdād that the Ottomans were planning to replace the Āl-Sabāh with others because of their sympathies with the Āl-Su'ūd.[13] The reason for this was apparently the refusal of the ruler of Kuwait to send to al-Hasā a few vessels requested by Farīq Pasha who had persuaded the authorities of Baghdād that Abd Allāh ibn Sabāh had influence on the Āl-Su'ūd. Farīq Pasha was further aggravated when Mubārak ibn Sabāh, who had left al-Hasā for Kuwait, refused to return there once again.

It would have been very difficult for Kuwait to avoid trouble with Baghdād, had it not been for the discreet and masterly politics exhibited by Shaikh Abd Allāh ibn Sabāh at those critical moments in the history of Kuwait. The ties between the Āl-Sabāh and the Āl-Su'ūd, mentioned briefly above, will be examined in somewhat greater detail.

Abd Allāh II and the Āl-Su'ūd

The Arab tradition of welcoming people who seek political asylum has been observed throughout Kuwaitī history. One may recall the cases of Thuwaynī, Chief of the Muntafiq Irāqī tribe and Mustafā Aghā, the *mutasallim* of Basra, who were protected by Shaikh Abd Allāh ibn Sabāh in the late 1780's. During the reign of Abd Allāh II and between 1871 and 1874, Kuwait received the three Su'ūdī brothers who alternated as rulers of Najd and al-Hasā, namely Abd Allāh, Su'ūd and Abd al-Rahmān, sons of Faisal ibn Turkī. Their reception by Abd Allāh ibn Sabāh must have been embarrassing to Kuwait because Kuwait had helped the Ottomans in their endeavours to restore their rule over the Su'ūdī territories in Najd and al-Hasā. However, the three Su'ūdī Chiefs frequented the neighbourhood of Kuwait either as visitors or as guests of its ruler.

Local Kuwaitī traditional historians refer to this matter frequently. On the other hand the same references indicate that some Arab tribes sought refuge at Kuwait when they were pursued by the forces of Su'ūd ibn Faisal who were trying to punish them. Such incidents could stand as testimony to the independence of Kuwait.

Official British sources give specific examples and dates for certain such incidents. Lorimer, for instance, states that Abd Allāh ibn Faisal sought refuge in Kuwait after being defeated by his brother Su'ūd in 1872,[14] despite threats to Kuwait by the latter. That threat was realised when Su'ūd staged an attack which was repelled by Mubārak ibn Sabāh's forces.[15]

Kuwait maintained a position of firm neutrality in relations between the Ottomans and the Āl-Su'ūd. During the period Abd Allāh ibn Faisal resided in the vicinity of Kuwait, Abd Allāh ibn Sabāh sent him two letters that had arrived from the Ottoman authorities in Baghdād. The first offered him the office of *Qā'immaqām* in Umān, which he refused to accept.[16] The second, which he also rejected, offered him the governorship of al-Qatīf and al-Hasā Oasis on the condition that he pay taxes to Istanbul.[17]

Kuwait and Bahrain

In similar circumstances, Kuwait played host to Muhammad Āl-Khalīfa of Bahrain, who, when driven from the Island by his brother Alī as a result of internal family strife, sought refuge at Kuwait with his cousins the Āl-Sabāh, in 1867. Soon after that, Alī suggested that the British should allow his brother to return to Bahrain. This having been accepted, Muhammad immediately initiated a plot against Alī, but the British intervened and sent him into exile outside the Bahrain Islands. Once again, Muhammad chose to seek asylum at Kuwait.[18]

Shaikh Abd Allāh ibn Sabāh, unhappy about the fraternal strife between his cousins, the Āl-Khalīfa, decided to send his brother Muhammad as arbitrator in the dispute. However, the mission failed and the struggle between Alī and Muhammad Āl-Khalīfa continued, thus becoming a part of the history of Bahrain.

This should not imply that Kuwait lost interest in the affairs of Bahrain, for later on in 1883 Shaikh Mubārak ibn Sabāh paid a friendly visit to the Āl-Khalīfa there and was very warmly received.[19] Contrary to

14. See Lorimer, *Gazetter*, I, i, p. 1015.

15. See Al-Rashīd, II, p. 35, where he states that Su'ūd's forces were camping in Wafra. See also *Letters from the Persian Gulf. L/P & S/P*, Vol. 23, p. 735. Perhaps Su'ūd wanted to attack Kuwait because its ruler allowed 'Abd Allāh ibn Faisal, Su'ūd's brother, to stay in Kuwait's neighbourhood after the two brothers had failed to reach agreement in their negotiations at Riyad in 1871.

16. See *Letters etc.*, in *L/P & 23/9*, Aug-Dec. 1873, pp. 1517-1520 and 1555-6.

17. See also *Letters etc.*, Vol. 24, a letter from Aghā Ahmad Vol. 24, a letter from Aghā Ahmad (news writer) to the (news writer) to the Resident, 20th Jan. 1874, p. 213.

18. Al-Rashīd, II, pp. 30-35.

19. See Lorimer, *Gazetteer*, I.

20.   See *Safaḥāt*, p. 21 and
Al-Rashīd, II, p. 17.
p. 21 and Al-Rashīd, II, p. 17.

21.   For the details of this
incident see Al-Rashīd, II, pp.
37-44 and also Dickson, *The
Arab of the Desert*, pp. 266-273.

22.   See Doughty, II, p. 312.

23.   See *ibid.*, pp. 46 and 438.

British suspicions that Mubārak was conveying a secret message from the Ottoman government to the ruler of Bahrain, the visit was of a purely personal nature. By 1892, the lengthy rule of Abd Allāh ibn Sabāh came to an end with the greatly lamented death of that leader.

Shaikh Muhammad ibn Sabāh ibn Jābir (1892-1896)

Abd Allāh ibn Sabāh was followed by his brother Muhammad ibn Sabāh who ruled until he was killed in 1896. Kuwaitī local historians, contemporaries of the new Shaikh, state that the affairs of government were shared with his brothers Jarrāh and Mubārak. While describing Muhammad as an extremely honest, modest person, who enjoyed the company of the *Ulamā'*, [religious scholars], they also state that he lacked willpower and aptitude for making decisions. They speak of how he trusted his brother Jarrāh with running the finances of the country and put Mubārak in charge of tribal forces outside the city wall.[20] Muhammad himself took charge also of affairs within the walls of the city of Kuwait. This division of power in government affairs, according to the same local historians, caused dissension among the three brothers and led Mubārak to eventually eliminate his brothers and assume complete charge of all the country's business in 1896.[21]

The four years of Muhammad's reign were a continuation of Abd Allāh's thirty years. During those thirty-four years, it became apparent that the foundations laid by Shaikh Abd Allāh I ibn Sabāh in the late 18th and early 19th centuries in political and economic fields were strictly adhered to. In the political arena, Kuwait retained its neutrality among struggling forces in the Gulf, and in this manner continued to be an independent country having no contractual agreements with either the Ottomans or the British, or even the Su'ūdī sides.

Economically, it enjoyed a flourishing trade and its fleet continued to grow. In his *Travels*, Doughty states that the people of al-Qasīm in Najd were dealing in merchandise carried by caravans from Kuwait.[22] When Doughty spoke of ibn Rashīd's trade in horses, he reported that those horses were exported to India via Kuwait. That trade seems to have been very extensive because ibn Rashīd covered all his government's expenses from it.[23]

As for the Kuwaitī fleet, its size and tonnage were on the increase, a fact substantiated by the vast number of vessels which participated in Midhat Pasha's 1871 expedition to al-Hasā.

This prosperity at Kuwait during the reigns of Abd Allāh and Muhammad was inherited by their brother, Mubārak, who was destined to play a major role at the international political level.

CHAPTER IX

COMMERCIAL ACTIVITIES OF KUWAIT IN THE EIGHTEENTH AND NINETEENTH CENTURIES

In this chapter we review some of the important factors that contributed to the development of Kuwait. First is its geographical position on the important trade-route of the Gulf which stimulated interest in that trade. In fact, the Kuwaitīs proved throughout the second half of the eighteenth century to be clever merchants who knew how to profit from the state of affairs in the Gulf. Kuwait's position at the extreme northwestern corner of the Gulf provided an opportunity to share in the caravan commerce between the Gulf and Aleppo.

An attempt will be made to study the trade-routes and merchandise to and from Kuwait, and to determine the type and amount of trade passing through the city itself.

Trade in and out of Kuwait must have followed the two old routes in the area: the Gulf sea-route and the caravan tracks. Kuwaitī vessels, together with other ships owned by Bahrain, Zubāra and Masqat,[1] almost monopolised the conveyance of goods in the Gulf by the former route. Ships owned by the merchants of Kuwait, Zubāra and Bahrain called at Masqat, Basra, Abū Shahr[2] and other ports of consequence in the Gulf.[3] Later in the eighteenth century, and after the Kuwaitī vessels were capable of trading with India, they ceased calling at Masqat and sailed directly from India back home to avoid paying duties to the Masqatī ruler. In short, the Kuwait and Bahrain fleet had a large share in the sea-trade of the Gulf second only to that of Masqat. By the end of 1790 "their Galliots and Boats are numerous and large and they have engrossed the whole of the freight Trade carried on between Muscat and the Parts of the Arabian shore,... and a Principal Part of the freight Trade, carried on between Muscat and Bussora".[4]

While boats provided one means of conveyance, it was left to the desert caravans to carry merchandise from Kuwait, as well as other Gulf ports, into the countries surrounding the Gulf and other remote areas.

The importance of the "Great Desert Caravan Route" in transporting goods between Asia and Europe in the eighteenth century has thus far gone unnoticed. No serious study has been made of the subject[5] in spite of the fact that the desert caravans were still used for commercial purposes between the Gulf and the Mediterranean. Here it is worth giving brief data on those caravans because of their effect on the trade of Kuwait.[6] The Kuwaitīs, as a people of increasing importance in Eastern Arabia, continued to use the customary caravan routes passing through their territories. Thus, goods that were unloaded at the ports of

1. With the exception of the vessels of Abū Shahr, it can be said that there were no other Arab cargo vessels in the Gulf in the second half of the eighteenth century. The merchants of Basra do not seem to have owned vessels at that time.
Since the capture of the Island of Bahreen by the Arabs of the Tribes of Beneattaba, an Enmity, rather however of an inactive and negative Kind, has uniformly subsisted between that Tribe and the Persians and has totally destroyed the commercial Intercourse, which previous to that Period, was advantageously cultivated by both Parties.

2. See Saldanha, *Selections from State Papers*, p. 409. Elsewhere in this report, p. 423, Manesty and Jones added that "little Intercourse has subsisted between the Inhabitants of the Opposite Shores of the Gulph" after the occupation of Bahrain.

3. When the Dutch established their Factory at Khārij Island from 1754-1765, the 'Utūb seem to have benefitted from that. There is no clear evidence on how much use the 'Utūb, especially those of Kuwait, made of that establishment. From Ives' account of the relations between the Shaikh of Kuwait and Baron Kniphausen, however, it becomes clear that the 'Utūb did have commercial intercourse with Khārij.

4. Saldanha, *Selections from State Papers*, p. 409.

5. Two distinguished scholars who wrote on "The Overland Route to India" in the period

under our consideration: Hoskins "The Overland Route to India" in *History* Vol. IX, 1924-25, pp. 302-318, and Furber, "The Overland Route to India in the Seventeenth and Eighteenth Centuries" in *J.I.H.*, Vol. 29, 1951, pp. 106-133. Both papers speak of the usage of both the Red Sea and the Persian Gulf routes for purposes of sending the English East India Company's dispatches. In neither of them can one trace any mention of goods conveyed by means of caravans; but both are extremely valuable for their information relative to the Company's mail.

6. Information on the desert-route and caravans in the second half of the eighteenth century comes from the Journals of the European travellers who used those caravans in journeying from Aleppo to the Persian Gulf, or vice versa. Most of these Journals were written by men who were in the English East India Company's service. Among those who crossed that desert in the 1750's and whose journeys were published: are Bartholomew Plaisted (his work is *Narrative of a Journey from Basra to Aleppo in 1750*) and John Carmichael (his work is *Narrative of a Journey from Aleppo to Basra in 1751*). These Journeys are published by D. Carruthers in his work *The Desert Route to India*, London, 1929. They were followed by Ives in 1758. The story of the caravan route subsequent to that, as told by Western travellers, is brief. In 1765 Niebuhr recorded an itinerary of this same caravan route, from information gathered from a bedouin who made the journey more than twenty times, and from a merchant of Basra *(Voyage en Arabie*, Vol. II, p. 193 ff). In 1774 A. Parsons set out from Alexandretta on "his voyage of commercial speculation" to Baghdād and Basra. In 1778 Colonel Capper went overland to India. In 1781, Mr. Irwin, of the Madras Establishment, "entrusted with dispatches too important to admit of delay", rode from Aleppo to Baghdād, Basra and India. In 1785-6 we have Julius Griffiths'

Eastern Arabia found their way into the inner parts of the peninsula through the traditional caravan routes from al- Uqair, Zubāra and al-Qatīf. There is no record of caravans carrying goods from Masqat along the Eastern shore of the Gulf to Basra. The fact that the 'desert express' was dispatched from Masqat by the East India Company's agent there to Basra to announce the arrival of the Company's ships at Masqat, seems to suggest that the ancient caravan route is still in operation. However, there is clear evidence that the desert caravans loaded at Kuwait and carried goods from there to Baghdad and Aleppo. The earliest reference to such caravans can be traced in Ives' *Voyage* of 1758. This continued until 1781, when for unspecified reasons they stopped calling at Kuwait until 1789, and perhaps for some time after.

Caravans usually consisted of merchants who hired camels, mules and donkeys from shaikhs who made this their business, and who accompanied them from starting point to destination. These shaikhs charged the merchants fixed amounts of money for services offered during the journey. These included the payment of duties to some chiefs of the Arab tribes on the caravan route and the hire of Arab guards or *rafiqs*,[7] besides the actual hire of camels. The cost of a camel was a matter of bargain. During the second half of the eighteenth century it ranged between thirty-five and fifty piastres for a loaded beast from Basra or Kuwait to Aleppo. This varied with the type of goods carried by a camel. For "in Arabia", say Manesty and Jones in their report of the trade of Arabia bordering on the Gulf,

> the usual load of a Camel is in Weight about seven hundred English pounds, and the Shaiks of the Caravans will in all Times by Customary Agreement, engage to convey from Grain to Aleppo and to pay the Arab the Jewaise or Duties thereon, that Weight of Piece Goods for a sum of Money equal to Bombay Rs. 130, and that weight of Gruff Goods for a Sum of money equal to Bombay Rs. 90.[8]

The shaikh of the caravan acted as guide and had absolute authority. The distance from Basra or Kuwait to Aleppo was covered in about seventy days.[9] Desert caravans sometimes broke their journey at Baghdad and oftentimes travelled directly between the Gulf and Aleppo. Other caravans often joined them enroute. The number of camels conveying goods[10] varied, depending on the amount of business in Aleppo, Basra, Baghdad and other commercial centres in the area. Plaisted estimated that the caravan with which he travelled from Basra to Aleppo consisted of 2,000 camels and about 150 'Musqueteers' at the start. These camels did not make a laden caravan, but were being taken to market.[11] Half-way, they were joined by the Baghdad caravan of 3,000 camels, bringing the total to 5,000 camels, 400 of which were laden, plus 1,000 men.[12] Carmichael's caravan consisted of fifty horses, thirty mules and 1,200 camels "600 of which were laden with merchandise valuing L 300,000". It was guarded by an escort of 140 Arab soldiers.[13] The caravan by which Ives and his colleagues attempted to travel from Kuwait to Aleppo in 1758, amounted to 5,000 camels accompanied by 1,000 men.[14] Parsons' caravan had 800 laden camels in addition to several mules, donkeys and horses; there were four European and twelve Turkish merchants as well as 105 Arab guards. Griffiths' caravan, which was composed originally of eight camels and a guard of thirty to forty men, included 200 camels before their departure from Aleppo on June 8th, 1786.

The number of camels varied because of the three types of caravans making the desert journey. The first was the light camel caravan coming from the south, up to Aleppo. This supplied that town with animals for carrying goods on one of the two other caravans. The second was the caravan for merchants who wished to carry their goods from Aleppo southwards without waiting for the arrival or departure of the third and largest one, called the Aleppo or Basra caravan, depending upon the place of departure. This last caravan travelled twice a year between Aleppo and Basra.[15]

In addition to these three, there was a fourth which could be called the travellers' caravan. English travellers at times hired a complete outfit, including both riding and baggage camels, as well as a small force of armed guards. Captain Taylor favoured travelling in comfort, by hiring a caravan at a cost from L 500 to L 600, engaging forty to sixty armed men, and twenty camels for water, tents, provisions, etc. The procedure of hiring and equipping these caravans, for men usually in the service of the English East India company, was done by the English Consul at Aleppo and members of the Basra Factory.

Travelling time between Aleppo and Basra or Kuwait depended upon the size of the caravan and the method of travel. While large caravans went slowly, (seven hours a day), and took from forty-five to seventy days, small caravans completed the journey in twenty-five days. Plaisted took twenty-four and a half days in a rather large caravan. Carmichael, averaging about seven hours a day, took 318 hours or forty-five days. Capper took 310 hours. The 'desert express' covered the same distance in about thirteen and a half to twenty days.

This operation of the desert-route no doubt had its effect on Kuwaitī trade and together with sea-borne cargoes, was vital to the expansion of Kuwait as a power in the region. Full understanding of the commercial activities of Kuwait would not be complete without a brief study of the conditions of the western side of Arabia, where the Red Sea trade-route remained a rival to the Arabian Gulf.

During the second half of the eighteenth century, the Red Sea was not a great competitor of the Gulf in the transport of Indian goods to the markets of the Ottoman provinces in Syria and Turkey. True, European vessels called at Suez carrying Indian goods to Egypt and other neighbouring countries until the 1770's, but the last decades saw a decline in that trade due to the Ottoman firman [imperial order] of 1779 prohibiting Christian vessels from trading with Suez.

These orders were contrary to the interests of the Mameluke Beys, the actual rulers of Egypt, who naturally tried to nullify its effect. Desert Arab attacks on caravans carrying articles for European merchants presented another danger to their trade. Until 1786, the Court of Directors of the East India Company preferred the Cape-route to that of Egypt for conveying Indian goods to Europe. "They were, therefore, quite

account of the same journey from Aleppo.
In 1789, Major John Taylor, "of the Bombay Establishment", went out to India by the same desert route and recorded his journey in great detail. Earlier, in 1785, Captain Matthew Jenour made the same journey, also from Aleppo. In 1797, Olivier, followed the northern section of the route, on his way from Aleppo to 'Irāq.

7.   These men usually belonged to the tribes through whose territories the caravan passed; this was the only way to guarantee unmolested passage.

8.   See Saldanha, *Selections from State Papers*, p. 409. Although this estimate looks too high, Manesty and Jones may be considered reliable after their long stay at Basra.

9.   Jenour, *op. cit.*, p. 27, allows sixty to seventy days. while Manesty and Jones, *Selections from State Papers*, p. 409, estimates about eighty days.

10.   Not all the camels in the caravan were carriers, especially when the caravan was travelling northwards to Aleppo. Many camels accompanied the caravan unloaded, to be sold at Aleppo to merchants to convey their merchandise southward. This was necessitated by the lack of camels in Syria.

11.   See his *Narrative of a Journey* in Carruthers, pp. 68-69 and 93.

12.   *Ibid.*, p. 80.

13.   Carruthers, *op. cit.*, p. xxxiii.

14.   From the context it appears that the caravan was coming to Kuwait from the south because Ives and his companions planned to hire camels at Kuwait to join that caravan. This might have been the same caravan dispatched annually from al-Hasā by the Shaikh of the Banī Khālid. It is described by Plaisted, p. 93, as "the caravan of light camels" contrasting it with the merchants' laden camels. It used to be made up of

young camels sent to Aleppo for sale. It had a guard of 150 men mounted on dromedaries, "which is a lighter and swifter sort of camel". Many merchants used to wait for its arrival at their stations to join it with their merchandise and thus they used to double or triple the original number setting out. Those merchants were Greeks, Armenians, Europeans and sometimes Turks (Arabs?).

15.   Latouche stated in one of his letters to the Court of Directors that such a caravan spent eight months performing this operation. See Latouche to the Court of Directors, Basra, 31.x.1778, *F.R.P.P.G.*, 17. No. 1160.

16.   Hoskins, *loc. cit.*, p. 307. In 1775 the English signed a treaty with the Beys of Egypt to facilitate their commercial activities. The Sultān and his advisers at Constantinople were against this because they were apprehensive that in time the governors of Egypt might find it to their advantage to throw off the Turkish yoke entirely, perhaps with English aid. See *loc. cit.*, p. 306.

17.   Parsons, *op. cit.*, p. 207. Muscat is a place of very great trade, being possessed of a large number of ships, which trade to Surat, Bombay, Goa, along the whole coast of Malabar, and to Mocha and Jedda in the Red Sea. It is the great magazine or deposit for the goods which they bring from those parts; it is restored to by vessels from every port in Persia, from Bussora, and the ports of Arabia within the gulph, and from the coast of Caramaina without gulph, as far as the river Indus, and many places adjacent to that river.

18.   This report covers the period from 1763 to 1789.

19.   The merchants in those parts did not normally keep registers of their trade. This practice is still continued by many merchants of Kuwait.

20.   See Saldanha, p. 405. The principal fishery is carried on during the months of May, June, July, August and September,

willing to support the point of view of the Turkish Government in opposing the navigation of the Red Sea by European vessels".[16]

French commercial rivalry and the conclusion of a treaty between Chevalier de Troquet for France and Murād Bey for the Mamelukes of Egypt at Cairo on February in 1785, revived British interests in the Red Sea Route. British diplomacy continued to prevail at the Porte, which in 1787 sent a successful Ottoman campaign against the Mamelukes. This victory did not mean that the Red Sea route was preferred to the Cape Route, or that of the Gulf. All three remained in use after that, both for trade and mail purposes, until the occupation of Egypt by Bonaparte in 1798.

If the French were able to compete in the markets of Egypt, they were not so successful in the markets of the Arabian Gulf. Kuwait was not affected in its commercial enterprises by the Anglo-French rivalry, nor did it rely on goods carried only by English or other European vessels. By the 1780's its own fleet sailed to India, returning with Indian goods to the Kuwait ports and Basra. Masqat was the emporium of trade in Arabia in the second half of the eighteenth century,[17] and Kuwait, Bahrain and Masqat monopolised the freight from Masqat and India to the Gulf.

Manesty and Jones began their reports on the trade of Arabia bordering on the Gulf[18] by showing how difficult it was for them to carry out this task because of the lack of available information from the people of the Arabian coast.[19]

It is uncertain how much trade was transported in the Utbī vessels and how much went through Kuwait and Zubāra from the Gulf trade. After considering the types of goods brought by the various trading vessels to the Utbī and other Gulf ports, one can assume that Kuwait conducted almost continual commercial activity all through the latter half of the eighteenth century. This trade was centralized at three places: Manāma in Bahrain, Zubāra in Qatar and Kuwait, with all sharing in the sea-borne as well as the desert trade. It seems more convenient to deal with each separately and try to establish what goods each imported and exported.

Bahrain's trade before the occupation of the Islands in 1782-1783 was mainly in pearls. After the arrival of the Āl-Khalīfa, the predominant businesses were fishery and marketing of pearls together with sea-trade with India, Masqat and the ports of the Gulf.

Concerning the pearl fishery, the Āl-Khalīfa seem to have made no changes in the customary practice of pearl-fishing which was "engaging the Attention of many rich Arabian Merchants resident at Bahreen" and which gave "Employments to many industrious People of the lower Arabs belonging to that Place".[20]

With the acquisition of large vessels from India, the Āl-Khalīfa of Bahrain, in the 1780's and later, sailed to Indian ports to purchase necessities for daily use of their people and to export to Baghdad and Aleppo. These goods found their way to market via both Basra and Kuwait.[21] It is interesting to note that the owners of those vessels were merchants who carried goods for their own profit. Goods from Surat were transported to Baghdad and Aleppo.[22] In addition, there was the trade with Masqat, where vessels loaded Mukha coffee for Bahrain, "partly intended for the Bussora Market", and a quantity of sugar, pepper, spices of Bengal, ghee and rice. Some of these imports were in turn sent to Basra. On their return, they carried to Bahrain dates, grain necessary for the local population, as well as other articles for the market of Surat. Though unable to state the exact amount of the imports at Bahrain during the 1780's, at the end of the century those imports "of Indian Goods" amounted annually to ten lakhs of rupees. These were "balanced by an export of pearls in an equal amount". [23]

The second centre of commerce of the Āl-Khalīfa was Zubāra, which because of its geographical location, played a role in carrying some of the above-mentioned cargoes from Bahrain to Eastern and Central Arabia. Before the occupation of Bahrain in 1782-1783, Zubāra was the centre of commercial activities of the Āl-Khalīfa and other Utbī families. There is no record as to the amount or nature of this trade before the 1780's. As a port on the pearl coast it must also have had a share in the pearl fishery, although it seems to have been a small one. After the Āl-Khalīfa bought large vessels for engaging in trade with India, Zubāra, together with al-Qatīf, served as a centre to distribute this merchandise among the Banī Khālid tribes.

The conquest of Bahrain did not seem to lessen the commercial importance of Kuwait. The ruling Utbī family there was faced with the rivalry of the Banī Ka'b and other Arabs from the Persian littoral, a fact which forced the Āl-Sabāh to own a strong fleet. As previously mentioned, in 1770, Kuwait served as a centre for the East India Company's mail. In addition, its geographical situation was advantageous to the town both as a seaport and as a station for the Aleppo and Baghdad caravans. In 1793, with the two-year establishment of the East India Company's Factory there, Kuwait held a special position equal to that of Bahrain.

It appears, therefore, that her commercial success was dependent largely upon transit trade. With the occupation of Bahrain, imports were made from Bahrain and Zubāra to Kuwait. These originated with merchants from Bahrain and Basra wishing to send goods either to Aleppo or Baghdad by desert caravans in order to avoid the heavy duties levied at Basra.[24] Dates and grain were imported from Basra for local consumption. It is interesting that the conveyance of property from Kuwait to Baghdad or Aleppo by desert caravans was in no danger. The caravan shaikhs were careful in their selection of *rafīqs* [guards] and in according the tribal shaikhs the necessary tribute. Griffiths, writing in 1785-1786, adds that the tribal shaikhs did their best to keep the caravans running regularly and free from harm, thus insuring their own reward.

The trade of Kuwait seems to have profited little from the presence there of the English Factory. Rather, the benefits were largely political, not economic. In the beginning, captains of the English ships refused to unload goods destined for Basra at Kuwait. As noted, Manesty did not

when the water is warm. The yearly catch was estimated at 500,000 Bombay rupees. This was divided in proportions settled by agreement between the merchants who were the proprietors of the vessels employed in the fishery, the people who navigated them and the divers. For a detailed description of pearl fishing, see Buckingham's *Travels in Assyria*, pp. 454-457, and Wellsted, *Travels in Arabia*, Vol. I, pp. 264-265, and his *Travels to the City of the Caliphs*, pp. 115-123. Al-Rashīd in his *Ta'rīkh al-Kuwait*, Vol. I, pp. 47-65, gives a detailed account of the present way of pearl fishing which has not changed through the ages.

21. See Saldanha, *Selections from State Papers*, p. 408. Manesty and Jones speak of those Indian goods as well as other European mercantile articles which were carried in 'Utūbī vessels to Bahrain. Those articles, in the present Times 1789 are however first conveyed in a direct Manner from Surat to Bahreen and from thence to Zebarra and Catiffe. The importations made from Surat to Bahreen for the consumption of that Island, principally consist of small quantities of Surat Blue and other piece Goods, Guzerat Piece Goods and Chintz, Cambay, Chanders, Shawls, Bamboos, Tin, Lead and Iron. *Ibid.*

22. These Surat articles in demand at Baghdād and Aleppo were described as "Sundry Gruff Articles of Commerce...Cotton, Yarn, Shawls, Surat Blue and other Piece Goods and Guzerat Piece Goods and Chintz". See Saldanha, *Selections from State Papers*, p. 408.

23. See Malcolm's "Report" in Saldanha, *Selections from the State Papers*, p. 445.

24. See Saldanha, *Selections from State Papers*, p. 409. Some of those imports from Bahrain, al-Qatīf, Zubāra and Masqat were for "the local Consumption of Kuwait and its immediate Vicinity". These consisted of "small Quantities of Surat Blue

Goods, Bengal Coarse white
Goods, Bengal Soosies, Coffee,
Sugar, Pepper and ca. Spieces,
Iron and Lead"..."and of more
considerable Quantities of
Bengal Piece Goods, Surat Piece
Goods, Cotton Yarns, Camby,
Chanders, Coffee, Pepper for the
Bagdad and Aleppo
merchants"*Ibid*. For the duties
collected on those goods both at
Basra and Baghdād, see above,
Chapter III.

25. See Saldanha, *Selections
from State Papers*, p. 445.

26. Griffiths, *op. cit.*, p. 389.

insist upon the enforcement of his orders forbidding the unloading of English vessels at Basra.

The principal entrepōts for the trade of the Arabian Gulf in this period were Masqat and Basra. The first was described by Parsons as a large store for European and Indian goods which were shipped to Basra and the Utbī ports by Masqat and Utbī fleets. Basra was the centre of the English East India Company's trade with the Gulf during most of the years from 1763-1800.

Although there are no statistics on the trade of the Arabian side of the Gulf apart from those of the English, it can only be described as prosperous. According to Malcolm, the Indian trade to Arabia amounted to forty lakhs of rupees, of which thirty were with Basra, and ten with Bahrain and its neighbourhood. "These great imports", says Malcolm,

> are answered by exports from Bussora of Dates, the Native Product, by Pearls (received from Bahrain and other neighbouring ports in exchange for grain) and Gold and Silver Lace brought from Europe by the Aleppo caravans and Copper from the mines of Diarbakr. Most of those exports pass through Muscat in their way to India.[25]

Griffiths said: "returns are made chiefly in specie or jewels; and a certain number of highly bred Arab horses".[26]

The Āl-Sabāh and Āl-Khalīfa's share in this flourishing trade was considerable, for they participated in its conveyance both by sea and caravan. They seem to have made use of both legal and illegal means to benefit from that flow of trade and did not hesitate to smuggle goods from Kuwait to the markets of Baghdād and Aleppo, in order to avoid the Basra customs.

The growth of Kuwait in the eighteenth century was a result of that enormous trade in the Gulf in which Kuwait played an active role. The word enormous is an inadequate expression in economic terms but affords the best description where the lack of records makes it impossible to obtain any statistics. Even references in contemporary English documents are rare. However, many changes occurred in the nineteenth century as will be revealed in the forthcoming pages of this chapter.

Trade in the Arabian Gulf in the Nineteenth Century

It has been noted in the first section of this chapter that the Gulf was the major link of communication between India and Britain during the eighteenth century, and that trade with the Gulf, mainly through the English East India Company, kept commercial life active in the major ports of the Arabian Gulf. Kuwait's prosperity depended, more or less, on its participation in that trade. In the nineteenth century the importance of the Red Sea route, at certain times, surpassed that of the Gulf. Yet despite this rivalry, the usual trade of the East India Company continued, and with the help of other factors the Gulf route maintained a profitable operation.

The East India Company's mail continued to travel via the Arabian Gulf during the first quarter of the nineteenth century except for dispatches that were sent via the Cape of Good Hope in South Africa. But by 1833 this mail ceased to be sent through the Gulf, and was carried instead to the Egyptian port of al-Qusair on the Red Sea. From there it was transported by land to Alexandria, from whence it continued its journey to Europe. The reason for this change is said to have been the better facilities for passengers travelling between India and Europe at both Alexandria and al-Qusair.[27] Public opinion in Britain was divided, however, and when Parliamentary committees were formed between 1833 and 1837 to discuss this matter, they decided in favour of the Red Sea route. Thus in August 1837, the first monthly mail from London to Bombay travelled this waterway and despite efforts of the Bombay Government to keep both routes open, the British Government decided that the Red Sea route would be used to dispatch original copies of letters, while only duplicates were permitted to be sent via the Arabian Gulf route.

Nevertheless, the Court of Directors in London decided to reactivate the Gulf route when they sent three commercial river boats to Basra specially made to carry the mail between that city and Baghdād. Later in 1843-44 the desert mail route between Baghdād and Beirut (with a stop at Damascus) was revived.[28] This route was used for local mail between Syria and Irāq. The Indian mail continued to suffer hardships and delays because mail between Abū-Shahr and Bombay, for example, had to travel from Abū-Shahr to Baghdād and thence to Beirut, Alexandria, al-Qusair, the Red Sea, and finally to India. Mail from Bombay to Abū-Shahr travelled in the opposite direction. These lengthy journeys continued until 1862, when, as a result of the establishment of telegraphic lines, the mail again crossed the Gulf on its way to Bombay. That year is described by Lorimer as the year of the inception of modern postal communications in the Arabian Gulf.[29] The beginnings were modest. Acquisition for "postal purposes" of a line of steamers to serve between Bombay and the Arabian Gulf, and to call at Karachi on the way, was sanctioned by the Secretary of State for India in 1862, the number of annual trips being limited at first to eight. The contract was undertaken by the British Indian Steam Navigation Company; in the same year the Secretary of State of India accepted an offer by the Euphrates and Tigris Steam Navigation Company to operate in consideration of a subsidy of L 2,400 a year, a monthly or six-weekly steamer between Basra and Baghdād, connecting at Basra with the new ocean service from Bombay. Postal services in the Gulf continued to improve after 1862, and the steamers made a trip every two weeks by 1868 and weekly starting in 1874.

Even though the conveyance of both mail and trade through the Gulf was bound to suffer with the opening of the Suez Canal in 1868, this route continued to be used during most of the nineteenth century for commercial purposes by the local powers as well as by the British in India. Any additional activity in the transport of mail added to the benefits

27. Lorimer, I, ii, p. 2439.

28. *Ibid.*, p. 2440.

29. *Ibid.*, pp. 2440-1.

30. Buckingham, BTravels in Assyria, etc., pp. 370, 462.

31. *Ibid.*, p. 463.

32. See "Memoir Descriptive of the Navigation of the Gulf of Persia" in *Bombay Selections*, Vol. XXIV, pp. 532-576.

33. *Ibid.*, pp. 522-23.

34. *Ibid.*, p. 566.

of the seaports located around the Gulf. Kuwait seemed to have continued its prosperous commercial endeavours as an important seaport of particular value to the British. This has been reported in the writings of several officials of the Bombay Government in the Arabian Gulf region, portions of whose commentaries on the trade of Kuwait will be reviewed in the following pages. Together with these official comments, useful information given by other travellers concerning this topic, will also be utilized. For the sake of historical chronology, these officials and travellers will be reviewed in accordance with the sequence of the years in which their remarks were presented.

Buckingham (1816)

First among those writers comes the traveller Buckingham who describes Kuwait harbour as "great",[30] its population made up mainly of merchants who handle local as well as international trade that is prevailing in the Gulf area. The Kuwaitī sailors are skilful, wise and brave,[31] who use about one hundred large and small vessels. Apparently Kuwait's traffic in horses was very extensive, and Buckingham gives interesting details of this trade between India and the Arabian Gulf seaports, especially Basra and Kuwait, as we see in a later discussion of this important commodity.

Captain Brucks' Memoir, 21st August 1829[32]

George Barnes Brucks was employed by the Indian navy and was asked by them to visit various ports in the Arabian Gulf for the purpose of submitting a report on their customs, religions, trade, and sources of wealth. That assignment proved to be rather difficult, for he introduced his report by offering apologies to his readers on account of the nature of the sources he had consulted in preparing his report. These were mainly the inhabitants of these ports, especially the Chiefs and other notables in those places. So whatever they told him in respect to the population must be taken at its face value. Brucks' information on Bahrainī trade will be related here for the sake of comparison with Kuwaitī trade.[33]

He estimated the population of Bahrain and its dependencies to be about 60,000, half of whom were working in the pearl fishing industry which employed 2,430 small boats, on board of each a number of workers ranging from eight to twenty men. This industry was supervised by the ruler of the Islands of Bahrain. Twenty large Baghlas whose tonnage varied from 140 to 350 tons each were the ships that were used in the trade of India. Smaller vessels - about 100 - with a tonnage between 40 and 120 tons were used in local trading in the Gulf area. The major port of Bahrain was Manama where shipments from India, Basra and Masqat were received. The duties collected at that sea port were 5% of the original price of the commodity.[34]

Exports from Bahrain for 1824 were estimated at 1,651,900 German crowns. Countries and cities to which these exports went were India, Persia, Basra, Turkey and Kuwait. The most valued were pearls for India, priced at 1,200,000 German crowns. Kuwait's imports from Bahrain were 5,000 crowns worth of sail materials and 800 crowns for the import of mattresses.[35] Bahrain's exports to Kuwait were given at 807,300 German crowns, and no mention of the imports from Kuwait to Bahrain was made.

Kuwait's Trade in Brucks' Report of 1829

Kuwait, in view of Brucks' report, was an important town which was known for its indulgence in local and international trade. Unlike other ports on the Gulf it had, because of its location, a "spiral" trade with inner Najd and northern Najd, which it supplied with wheat, coffee and Indian produce. Its merchants owned fifteen large vessels - *Baghlas* and *Dhows* - whose tonnage averaged between 100 and 400 tons, and twenty ships of the previous type with a tonnage of 20 to 150 tons. There were other types of vessels in the Kuwaitī merchant fleet numbering one hundred and fifty, averaging in freight capabilities from 15 to 150 tons each. These sailed to Gulf ports and countries around the Red Sea and Indian sub-continent.

Kuwait imported a wide assortment of goods. Among the list, Brucks included cloth, rice, sugar, wood, spices and cotton. Evidently Kuwait at the time of his visit was an importer of coffee from the Yemen, tobacco and dried fruits from Persia, wheat and dates from Basra, and cloth, dates and fish from Bahrain.

Kuwait exported ghee and horses which were brought from neighbouring bedouin tribes, and for which they bartered certain commodities which the bedouins could not get at home. The total amount of imports "was almost 500,000 dollars (riyals)" while the exports were less than one hundred thousand riyals. Most of the Kuwaitī catch of pearls found its way to local markets.[36]

Stocqueler in Kuwait, 1831

Whereas Brucks was specific in mentioning the names of the countries and ports Kuwait's ships had been travelling to, Stocqueler personally travelled on board one Kuwait vessel (Buggala), i.e. *Baghla*, from Bombay and Kuwait in 1831 and gave a description of the "Nasserie", as his Buggala was named. He even stated that passengers for that journey paid 150 rupees.[37] That Arab boat was carrying passengers as well as freight. The "Nasserie" called at Masqat and carried from that city a load of leather and mats. Perhaps it is worth mentioning that Stocqueler stated that Kuwait collected 2% duties on all its imports. He was also very knowledgeable about the town and its social life.

35. *Ibid.*, pp. 568-569.

36. *Ibid.*, p. 576.

37. See Stocqueler, *Fifteen Months of Pilgrimage* etc., pp. 1-2.

38.   Jones stated that watermelons were planted locally in Kuwait. See his report in *Bombay Selections*, XXIV, p. 52.

39.   See Appendix No. III, for the full text of Hennell's report.

40.   See Kemball's report, "Measures adopted by the British Government between 1820 and 1844 for the effecting of the suppression of the slave trade in the Persian Gulf", in *Bombay Selections*, XXIV, p. 648 ff.

Lieutenant Felix Jones, 1839

Eight years after Stocqueler's visit to Kuwait, Lieutenant Felix Jones of the Indian Navy paid a visit to Kuwait harbour and the island of Failaka in November 1839. His report on the trade of Kuwait is an interesting one. He states that Kuwait was an importer of fruits, such as dates, citrus fruits, pomegranates, and watermelons which came from Basra and Abū-Shahr. From India the imports were wheat, barley and rice. Basra and Abū-Shahr also supplied Kuwait with lentils. Cattle and poultry were supplied by the bedouin neighbours whose prices varied according to seasons. Teak plank essential for shipbuilding was imported from Bombay.[38]

Captain Hennell, 1841 [39]

After Jones' visit to Failaka Island and Kuwait town, the Bombay Government asked Captain Hennell, a British Resident in the Gulf, to proceed from Abū-Shahr to Kuwait for the purpose of reporting on its harbour and the feasibility of the British moving its forces from the Island of Khārij to Kuwait if compelled to do so. Though Hennell did believe that Kuwait would be a good substitute for Khāraj, he recorded a few notes pertaining to Kuwait's trade which are useful in this study.

> This Town presents a singular instance of communnal prosperity, although wanting in almost every advantage, excepting its magnificent harbour. Its population is large, as it can produce about six thousand men capable of bearing arms, . . . of inhabitants nearly twenty five thousand individuals. They possess thirty one Buglas and Bateels, from one hundred and fifty to three hundred tons burthen, which trade constantly with India. Fifty smaller vessels are employed in the coasting commerce of the Gulf, and about 350 boats engaged in fishing and on the pearl banks.

Hennell presents the view that the Shaikh of Kuwait collected no taxes or customs, the port being entirely a free one. The Shaikh's income was approximately 3,000 dollars, and he spent that revenue together with the profits from his trading vessels on keeping up "a public table of plentiful but coarse description to which every one appears to be welcome."

Kemball's Three Reports, 1844, 1845, 1854 [40]

In all three reports written by Lieutenant Kemball, some light is shed on the slave trade in the Gulf and other aspects of the Gulf's commercial life.

The first of three reports by Kemball, who was assistant British Resident in the Gulf, was written in October 1844 and concentrates on the slave trade in the regions of the Arabian Gulf and the Indian Ocean. The report records that during the months of August, September and

October of 1841, the number of vessels carrying slaves in the Gulf region was 117, six of which were of Kuwaitī ownership. The total slave load for all vessels was 1,217, 103 being carried by Kuwaitī boats. These slaves would be unloaded at Kuwait, Basra and Muhammra. Muscat was, according to Kemball, the principal slave market in the area.

It is interesting to note that Kemball was of the belief that vessels carrying human cargo from Gulf ports to India were owned by horse merchants as well as merchants from Basra, Kuwait, Abū-Shahr, Bahrain, several places on the Gulf coast and Bombay.

In the second of his reports which was written on January the 6th, 1845, Kemball reproduces most of Captain Hennell's report of 1841.

In his last and third report dated February 17th, 1845, he estimates the population of Kuwait at 22,000 individuals, and its income is put at 22,000 German crowns.

Colonel Pelly, 1863 & 1865

Perhaps the fullest reports dealing with the subject of this chapter can be found in John Lewis Pelly's three reports on the region. Pelly, British Resident in the Gulf for some time, in his long and detailed reports, mentions Kuwait within the context of trade in the entire Gulf region. It is important to note that he was writing of Kuwait from first-hand knowledge.

Upon reaching Kuwait town, he noticed small boats, 60-70 tons each, bringing in commodities from northern ports of the Gulf to be conveyed by the large Kuwaitī *Baghlas* to Bombay. Similarly, he stated that produce from India was transported on those large ships to Kuwait where it was distributed by smaller vessels to neighbouring northern ports of the Gulf. Heading the list of those imports from India (Bombay) was teak plank, the wood essential to the ship building industry.

In a following report[41] Pelly wrote that yearly imports at Kuwait from Malabar and Bombay were estimated at 200,000 rupees, money paid for cloth, rice, coffee, wood and spices. Kuwait exported 800 horses to India every year at an average of 300 rupees each. Exports to India included wool for 40,000 rupees, dates for 60,000 rupees and perhaps other commodities in the range of 40,000 rupees a year. Horses were bought for Kuwaitī merchants by agents among the Arabs of Shammar in northern Arabia. They were then brought to Kuwait rather than Basra for export in order to avoid paying duties.[42]

Kuwaitī vessels were manned by 4,000 Kuwaitī sailors who were highly regarded for their pleasant disposition and hard work. Thirty of those vessels averaging 100 tons were sent to Bombay from the Shatt al-Arab every year, each loaded with 2,000 baskets of dates priced at one thousand French riyals with a total value of 30,000 French riyals or the equivalent of 60,000 rupees. These dates were shipped from the Shatt al-Arab on Kuwaitī boats. They imported part of the fodder for the horses from Zubair, a town between Basra and Kuwait-town. Sheep, ghee

41. See Pelly, "Recent Tour, etc.," p. 118.

42. *Ibid.*, pp. 119-120.

43. See Pelly, "Remarks on the
     Tribes,etc." p. 73.

44. Pelly,"Remarks", p. 109.

and milk were purchased from Kuwaiti bedouins who brought their animals to the main gates of the town to sell. Among the numerous tables Pelly produced in his *Remarks*, the following shows Kuwait's annual export trade with Abū-Shahr. [43]

APPROXIMATE ANNUAL IMPORTS BY SEA INTO BUSHIRE FROM KUWAIT, PRESENT AND FUTURE

	Approximate Present Annual Exports			Approximate Future Annual Imports			Amt. of duty leviable in Bombay Rupees	Remarks as to cause of increase or decrease
Article	Quantity in Tabreez Mds.	Value in Bombay Rupees	Article	Quantity in Tabreez Mds	Value in Rupees			
Coffee (Malabar)	4,000	8,000	Coffee	4,000	8,000	60		
Pepper (do.)	5,000	6,250	Pepper	5,000	6,250	120		
Cotton Piece Goods (Eng.)	1,500 pieces	18,000	Cotton Piece Goods (Eng.)	1,500 pieces	18,000	750		

Kuwait's imports from Abū-Shahr were as follows:[44]

APPROXIMATE ANNUAL EXPORTS BY SEA INTO BUSHIRE TO KUWAIT, PRESENT AND FUTURE

	Approximate Present Annual Exports			Approximate Future Annual Exports			Amt. of duty leviable in Rupees	Remarks as to cause of increase or decrease
Article	Quantity in Tabreez Mds.	Value in Rupees	Article	Quantity in Tabreez Mds	Value in Rupees			
Tobacco	14,000	8,750	Tobacco	14,000	8,750	275		
Madderroot	2,000	1,250	Madderroot	2,000	1,250	$27\frac{1}{2}$		
Ahlook (Nuts)	3,000	750	Ahlook (Nuts)	3,000	750	20		
Nokhod (Gram)	3,000	750	Nokhod (Gram)	3,000	750	20		
Carpets different sorts	500 pieces	5,000	Carpets different sorts	500 pieces	5,000	150		

On March the 3rd of 1863, Pelly was at al-Jahra village where horses were brought for fodder until their shipment to India.[45] On his way to Riyād in February 1865, he again passed through al-Jahra; in discussing Kuwait's trade in horses, he emphasized its value as an important source of income for the town. Since this trade had an important place in the commerce of Kuwait, it is useful to consider what Buckingham had to say about it.

45. *Ibid.*, p. 110.

46. Buckingham, *Travels*, p. 385.

47. It should be noted that half of the horses were sold in Bombay, one quarter in Calcutta and the last quarter in Madras.

48. See Buckingham, p. 389. For table see end of this chapter.

Trade in Horses

When the British were building up their Empire in India, horses were in great demand by the army, especially when they were waging war against their enemies in the northern provinces of the Indian sub-continent during the first half of the 19th century and part of the second half.

Buckingham gives the figure of 1,500 for the number of Arabian horses exported from Basra and Kuwait to Bombay, Madras and Calcutta in 1816. The price of each horse at the port of export was 300 rupees, but by the time it reached its destination, the amount spent on fodder and transportation increased costs by 200 rupees.[46] In other words the total amount of one year's trade in horses was 750,000 rupees. In addition, a gift of fifty piastres was made to the *mutasallin* at Basra for each horse exported from there and 100 rupees per horse paid for miscellaneous expenses bringing the grand total to 900,000 rupees.

The prices for which these horses were sold varied from one city to the other and also from one horse to another. At Bombay the horse was sold for 800 rupees, giving the merchant 100 rupees in net profit.[47] Horses sold in Bengal were more expensive because they were always the best among the shipment. These sold for 1,000 rupees each. If other expenses were added, each horse would be sold for 2,500 rupees although the average price was usually 2,000 rupees or L 200. It should also be mentioned in relation to this trade that vessels especially equipped for this type of shipment were capable of carrying between eighty and one hundred horses each. The accompanying table shows the importance of the horse in the Bombay trade.[48]

The reader of this chapter will be able to conclude from information supplied by travellers and officials of the Bombay Government that Kuwait's economic policies devised by Shaikh Abd Allāh I ibn Sabāh concerning free trade, were continued under his successors Jābir ibn Abd Allāh and Sabāh ibn Jābir.

It is clear that Kuwait's participation in the Gulf trade with India continued and the amount of trade carried by Kuwaitī vessels remained high. Kuwait seems to have kept its place among the Gulf ports in the number of its large vessels (*Baghlas* and *Buteels*) and tonnage. A glance at what Bahrain owned of these large vessels and what Kuwait had substantiates what has just been said. For Bahrain had twenty large vessels whereas Kuwait owned thirty one.

Kuwait's horse trade with India was indeed a lucrative one and her continued active role in the Gulf contributed to a position of distinction which perhaps helped avoid an attack on its territory by the Egyptians, as already explained. With numerous vessels at Kuwait's disposal, shipments to al-Hasā of whatever the Egyptians needed of food to fodder and ammunition were expedited. In short, Kuwait's trade continued on the rise during the 19th century, as it had in the second half of the 18th century under Abd Allāh I ibn Sabāh. There is no doubt that what Pelly observed in Kuwait's political stability during his visits of 1863 and 1865 was a result of this commercial success.

The growth in the size and capacity of the Kuwaitī fleet was noticeable in the 1871 Turkish expedition into al-Hasā. This role of their fleet in the war, under the command of Abd Allāh II ibn Sabāh ibn Jābir, was clearly explained in the preceding chapter.

The next chapter will take Kuwait into the twentieth century when it stands at the threshold of dealing directly with the big powers of Europe. Mubārak, referred to by the Kuwaitīs as Mubārak the Great, was to assume the role of chief architect in the modern state of Kuwait.

ABSTRACT ACCOUNT OF THE VALUE OF ALL IMPORTS INTO, AND ALL EXPORTS FROM BOMBAY IN THE OFFICIAL YEAR, 1836/37

	Value of Imports				Value of Exports			
	Merchandise	Treasure	Horses	Total Imports	Merchandise	Treasure	Horses	Total Exports
Great Britain	1,32,41,910			1,32,41,910	1,35,29,317			1,35,29,317
France	5,25,853			5,25,853	2,37,443			2,37,443
Madeira	24,725			24,725				
Cape of Good Hope	9,752			9,752	612			612
Brazils	92,490			92,490				
Coast of Africa	3,49,538	911		3,50,449	5,93,331	25,000		6,18,331
Isle of France	1,39,863			1,39,863	26,771	80,900		1,07,671
America	46,289			46,289	2,34,756	56,250		2,91,006
China	40,05,669	1,00,74,283		1,40,79,952	3,26,66,247	8,800		3,26,75,047
Manilla	31,410			31,410				
Penang, Singapore and the Straits	7,17,721	2,35,442		9,53,163	6,84,986	19,720	751	7,05,457
Calcutta	25,38,101			25,38,101	8,76,884	10,200	2,49,900	11,36,984
Coast of Coromandel	1,11,648			1,11,648	2,95,249	5,65,000	500	8,60,749
Ceylon	55,340	53,000		1,08,340	37,818	48,658	15,000	1,01,476
Persian Gulf	11,02,897	20,10,892	4,45,800	35,59,589	34,57,341	42,900		35,00,241
Arabian Gulf	7,81,404	11,02,290		18,83,694	12,47,340	17,790		12,65,130
Malabar and Canzra	75,80,673			75,80,673	9,11,547	11,11,581	2,95,400	23,18,628
Cutch and Sciende	14,99,590	550	72,500	15,72,640	23,27,347	2,000		23,29,347
Goa, Demaun, and Diu	3,94,030	1,000		3,95,030	1,61,259	67,280		2,28,638
Rupees	3,32,48,903	1,34,78,368	5,18,300	4,72,45,571	5,72,88,248	20,56,079	5,61,651	5,99,05,978

Total Imports – Rupees 4,72,45,571

Total Exports – Rupees 5,99,05,978

Shaikh Mubārak al-Ṣabāḥ 1896–1915

CHAPTER X

MUBĀRAK IBN SABĀH 1896-1915

Mubārak "The Great", seventh ruler of Kuwait from the Sabāh family, is considered the founder of modern Kuwait by local historians. This title reflects, in the view of those historians, the major role he played in the establishment of his authority among contemporary rulers in the Gulf area in general and Arab shaikhs of Eastern Arabia in particular. The road to fame and distinction in Arabia and the Arabian Gulf region was not a smooth one. On the contrary, it was strewn with great obstacles created by both local and international rivalries. To understand and appreciate those difficulties, a brief description of the political situation in the Arabian Peninsula on the one hand and the European continent on the other must of necessity be given.

When Mubārak rose to power towards the closing years of the 19th century, most of the Arabian Peninsula, of which Kuwait is a part, was under the rule of independent chiefs who did not always acknowledge the authority of the Ottoman Sultan. Long before the days of Mubārak, the Ottoman Empire was known as the sick man of Europe, an indication of its declining power. At the onset of the twentieth century, Eastern Arabia was governed by independent shaikhs who had entered into treaty relations with Great Britain. But other than the Sultans of 'Umān, not one of those chiefs had control over clearly-defined territories. Even 'Umān's borders with some of the Trucial shaikhdoms were not clearly defined. Najd and al-Hasā which were united under Su'ūdī rule were partially controlled by the Āl-Rashīd of Shammar. After the return of Ottoman rule to Najd and al-Hasā as a result of Midhat Pasha's expedition in 1871, the Su'ūdī dynasty sought refuge in Kuwait and other places in eastern Arabia.

Before the turn of the twentieth century, European powers seemed eager to divide the Ottoman Empire among themselves, but this was delayed until after the end of the First World War in 1918. However, the Arabian gulf region began to draw the attention of other European powers besides the British. German-Ottoman relations grew closer as was apparent from German plans for a Baghdād-Berlin railway. The Russians, in their turn, had hopes of reaching the warm waters of the Arabian Gulf. This combination of Ottoman decadence and European rivalry for supremacy in the Gulf area, led Shaikh Mubārak, a man of

1. See al-Rashīd, II, pp. 37-47,
    and al-Qinā'ī, pp. 21-23. See
    also Dickson, *The Arab of the
    Desert*, pp. 266-272.

2. In explaining the connection
    between Yūsuf al-Ibrāhīm and
    the two brothers Muhammad
    and Jarrāh, Lorimer had to say
    this in his *Gazetteer*, I, i,
    footnote to page 1017:
    The relationship was rather
    complicated. 'Ali bin Jābir, who
    was the youngest brother of
    Shaikh Subāh of Kuwait,
    married the youngest daughter of
    'Alī bin Muhammad bin
    Ibrāhīm, and had by her three
    daughters, of whom the eldest
    married Shaikh Muhammad and
    became the mother of his sons
    Subāh, Sa'ūd, Khālid and
    'Adhbi, while the second married
    Jarrāh and bore a son Hamūd
    and a daughter who married her
    own first cousin Subāh bin
    Muhammad. An elder daughter
    of 'Ali bin Muhammad bin
    Ibrāhīm married 'Abdullah, a
    first cousin of her own father,
    and became the mother of Yūsuf.

3. Al-Qinā'ī, p. 25 and
    al-Rashīd, II, pp. 52-56. See also
    Lorimer, I, i, pp. 1017-1018, and
    Dickson, *Kuwait and her
    Neighbours*, p. 136.

perseverance and determination, to think of ways and means of ensuring the independence of Kuwait immediately after assuming leadership of the country in 1896.

Muhammad, Jarrāh and Mubārak (1892-1896)

Mubārak's greatest concern was dissension at home with his two brothers, Muhammad and Jarrāh, a few years before 1896. After the death of Shaikh 'Abd Allāh II ibn Sabāh in 1892, Muhammad became the ruler of Kuwait. According to contemporary Kuwaitī historians, Muhammad, in cooperation with his brother Jarrāh, managed the financial affairs of the shaikhdom, while Mubārak was entrusted with keeping peace among the bedouins of the desert who were subjects of the Shaikh. This arrangement served apparently to keep Mubārak out of sight. When local historians speak of the limited allowance allocated for Mubārak's duties, it becomes clear that he was not only excluded from the city, but also relegated to a position of minimal influence among the bedouins. Lengthy accounts of this situation have been related by local historians and by Colonel Dickson in his two books, *The Arab of the Desert* and *Kuwait and Her Neighbours*.[1]

There is no doubt that Mubārak sensed that his two brothers sent him from Kuwait town on the advice of the most influential and extremely rich Kuwaitī merchant, Yūsuf ibn 'Abd Allāh al-Ibrāhīm. The latter was 'Irāqī (from Basra) by origin and related to Muhammad and Jarrāh through marriage.[2] Because of Yūsuf's association with the Ottoman Governor of Basra, it was suspected that he was conspiring with the Governor to become the ruler of Kuwait.[3] Mubārak felt that the time had come when he should replace his brother Muhammad as ruler of Kuwait, and the only way to achieve that was by getting rid of both brothers, which he did in June 1896.

However, this was not the end of Mubārak's internal troubles, for shortly after the arrival of Yūsuf al-Ibrāhīm in Basra, he arranged for the sons of the deceased Muhammad and Jarrāh to join him there. Since Yūsuf depended on Ottoman representatives in 'Irāq and Najd while planning his attacks on Kuwait, his activities will be dealt with as a part of Mubārak's relations with the Ottomans.

Mubārak and the Ottomans

With the arrival of the sons of Muhammad and Jarrāh the political and military struggle between Yūsuf and Shaikh Mubārak began. It is interesting to note that the two men followed similar tactics in trying to win that dispute. Yūsuf made immediate contact with Hamdī Pasha, the Ottoman *wālī* (Governor) of Basra, to gain his support in the cause of the deceased ruler of Kuwait, while Mubārak, on the other hand, approached Rajab Pasha, the Ottoman Governor of Baghdād. While Yūsuf sought help from the British consul at Basra, Mubārak hastened to the British

Resident at Abū Shahr, hoping to ensure British protection for Kuwait. Mubārak went one step further by approaching the Grand *Muftī* at Istanbul, Shaikh Abū al-Hudā. He spent money lavishly in hopes that the Sultan would sanction his position and recognize him as *Qā'immagām*, a title which the Sultan had conferred upon his father, Shaikh 'Abd Allāh II ibn Sabāh, in 1871 in recognition of Kuwait's participation in Midhat Pasha's expedition to al-Hasā.[4]

Both men were preparing for a military showdown. From the start it appeared that Mubārak's moves were more shrewdly planned and organized at higher levels, both in the neighbouring Gulf region and at Istanbul, the capital of the Ottoman Empire. However, because of Yūsuf's immense wealth and the possibility that he might hire an army to fight on his side, Mubārak prudently kept his vessels and land forces on the alert. The money which Mubārak spent in both Baghdād and Istanbul secured for him the approval of the Ottomans in December 1897, when a cable was relayed to him by the new Pasha of Basra, Muhsin. Thus, the battle for Ottoman support was won by Mubārak, who was anxious to avoid conspiracies and plots made at Istanbul or its dependencies in Baghdād and Basra against his new regime. As for the British, it was not until two years later, in 1899, that they signed a treaty with Mubārak. It is important to point out that at this time a struggle was being waged between the British and Ottomans to gain the upper hand in matters relating to the affairs of Kuwait. Kuwait's status in international diplomacy will be taken up when the question of a railway between the northern Arabian Gulf and Europe comes under discussion.

Yūsuf al-Ibrāhīm's War Against Mubārak[5]

Yūsuf was secretly preparing a sea invasion of Kuwait. By June 30, 1897, preparations were not only completed but the expedition which he had been equipping at Hindiān, on the Persian coast of the Gulf, advanced toward Kuwait. Despite the utmost secrecy in Yūsuf's plans, Mubārak's intelligence became aware of what was happening on the other side of the Gulf and his fleet was ready for Yūsuf's men at sea. When Yūsuf discovered that Kuwait was prepared for the war, he ordered his vessels to sail away, south to Bahrain Island which they reached in August 1897.

Yūsuf was hoping to persuade the Bahrainī ruler to join him in battle, but Mubārak had already invited Shaikh 'Isā Āl-Khalīfa to act as an arbitrator between Mubārak and his brothers' sons. Shaikh 'Isā, for reasons which he did not disclose, refused to mediate in the dispute, though the Government of India was hoping he would. The departure of Yūsuf's fleet from Kuwait and the negative response he received at Bahrain did not put an end to his attempts to invade Kuwait. That danger continued for the remainder of 1897 and throughout the following year.

4. See above, Chapter VIII, pp. 89-90.

5. This subject has been treated by Kuwaitī local historians and by other contemporary British sources. See Al-Qinā'ī pp. 25-26; al-Rashīd, II, pp. 51-62. See also Lorimer, I, i, pp. 1017-1018, and pp. 1027-1028. For other contemporary British reports see *Foreign Office Confidential Prints: Correspondence Respecting Affairs at Kuwait, 1896-1905*, published by R. Bidwell in *The Affairs of Kuwait, 1896-1905*, Vol. I, pp. 13-22. See also Dickson, *The Arab of the Desert*, pp. 271-272.

6.   See Lorimer, I, i, p. 1019;
See also al-Rashīd, II, pp. 61-62.

7.   See al-Rashīd II, pp. 63-65;
and Lorimer, I, i, pp. 1027-1028.

Yūsuf and Jāsim Āl-Thānī (1897-1898)[6]

After the failure of his mission at Bahrain, Yūsuf sailed to Dōha in Qatar where its Shaikh, Jāsim Āl-Thānī, agreed to a joint attack on Kuwait. Historical documents tell that Jāsim equipped a sea as well as a land force to march simultaneously against Kuwait. Moreover, he even approached Ibn al-Rashīd, Amīr of Shammar, with a proposal to join in the fighting against Mubārak. However, this venture, which was to commence in November 1898, did not materialize.

Although all of these attempts were unsuccessful, Yūsuf persisted and travelled to Hā'il, the capital in northern Najd, to conspire with Ibn al-Rashīd against Mubārak. It seems that that plot against Kuwait came as a result of advice rendered to Yūsuf by Ottoman authorities in Basra and Baghdād because of Ibn al-Rashīd's friendship with the Ottomans and because the Ottomans knew of his contempt for Mubārak.

Yūsuf al-Ibrāhīm and 'Abd al-Azīz Āl-Rashīd[7]

Ibn al-Rashīd was bound to suspect Mubārak for two reasons. 'Abd al-Rahmān ibn Faisal Āl-Su'ūd sought asylum with Mubārak upon losing his fight against Ibn al-Rashīd, also Najd had become a dependency of Jabal Shammar, Ibn al-Rashīd's land in northern Najd. Yūsuf travelled to Hā'il accompanied by the sons of the late Muhammad and Jarrāh. At Hā'il, Ibn al-Rashīd was hoping, with some assistance from the Pasha of Basra and Baghdād, to subject Kuwait to Ottoman rule, thereby, abolishing Mubārak and his guest, 'Abd al-Rahmān Āl-Su'ūd, who had been residing in Kuwait since 1897.

Though it is not possible to ascertain how the skirmishes between Mubārak and Ibn al-Rashīd began, it is a fact that Sa'dūn Pasha, exiled Shaikh of the Muntafiq tribe of 'Irāq, accompanied by 'Abd al-Rahmān Āl-Su'ūd, raided Najd in August 1900 after the latter had left Kuwait and joined Sa'dūn. It has also been established that Mubārak had sent reinforcements in September to 'Abd al-Rahmān Āl-Su'ūd upon the latter's request. In October, Mubārak joined the invaders in the hope of re-establishing 'Abd al-Rahmān in Riyād, the former capital of the Āl-Su'ūd. At this stage of the fight, Muhsin Pasha, the Ottoman Pasha of Basra and a friend of Mubārak, asked Sayyid Ahmad and Sayyid Tālib al-Naqīb, notables of Basra, to act as mediators in the conflict. The Naqībs managed to bring peace to the area, but only temporarily.

By that time, 1900, Mubārak's agreement with the British had been in effect for one year. Though relations between Mubārak and the British will be dealt with later, it should be pointed out that the British were not in favour of Mubārak's desert wars. But because Mubārak could not tolerate the presence of Yūsuf and the sons of Muhammad and Jarrāh at Hā'il as guests of Ibn al-Rashīd, the next round of fighting was inevitable.

The Battle of al-Sarīf (March 17, 1901)

Mubārak decided to attack Ibn al-Rashīd in Najd and Shammar without delay. For this expedition, he mustered a large army from among the settlers of Kuwait City and tribes of the Kuwaitī deserts: 'Awāzim, Rashāyida, Mutair, 'Ajmān, Banī Hājar and Banī Khālid.

In December 1900, Mubārak, accompanied by 'Abd al-Rahmān Āl-Su'ūd, marched at the head of his army to Najd which was conquered without any resistance. At Riyad, Mubārak reestablished the Su'ūdī rule with 'Abd al-Rahmān returning to his former seat as the Amīr of Najd. The victorious army advanced from there to mount an attack at Hā'il in Jabal Shammar. Unfortunately, before reaching their objective, on March 17, 1901, 'Abd al-'Azīz ibn al-Rashīd met the invaders at al-Sarīf, twenty miles northeast of Burayda in al-Qasīm district of Najd. The Kuwaitī army was routed and almost completely destroyed by Ibn al-Rashīd's army. Seven hundred out of a total of one thousand Kuwaitī settlers were killed as were another hundred from the Kuwaitī tribal forces. Mubārak managed to reach Kuwait safely after rumors had circulated that he had lost his life in battle. The disaster of al-Sarīf was viewed by many as the battle that destroyed Mubārak's dreams of establishing a great state in Arabia.[8]

Continued Enmity with Yūsuf (1902)

With Mubārak weakened militarily, Kuwait became potential prey to any strong aggressor such as 'Abd al-'Azīz Āl-Rashīd who would be tempted to attack at the instigation of the Ottomans in Basra, directly by the Governor of Basra himself, or by Yūsuf al-Ibrāhīm. Indeed, Yūsuf thought that the time was opportune for deposing Mubārak. His first tactics were to direct raids upon the bedouin tribes who were subjects of Mubārak. Using Zubair as a starting point, the raiders were not stopped by the Ottoman soldiers whose duty it was to enforce law and order in that area. Safwān and Sabiyya neighbourhoods were attacked and camels and sheep belonging to Kuwaitī bedouins stolen. These incursions were not serious enough to arouse the anger of Mubārak until Yūsuf planned a nocturnal attack on Kuwait town itself. By outfitting two *booms* [large local boats] with his armed men, Yūsuf hoped to surprise Mubārak at night and do away with him in the same way that Mubārak had disposed of his two brothers, Muhammad and Jarrāh.

To assure the success of this plan, Yūsuf convinced 'Adhbī ibn Muhammad Āl-Sabāh and his cousin, Humūd ibn Jarrāh Āl-Sabāh, to participate in this plot to avenge the deaths of their fathers. Unfortunately for Yūsuf, the two *booms* were spotted at night on the coast of al-Fāo Island in the north of Kuwait by the British warship, the "Lapwing", which hastened to alert Shaikh Mubārak of the impending danger. The Captain of the "Lapwing" learned that Mubārak knew of the conspiracy and that Kuwait was ready for the encounter.

8. Kumar, *India and the Persian Gulf Region*, p. 195. For vivid description of the effect of the defeat of Mubarak at al-Sarīf see al-Rashīd, *History of Kuwait*, II, pp. 66-73; See also al-Qina'ī, pp. 27-29.

9. See Lorimer, I, i, p. 1044.

However, by the time the "Lapwing" returned to its station off the coast of al-Fāo, the two *booms* had disappeared in Knōr 'Abd Allāh, a creek near al-Fāo. It should be recorded that the two *booms* moved to the coast of al-Fāo from al-Dawraq near Shatt al-'Arab the night of September 3 and remained there out of sight until September 5 when they were discovered and pursued by the Lapwing. Each had on board from 100 to 150 men armed with guns and not hoisting any flags. When the *booms* were grounded in the mud, the armed men jumped into the long grass of the marshes and started firing at the "Lapwing". One British soldier was killed and two wounded in the ensuing fight. Both *booms* were completely destroyed; one of them had been the property of Yūsuf al-Ibrāhīm, who was thrown out of Zubair and Basra as a result of a British protest to the Governor of the latter city. As expected, Yūsuf ibn 'Abd Allāh al-Ibrāhīm sought refuge with 'Abd al-'Azīz al-Rashīd at Hā'il, where he remained until his death in January 1906.[9]

Mubārak's Relations with the British

The "Lapwing" involvement in foiling the last attempt of Yūsuf al-Ibrāhīm to oust Mubārak from the seat of government in Kuwait invokes an in-depth study of Kuwaitī-British relations in Mubārak's era.

It has previously been stated that shortly after he assumed power in Kuwait, Mubārak hastened to contact the British Resident at Abū Shahr. Before reviewing Mubārak's relations with the British, a general survey of the political conditions in Europe as well as the state of affairs in the Gulf area in the late nineteenth and early twentieth centuries, may help in understanding why he chose to sign an agreement with the British.

By the nineteenth century, the political arena in Europe was dominated by imperial Britain and France, the newly rising power of Germany and the ambitious czarist Russia. Great Britain was at its political peak with colonies scattered across the globe and its position bolstered in the Arabian Gulf area by the presence of a strong naval contingent and standing treaties with many Gulf states. France had been able to acquire similar colonies in Africa and Asia but with less influence in the Gulf area. The Germans were late in achieving their national unity which was completed by 1870, a rather late date to acquire any significant colonial power, but eager to do so. The Russians still had hopes, however slim, of reaching the warm waters of the Mediterranean and the Arabian Gulf in the south. "The sick man of Europe", the Ottoman Empire, was still weak and waiting apprehensively for its territories to be divided among the European powers who could not agree among themselves on a way to do this. Kuwait, as well as most of the countries of the Arab Middle East were bound to suffer if the Ottoman Empire failed, because most of them were in some way linked to it. Some of them came under direct Ottoman rule, while others, like Kuwait, nominally recognized Ottoman supremacy. It was, therefore, natural for a shaikhdom like Kuwait to seek to establish a clearly independent status after or even, if possible, before the Empire's decline. And this was what Mubārak decided to accomplish.

To understand the strategem of Mubārak, one must be familiar with the state of affairs in Eastern Arabia during this same period, and Kuwait's efforts to maintain its independence under the Sabāh rule until Mubārak's rise to power. Most of the Arabian Peninsula was added to the Ottoman Empire during the sixteenth century. Eastern Arabia, as previously mentioned, was conquered in 1555, at which time Kuwait was not in existence. However, Ottoman rule in Eastern Arabia lasted until the end of the sixteenth century with the rise of the Banī Khālid who dominated the political scene in Eastern Arabia until they lost to the Wahhābīs. Concerning Wahhābī rule in Eastern Arabia *vis-a-vis* Ottoman rule, it is important to note that they and the Banī Khālid before them, ruled the area directly and, therefore, effectively. The Ottomans on the other hand, in most of their acquired territories, allowed former rulers to continue in power on condition that they acknowledge the Ottoman Sultan as their superior and pay tribute to the treasury in Istanbul.

When the Wahhābī power was destroyed by the Egyptians in 1818, the latter reestablished Banī Khālid rule in Eastern Arabia. The Wahhābīs or the Āl-Su'ūd came to power in 1840 after the withdrawal of the Egyptians from the Arabian Peninsula, and continued to rule Najd and al-Hasā until the Ottomans made a comeback under Midhat Pasha, Governor of Baghdād in 1871. But the situation in Eastern Arabia in 1871 was much different from that in 1555 when the Ottomans first arrived. Most of the chiefs of Eastern Arabia had signed treaties with the British who were annoyed to see the Ottomans once more gain a foothold along the shores of the Gulf. For specific details on Wahhābī, Ottoman, Egyptian and British activities on the eastern Arabian coast between 1800 and 1871, the reader is referred to preceding chapters.

The rule of the Āl-Sabāh in Kuwait began in 1752, at a time when the region from Qatar in the south to Basra in the north was under the Banī Khālid rule. It was in that year (1752) that the Banī Khālid began to lose control over their domains due to internal feuds among members of the ruling family. Thus, Kuwait gradually established its independence and by the 1760's seemed to have become completely free of the Banī Khālid who, in their turn, were no longer under the domination of the Ottomans. Whereas most of the shaikhdoms on the eastern coasts of Arabia, from Rās al-Khayma in the south to Qatīf and 'Uqair in the north, acknowledged the authority of the Wahhābī ruler by the end of the 18th century, Kuwait did not and successfully defended itself against the Wahhābī attacks. From 1800 and until 1896, when Mubārak became ruler of Kuwait, it seems that the town did not acknowledge the authority over its territories of any of the powers which held control of Eastern Arabia. The title of *Qā'immaqām*, bestowed on Shaikh 'Abd Allāh II by Midhat Pasha for services rendered during the latter's expedition to al-Hasā was nothing more than an honorary title and did not signify any form of dependency or servitude.

10. See Kumar, *India and the
     Persian Gulf Region*, p. 140.

Mubārak must have been aware of that when he became ruler in 1896, and in fact, must have realized something was in the offing as he observed conditions in the Ottoman Empire steadily become worse. He foresaw the dismemberment of Ottoman possessions in Arabia where local governors were becoming more independent in the management of their governments and where the authority of the Sultan was diminishing to the point where he was a leader in name only. Since the Sultan no longer represented a threat to the governors of his provinces, Mubārak felt that any obstacle to Kuwait's independence would inevitably come from her neighbours. It was then that he undertook the search for a strong ally on whom Kuwait could depend if attacked by a greedy and vicious neighbour who might also become completely independent of Ottoman rule. The strongest among those powers with vested interests in the Gulf region was Great Britain, and it was to her that Mubārak turned for talks of mutual interest to both parties.

Mubārak Seeks British Protection (1896-1897)

The reader's attention is drawn to the fact that certain Ottoman Pashas appointed to the Provinces of Baghdād and Basra were ambitiously planning expeditions to al-Hasā to revive interest in a former province of the Sultan. Among those was Midhat Pasha who sent an expedition in 1871, and Hamdī Pasha, Governor of Basra Province, whose attention in 1896 was focused on Kuwait, a territory within closer range. Mubārak's couriers in Istanbul kept him informed of such plans well ahead of time. The British who had interests in this area were also anxious to curb these renewed efforts of the Ottomans. After the opening of the Suez Canal by the French in 1869, to the exclusion of the British, it became imperative for Great Britain to seek an alternative trade route to India. Hence the appointment by the British Parliament of a Committee in 1871 to investigate the feasibility of a railway connecting the Mediterranean Sea and the Arabian Gulf.[10] The Committee recommended that a railway be built between Alexandretta on the Syrian coast and Kuwait on the Arabian Gulf. This, in their view, would be a faster way for transporting soldiers, when necessary, to the Arabian Gulf to repel any Russian forces which might reach the Gulf via Persia. However, because it was not economically viable, the project was not carried out. Yet, a few years later, similar railway projects by the Russian Count Kapnist and the German Berlin-Baghdād railway, were approved by the Ottoman authorities. The Germans also favoured Kuwaitī territory as the terminus.

The aborted British project is of special importance to this narrative because of the choice of Kuwait as its terminal point on the Gulf end. It should also be recalled that Colonel Pelly, the British Resident in the Gulf, in a report on Kuwait harbour written after his visit there in 1863, pointed out the suitability and importance of the port for the British navy. This must have attracted the attention of the Foreign Office when approached by Mubārak who was seeking to sign a treaty with the British Government in 1896. That treaty was not signed until the 23rd of January, 1899, a delay prompted by the international political scene.

Due to certain events which were taking place in the last decade of the nineteenth century, Britain was inclined toward drawing up agreements with the rulers of the Gulf region aimed at excluding other European powers.

Upon learning that the French and the Russians were establishing cordial relations and cooperating in the Mediterranean Sea, and in view of the developing friendship between the Germans and Ottomans, the British decided to shut the doors of the Arabian Gulf to those three major European powers.

Masqat, at the southern entrance of the Gulf, had already signed treaties of friendship with Great Britain as had the Arabs of Trucial 'Umān and of Bahrain. The only country without a contractual agreement with Britain and whose geographic location was of extreme importance to British policy was Kuwait. Thus, when Britain was looking for an opportunity to sign an agreement with Mubārak, she could find no better reason than the Ottoman's concession to Count Kapnist in 1898, and the desire of Istanbul to ask the Germans to build the Berlin-Baghdād Railway. As previously stated, both projects viewed Kuwait or Kāzima in Kuwait as the railway terminal on the Arabian Gulf. The British were, at long last, ready to negotiate an agreement with Mubārak.

Prelude to the 1899 Agreement

In fact, it could have been Istanbul's false accusation of the British that led both Mubārak and the British to see eye-to-eye on the question relating to Ottoman plots against Mubārak. For when Mubārak succeeded in staging the coup against his brother, Muhammad, Istanbul accused the British Resident in Abū-Shahr of planning the coup. The Resident made it quite clear to the Foreign Office that the charge was untrue. An act of piracy which took place off the coast of Kuwait shortly after the coup, forced the British to choose between holding either the Ottoman authorities in Basra or Shaikh Mubārak responsible for the attack.[11] The Foreign Office decided to hold Shaikh Mubārak accountable seeing as it took place in the territorial waters of Kuwait. The Shaikh of Kuwait was treated, in this instance, "as an independent ruler" who recognized the nominal authority of the Ottomans in Kuwait.[12] This decision by the Foreign Office was a *de facto* recognition of Mubārak's independence. Official British acknowledgement, however, did not come until two years later when they were forced to do so as a result of Count Kapnist's railway project.

Count Kapnist's Railway Project

On the 30th of December, 1898, the Ottoman Government granted Count Kapnist the concession of building a railway starting at Tripoli on

11. The vessel concerned was the India *Baghla* "Haripasa". For correspondence relating to this incident, see pages 1, 8, 9 and 10 in *The Affairs of Kuwait*, Vol. I. See also an interesting discussion of the same incident in *Gazetteer of the Persian Gulf*, I, i, pp. 1019-1020.

12. See Kumar, *India and the Persian Gulf*, p. 138, who argues that Shaikh Mubarak was in fact an independent ruler.

13.   For the text of Exclusive
Agreement see Appendix No. IV.
For a discussion of the terms of
the Agreement, see Lorimer, I, i,
pp. 1022-1023.

the Syrian coast, via Homs and Baghdād, and ending at Kuwait. Salisbury, Secretary of the Foreign Office, realized that if Kapnist's project was put into operation, Syria, 'Irāq and Eastern Arabia would be lost to the Russians. Consequently he decided to sign with Mubārak an agreement similar to that which Britain had signed with the Sultan of Masqat in 1891.

Colonel Meade, the British Resident in the Gulf, was instructed to proceed to Kuwait and sign an exclusive treaty which made it quite clear that Mubārak would agree not to sell or lease any part of his domains to a foreign power without prior permission granted by the British Government.[13]

When the agreement was given to Mubārak for his signature, he refused to sign unless the British Government added a clause explicitly stating that Great Britain would insure the defense of Kuwait if attacked by a foreign power. Meade informed Mubārak that he was not authorized by his Government to add any new item to the treaty. He also added that Britain had not promised protection of that kind to any of the Arab rulers who had previously signed similar treaties with her, though those rulers would receive assistance if necessary. It was finally decided that Meade would write a letter to Mubārak in which he would guarantee, on behalf of his Government, such protection as long as Mubārak continued to respect that agreement.

Because Britain was determined to keep the Russians out of the Gulf area, Mubārak was able to obtain from Meade the security he was seeking. As a result of that treaty, Great Britain, by virtue of its influence in Kuwait, succeeded at last in enhancing her political, military and commercial interests in this strategic northwestern corner of the Arabian Gulf. The history of the European rivalry in the Gulf region would not be complete without a brief review of the Berlin-Baghdād Railway, the German project.

The Berlin-Baghdād Railway

Friendly relations and stronger ties between Germany and the Ottoman Empire seemed to have been greatly enhanced by the two visits paid to Turkey by the German Emperor in the latter part of the 19th century. One of the most important issues for discussion was the desire of the Germans to open the Levant as a market for their industrial products. This could be facilitated by building an extension onto the existing Berlin-Istanbul railway which would pass through Asia Minor and Syria to Baghdād in 'Irāq.

The British, who preferred the Germans to the Russians, favoured the new project because the Germans, if their plan were executed, would stop Russian penetration into the Levant territories of the Ottoman Empire. The Russians, on the other hand, suspecting it was backed by a British-German alliance, opposed the plan.

An *Irādeh* announcing approval of the German plan was issued by the Sultan in Istanbul on November 25, 1899. Early in 1900, after the agreement had been signed by the Germans and Ottomans, a team of German surveyors reached Basra and began its work. Wratslaw, the British Consul, heard that the German team was on its way to Kuwait and soon after learnt that they had reported that the success of the project would depend on two factors; first, that its terminal point should be Kuwait rather than Basra, and second, that the Ottoman Government should back it financially.[14] The German team advised the Company to discuss the first point directly with the Sultan and not with Shaikh Mubārak. This disturbed the Government of India which felt that any agreement reached directly with the Sultan would weaken its position in the Gulf region. Since the 1899 Exclusive Treaty with Mubārak had been kept secret, the Government of India suggested that the Foreign Office should inform the German Government of its existence. This advice was followed.

The German team had had an audience with Shaikh Mubārak, and the Government of India was informed of their discussions. Mubārak told them that the people of Kuwait would not sell or rent any piece of their land to a foreigner, and that he did not acknowledge the authority of the Ottomans over Kuwait.[15]

The British Ambassador to the Ottoman court paid a visit to the Ottoman minister of external affairs and explained their position with respect to the Berlin-Baghdād Railway, emphasizing that they did not want the *status quo* in the Gulf to be disturbed. He made it clear that any agreement with a foreign power to extend the railway beyond 'Irāq to Kuwait would not be acceptable to the British Government. Immediately after that call, the Ambassador proceeded to the German Embassy where he disclosed to the German Ambassador the hitherto secret 1899 agreement with the Shaikh of Kuwait, making it clear that no agreement affecting Kuwait and its territories would be acceptable to the British without the prior sanction of the latter, or in any case without British companies' participation in the project. The Germans accepted the British points of view, but the project did not materialize due to circumstances linked to the international struggle among the four major European powers. As far as the modern history of Kuwait is concerned, the projects of Baron Kapnist and the Germans called attention to Kuwait's importance at the international level. Mubārak's position, in honoring the terms of the Exclusive Treaty in his deliberations with the German team of surveyors, gained him the respect of the British Government and its support of Kuwait's independence against foreign aggression. In ensuing years, other agreements were negotiated reinforcing British-Kuwaitī relations to an even greater degree.

Other Agreements with the British

On the 24th of May, 1900, Shaikh Mubārak signed an agreement with the British pledging to curtail the prosperous trade of arms

14. For a thorough discussion of the German Berlin-Baghdad Railway Project, see Kumar, *India and the Persian Gulf Region*, pp. 154-188. See also Lorimer, I, i, pp. 1545-1547. For the question of Kuwait and Baghdad Railway extension to Kazima, see *The Affairs of Kuwait*, Vol. II, pp. 55 and 61.

15. Kumar, *India and the Persian Gulf Region*, p. 157.

Lord Curzon's visit to Kuwait, 1903

The Shaikh waiting

Bodyguard of Mailed Sowars

Landing at Koweit

Camel Guard of Honour

A Few Words of Welcome

trafficking (smuggling) to Afghanistan, a practice common at some Gulf ports, including Kuwait. Four years later on February 18, 1904, Shaikh Mubārak signed another agreement with the British allowing them to establish a postal service. On June 24 of the same year, he gave his consent to have a British Political Agent in residence to look after British interests. Captain Knox, the first to hold that post, arrived on the 6th of August of the same year and was warmly received by Shaikh Mubārak. The major tasks of the new Political Agent were the curtailment of Mubārak's activities outside the borders of Kuwait, especially in his relations with the Āl-Rashīd of Jabal Shammar, and easing of tensions on Kuwait's northern borders with 'Irāq at Umm Qasr, Safwān and Bubiān Island.

Another step towards establishing the British in Kuwait was the treaty which made it possible for the British to rent the port of Shuwaikh (Bandar al-Shuwaikh) in the vicinity of Kuwait. Although it was stated in the agreement[16] that Bandar al-Shuwaikh was going to be used as a coaling station for the British fleet, the main objective was to enable British guns to fire at the German encampment at Kāzima should the Ottomans and Germans decide to bring the Berlin-Baghdād Railway to a terminal in that place without Mubārak's permission.

The series of agreements between Mubārak and the British continued. On July 29, 1911, Shaikh Mubārak agreed not to allow foreigners to dive for sponges and pearls in the Kuwaitī territorial waters before consulting with the Political Agent. In a letter dated July of the following year, addressed to Sir Percy Cox, the British Resident at Abū Shahr, Mubārak gave his approval of the establishment of a telegraphic cable line in Kuwait. This was followed by another agreement on October 27, 1913, in which Mubārak wrote to Sir Percy confirming a previous discussion between them relating to oil exploration and production in Kuwait. That operation, according to the agreement, became a British monopoly.

The reader of the texts of these agreements soon comes to realize that the main objective of the British was to keep Mubārak so occupied and engrossed in these matters that he could not establish any relations with foreign powers other than the British. These agreements continued to be honoured by Kuwait long after the death of Mubārak on January 3, 1916. It is obvious that the British realized benefits from these agreements. The question that arises is: How much did Kuwait gain from them?

To answer this, one has only to remember the turbulent and unstable state of affairs in the regions surrounding Kuwait at that time. The 1890's was a period of European competition not only among the powers of that continent but overseas as well. One of the most vulnerable areas was the territory of the Ottoman Empire in Western Asia; without a dependable ally chosen from among those powers, a small country like Kuwait could not have survived the struggle among these European powers to reach the northern head of the Arabian Gulf. Even on the local scene, Kuwait was

16. See the agreement concerning Bandar Al-Shuwaikh in the Appendix No. IV.

17.   See Lorimer, I, i, pp.
1546-1547; see also Kumar,
pp. 155-156.

either being threatened by the Ottoman Pashas in 'Irāq, or by Ibn Rashīd in the Shammar area and northern Najd.

At a later date, when the world was involved in the Great War of 1914-1918, the benefits of Mubārak's alliance with the British were of crucial importance to the continuation of Kuwait's independence. After the Allies, Britain and France, defeated the Germans and the Ottomans, the Ottoman territories of Greater Syria and 'Irāq were divided between the British and French. Britain became the mandatory power over Palestine, Jordan and 'Irāq, while Lebanon and Syria became mandates of the French. Britain guaranteed Mubārak's northern borders with 'Irāq which were his main concern. Even before the War of 1914, the British, in accordance with the 1899 agreement with Mubārak, kept the Ottoman Provincial Governors of Basra from these borders by denying them the use of Kāzima as the terminal point of the Berlin-Baghdād Railway.[17]

Disadvantages of Alliance with Britain

However, the 1899 agreement did not prove to be advantageous to Kuwait at all times. To understand this statement, the relationship between 'Abd al-'Azīz Āl-Su'ūd and Mubārak should be recalled. These two great Arab leaders shared, among other things, great ambitions. No sooner had Mubārak become aware of the decline of the power of the Su'ūdī state in the 1880's, than he began contemplating the extension of his domains to al-Hasā and Najd upon his accession to the seat of power in Kuwait in 1896. Mubārak helped the Āl-Su'ūd regain Riyād in 1902, but when 'Abd al-'Azīz was besieged at al-Hufūf, Mubārak sent his son Sālim to the rescue with instructions not to destroy the besieging tribes of al-'Ajmān completely after defeating them in battle, but to allow them to retreat to the neighbourhood of Kuwait. Thus, 'Abd al-'Azīz was made to realize that he would always need the patronage of Mubārak.

With the appointment of the British Political Agent at Kuwait since 1904, Mubārak's hopes and aspirations seemed to gradually diminish. He was not being given a free hand in dealing with his neighbours such as the Āl-Su'ūd, Ibn al-Rashīd or the Governors of Basra, and he was not going to be allowed to expand beyond certain borders, expecially in the south. In 1913, the British negotiated with the Ottomans an agreement on the borders of Kuwait, Najd and 'Irāq. Mubārak agreed to the British-drawn borders only because he could not afford to disagree. The British, after all, had been authorized by the 1899 agreement (and others that followed) to handle Kuwaitī foreign affairs, which they were doing.

One must also bear in mind in conjunction with this that British policy, since the 1820 General Treaty of Peace with the Qawāsim, was to maintain peace in the waters of the Gulf, that is at sea, and not on land. This policy, adopted by the British Government of Bombay as early as 1800, was upheld by the British Government of India after that date and no exceptions would be made for Mubārak. In another instance, during the reign of Ahmad al-Jābir, Mubārak's grandson, the British signed on behalf of Kuwait an agreement at 'Uqair, resulting in the loss of two-thirds of its territory to 'Abd al-'Azīz Āl-Su'ūd. This matter will be the subject of further discussion in the following chapter. Even though the 1899 agreement with Britain was not a total success for her, Kuwait, under Mubārak, passed through what may be described in current terms as a period of modernization.

Progress under Mubārak

Ever since its establishment as the capital of the Āl-Sabāh in the 1750's, Kuwait has never been a neglected port. Her fleet, built in the 1770's, was the second largest Arab fleet in the Gulf, Masqat being first. Prosperity in a major town depends not only on an active merchant establishment and daring commercial enterprises but also on the preservation of law and order.

During Mubārak's rule, Kuwait enjoyed peace at home and prosperity abroad. Allowance must be made for the first few years of Mubārak's rule, when he was engaged in trying to defeat his enemy, Yūsuf ibn 'Abd Allāh al-Ibrāhīm. Despite these wars, Kuwait was a very prosperous seaport, supplying Najd and Jabal Shammar in the east and northeast with food and necessary clothing. Perhaps this explains why Ibn al-Rashīd had hoped to annex it to his domains in Jabal Shammar which had no other outlet to the sea. Kuwait's customary trade with 'Irāq, Persia, India and East Africa continued to flourish under Mubārak and British steamers sailed into its port once each week.

Mubārak, as stated previously, agreed to establish postal services as well as cable lines for telegraphic communications. These two services not only helped promote modernization, but aided in the growth of trade.

Mubārak's major achievement in social services was the introduction of modern medicine to his country. The first medical officer to practice in Kuwait was the Assistant Political Agent, who was appointed shortly after the arrival of the Political Agent himself in 1904. But credit for laying the foundations in that field should be given to the Arabian American Mission [18] whose first medical services started at Kuwait in 1911. This group initiated its work in Arabia late in the 19th century, but was not allowed to come to Kuwait until much later. Mubārak had learned of their medical services earlier than 1911 when he was on a visit to his friend, Shaikh Khaz'al of Muhammara. Mission records kept in New Brunswick, New Jersey, in the United States of America, blame him for the delay in their arrival. It seems, however, they were not aware of the terms of the 1899 agreement between Mubārak and the British which did not allow the sale or rental of Kuwaitī territory to foreigners. The British, however, eventually allowed the mission to get in touch with Mubārak who granted them permission to come to Kuwait as a medical mission, but not as evangelists. This is clear from the original draft of their agreement with Mubārak.

Upon the Mission's request, the word medical was omitted by the

18.   American Arabian Mission which started its medical activities first in Basra in 1892, tried to gain footing in Kuwait as early as 1898, but its doctors were not able to practise there until 1911. In 1910, Dr. Bennett wrote to his headquarters in New York City from Kuwait (8th December, 1910) informing them that Shaikh Mubārak had agreed to sell the "Mission" a piece of land for building a hospital (see *Arabian Mission Series*, Box 4, no. 783). This visit was a follow-up on an earlier visit to Kuwait in August, 1910. Medical work at Kuwait by the American Mission doctors started in 1911. Bennett was apparently the explorer, but soon Dr. Paul Harrison was appointed and so was Dr. Eleanor T. Calverley in 1912 and the latter two were appointed to Kuwait after Dr. Stanley Mylrea, the resident doctor had left in 1911 on a furlough to America. For details of the Mission's medical activities see scattered information in Dr. Eleanor Calverley's book *My Arabian Days and Nights*, and Dr. S. Mylrea's *Kuwait before Oil*, pp. 39 ff.

19. See Appendix No. VI. A copy of the agreement signed by the British resident (on behalf of Shaikh Mubārak) and Modrdyk and Dykstra of the Mission was sent to the headquarters rk City from Bahrain on 18th November, 1910. See *Arabian Mission Series*, Box 4 no. 753.

20. For medical work in Kuwait between 1912 and 1929, see Dr. Eleanor T. Calverley's book *My Arabian Days and Nights*; and for the period from 1911-1945, see Dr. Stanley Mylrea's manuscript, *Kuwait before Oil*. Information in the two books is not restricted to certain chapters, but can be found throughout the works.

21. See Barclay Raunkiaer, *Through Wahhabiland on Camelback*, pp. 33-39.

British Resident at Bahrain where their secretariat was located.[19] The agreement was signed at Bahrain and Kuwait in 1910. Of special interest to the historian of Kuwait are the British files kept at the India Office Records in London. These documents, including correspondence from the British Resident in the Gulf, indicate that the British viewed the mission's work with great political suspicion, especially when they went on tours across the Gulf to countries like Najd, Qatar and interior 'Umān. The delay in the opening of the Kuwait station, therefore, cannot rightfully be blamed on Mubārak, but on the British.

The medical team of the Arabian mission at Kuwait was, indeed, very dynamic. The first building of the hospital for men was put up immediately after their arrival. This was followed by a hospital for women. Mubārak, in appreciation and encouragement for their medical services, gave them as a gift another parcel of land, equal in size to the one they had bought for £1,500. Among the early doctors who joined the American team was a woman, Eleanor Calverley, who stayed in Kuwait between 1912 and 1929.[20] Another who served with distinction was Dr. Stanley Mylrea, who is buried at Kuwait.

Mubārak's efforts in the area of modern education were also outstanding. It was under his direction, in 1911, that al-Mubārakiyya School was built for the instruction of classical as well as modern subjects.

In conclusion, Mubārak's role in the history of Kuwait laid the foundations of what is today referred to as modern Kuwait. His futuristic policy guaranteed his country political stability in a troubled area during turbulent times. Mubārak, a diplomat of both the 19th and 20th centuries, was proficient in handling the big power politics of his era in the European style. The net result was the establishment of an internationally recognized country. While it is true that Mubārak was a merciless ruler, this should not discredit him by any means because human actions are so often controlled by their environment; in this case, the desert and the sea both of which can also be merciless. Yet, Mubārak was always in close touch with his people. His daily *majlis* [diwan meetings] in the market place exemplifies this side of his nature, which was well described by Raunkiaer.[21] In this manner, Mubārak retained an honored tradition which his ancestors had established long before his time and which to this day is adhered to by other members of the Sabāh family.

Mubārak was succeeded by his eldest son, Jābir, who in turn was followed by his brother, Sālim. The coming chapter will deal with the rule of these two brothers as well as that of Ahmad, son of Jābir.

My escort in Koweit Desert, November 1909. (Shakespear)

Mid-day halt in desert Koweit hinterland, November 1909. (Shakespear)

*Breaking camp, Koweit
Desert. Thamila al Ga'a,
7 December 1909.
(Shakespear)*

*'Dhabia' with owner Khalaf
and 'Shalwa', Koweit Desert,
7 December 1909.
(Shakespear)*

*Breaking camp, Koweit
Desert. Thamila al Ga'a,
7 December 1909.
(Shakespear)*

*Shaikh's palace, Koweit.
(Shakespear)*

Shaikh's palace, Koweit.
(Shakespear)

The British Agency, Koweit.
(Shakespear)

Shaikh Sālim ibn Mubārak 1917–1921

CHAPTER XI

KUWAIT AFTER MUBĀRAK
1915-1965

It has already been noted that in 1899, Mubārak signed the Exclusive Agreement with Great Britain and that it had been put into effect immediately.[1] However, the crucial point came in 1914 with the beginning of the First World War when Britain was fighting the Ottomans, allies of the Germans. Mubārak's position was clear. He stood by the agreement on the side of the Christian British who were fighting the Moslem Caliph, the Ottoman Sultan.

After Mubārak's death, Kuwait was ruled by Jābir his eldest son (1915), followed by Sālim in 1917. The reigns of these two brothers were brief but eventful. Though Jābir and Sālim followed the example set by Mubārak in allying themselves with the British, Sālim did not back the British wholeheartedly.[2] It was, indeed, very difficult for any ruler in the Arabian Peninsula to side with the British against the Ottoman Sultan, since the subjects of those rulers were also Moslems. It was even more difficult if that ruler had no real grievance against the Sultan.

The Āl-Sabāh were not the only Arab ruling family in the Peninsula who took the side of the British. 'Abd al-'Azīz Āl-Su'ūd, *Amīr* of Najd, as well as the *sharifs* of Makka did likewise. As mentioned earlier in this book, the Āl-Su'ūd had been on unfriendly terms with the Turks over a long period of years. In 1818, their capital, al-Dir'iyya, was destroyed by an Egyptian-Turkish expedition and in 1871, Midhat Pasha, Ottoman Governor of Baghdād, succeeded in re-establishing Ottoman rule over al-Hasā and Najd.[3] As a result of Midhat's campaign, many Su'ūdī *amīrs* sought refuge in the neighbouring towns. Among those fleeing to Kuwait was 'Abd al-Rahmān ibn Faisal, the father of 'Abd al-'Azīz. It has already been related how 'Abd al-'Azīz managed, with the help of Shaikh Mubārak of Kuwait, to capture al-Riyād in 1902 by staging his attack from Kuwait. Therefore, it was only natural for 'Abd al-'Azīz to join the British in their war against the Ottomans.

Jābir ibn Mubārak (1915-1917)

Under Jābir, Kuwait seemed to have flourished immensely as a result of the increase in volume of trade with Syria. Caravans carried from Kuwait to Syria almost every commodity the natives there needed.[4] These

1. See above, Chapter X, pp. 117-119.

2. See al-Rashīd, II, pp. 150-151 and 159-162.

3. See above, Chapter VIII, pp. 85-87.

4. Al-Rashīd II, pp. 161-162.

5. *Ibid.*

6. *Ibid.*

7. See above, Chapter X, pp. 236-237.

8. For the siege of al-Jahra see al-Rashīd, II, pp. 178-192. Al-Rashīd participated in the actual fighting. See also Mylrea, *Kuwait before Oil*, pp. 86-100; and Dickson, *Kuwait and her Neighbours*, pp. 253-256

commodities reached the hands of the Turks as well, a fact which indicates that the British blockade of the Ottomans was broken by Kuwait. It seems that Shaikh Jābir made no effort to stop these caravans from trading with Syria. However, the British were sure that his policy was to discourage the smuggling of goods to Syria. Jābir had, of course, declared officially, after his succession to the seat of Governor, that he and his people were on the side of the allies. Jābir's rule lasted just a year and two months and he was succeeded by his brother, Sālim.

Sālim ibn Mubārak (1917-1921)

Since the new ruler was a strict observer of the Moslem faith, the British were afraid he might openly join the Ottomans or try his best to help them against the allies.[5] Sālim seems to have preferred putting his efforts towards aiding the Ottomans. And though he did not declare his intentions for fear of the British intervening in the internal affairs of Kuwait, it appears that he did encourage the continuation of the illegal trade with Syria and the Ottomans. This action provoked the British to such an extent that they threatened Sālim by declaring that they would not come to the rescue of Kuwait if it were subjected to a foreign attack unless he changed his stand towards their enemy, the Ottomans.[6]

Sālim remembered the impending danger of 'Abd al-'Azīz Āl-Su'ūd whose attack on Kuwait was expected at any time, now that Sālim had become ruler. The animosity between these two men dated back to December 1915, when Sālim, accompanied by Ahmad al-Jābir al-Sabāh, grandson of Mubārak, was sent at the head of a Kuwaitī army and instructed by Mubārak, his father, to rescue the besieged 'Abd al-'Azīz from the 'Ajmān tribe. The 'Ajmāns were on the verge of capturing Hufūf in al-Hasā and seizing 'Abd al-'Azīz. The Kuwaitīs, as previously alluded to, defeated the 'Ajmāns, routed their forces and relieved the besieged town. 'Abd al-'Azīz wanted Sālim and the army under him to pursue the 'Ajmāns and deal them a blow from which they could never recover. But Sālim, acting on instructions from his father, Shaikh Mubārak, allowed the defeated 'Ajmāns to travel northward to Kuwait and seek shelter in its neighbourhood. This enraged 'Abd al-'Azīz who was unable to contend with the 'Ajmāns and punish them on his own.[7] That incident marked the beginning of the enmity between the two men, an enmity which led later to the siege of al-Jahra town by the forces of the fanatic Wahhābī Ikhwān (brothers) under the command of Faisal al-Duwaish in 1920.[8]

The Siege of al-Jahra (October 10, 1920)

The battle of al-Jahra is considered by far one of, if not the most important, events in the modern history of the shaikhdom of Kuwait. Not only did it reflect the tenacity of Sālim's courage, but it also showed that Sālim meant to defend the entire territory of his shaikhdom against the aggressors, not only Kuwait town, its capital. But before we deal with that battle, let us examine the relations between Kuwait and Riyād prior to the Ikhwān's attack on al-Jahra.

These relations must have been favourable, for in November 1915 Sālim was sent to the rescue of 'Abd al-'Azīz. It can, therefore, be concluded that up until the death of Mubārak in November 1915, relations with 'Abd al-'Azīz were friendly. Mubārak died. During his son Jābir's rule, still no tensions in the relations between Kuwait and Riyād were reported. In the five years that elapsed between the death of Mubārak and the siege of al-Jahra in 1920, 'Abd al-'Azīz was busy consolidating his own authority over Najd and al-Hasā when al-Ikhwān challenged his leadership of the community.[9] Soon after he had solved that internal problem, he directed his attention toward Kuwait, a major center of trade which was essential to the population of Najd. The economic prosperity of Kuwait during the First World War did not go unnoticed by 'Abd al-'Azīz nor did he forget how Sālim refused to help him destroy the 'Ajmāns, his bitter enemies.

After 'Abd al-'Azīz's success in curbing the influence of the Ikhwān at home, when they accepted him as their *Imām* [religious leader] and political chief, he apparently wanted to settle that old feud with Sālim and his father, Shaikh Mubārak. His weapon in achieving this end was the Ikhwān whose wrath he directed at Kuwait. It was a simple matter for him to claim that the Ikhwān were attacking Kuwait on their own initiative on the basis of their reputation as an unruly group of zealous Moslem tribesmen.

Sālim was evidently aware of 'Abd al-'Azīz's intentions and before the Ikhwān's attack on Kuwait's territories, sent some soldiers of his tribal forces to encamp near Manīfa Mountain, Kuwait's southern border as designated by the unratified treaty of 1913, which had been negotiated between Great Britain and the Ottomans in Istanbul. Sālim's tribal soldiers were surprised by a sudden attack by the Ikhwān who massacred most of them on the 4th of April, 1920.[10] Those who managed to escape found their way to Kuwait. This incident shows quite clearly that 'Abd al-'Azīz was not willing to accept the 1913 demarcation of boundaries between Kuwait and his domains.

On the other hand, Sālim, as a result of all this, discovered that his suspicions of 'Abd al-'Azīz's intentions towards Kuwait proved true. He therefore embarked on an immediate plan for the defence of Kuwait town and other Kuwaitī territories.[11] At Kuwait itself, he ordered a wall to be built around the city to protect it from the Ikhwān raids. His ambitious project was completed in a record time of two months. The wall could not have been completed had it not been for the unfailing support and personal involvement of each and every individual Kuwaitī, man or woman, in the construction of that wall, which remained intact until its demolition in 1956 in accordance with the new town planning.[12] Many residents of the town, including the author, were saddened to see the disappearance of that monument. However, the main gates were left untouched and are preserved as a reminder of the near past.[13]

9.   For *al-Ikhwān* see Hafiz Wahba, *Jazīrat al-'Arab fi al-Qarn al-Ishrīn*, pp. 273-289; and see also Dickson, *Kuwait and her Neighbours*, pp. 148-150.

10.   See al-Rashīd, II, pp. 178-192; see also Freeth and Winstone, *Kuwait - Prospect and Reality*, pp. 84-86; and Mylrea, *Kuwait before Oil*, pp. 86-93.

11.   See Freeth and Winstone, *Kuwait - Prospect and Reality*, pp. 82-84; see also Mylrea, *Kuwait before Oil*, pp. 86-87. Mylrea was an eyewitness to the building of the new city wall which began on 22nd May, 1920 and was completed in Septd6ber, 1920. See *ibid.*, p. 87.

12.   The demolition of the wall took place at the time when the city was outgrowing its size within its wall. Mr. Said Breik, Chief Municipal Engineer was then in charge of the planning, and he explained to me in 1956 and later in 1978 why the wall had had to be razed.

13.   These main gateways, however, look different in colour from the old ones because they were covered with a thin layer of cement.

14. See al-Rashīd II, page 180
     ff. for a description of the
     situation of the besieged
     Kuwaitīs in the Red Fort of
     al-Jahra. For the British
     participation in repelling the
     Ikhwān, see Mylrea, *Kuwait
     before Oil*, pp. 97-100; Dickson,
     Kuwait and her Neighbours,
     pp. 255-256.

15. See above, pp. 95-100.

16. See Appendix No. IV.

17. See Mylrea, *Kuwait before
     Oil*, p. 99.

The Ikhwān Attack

Soon after the completion of that wall, Sālim sensed the impending danger from the Ikhwān who started their march northwards to Kuwait under the leadership of Faisal al-Duwaish. It was evident that Kuwait town was their objective. Sālim realized that his first line of defence must not be Kuwait city, but the town of al-Jahra which was protected by a strong fort. He proceeded to that town, at the head of well-armed Kuwaitī citizens, where they were joined by additional tribal forces. Faisal al-Duwaish led the attack on al-Jahra with an army that outnumbered the Kuwaitīs. The battle fought outside al-Jahra resulted in catastrophic losses for Sālim's forces. With the remainder of his men, he retreated to the Red Fort of al-Jahra where it was decided to put into action delaying tactics in order to exhaust al-Duwaish's forces on the one hand and to postpone their attack on Kuwait town on the other. Though details of this famous siege of the Red Fort will not be given, it should be noted that Sālim's strategy succeeded and the final battle did not reach Kuwait; the fate of the war was decided at al-Jahra after the intervention of the British.[14]

The Position of the British

The conflict in al-Jahra had far-reaching effects on the internal situation in Kuwait itself and on the position of the other powers in the region.

Kuwait, before and during the crisis, knew that the only means of survival was to strengthen the ties of cooperation among its population. The battle of Jahra for the Kuwaitīs was a matter of life and death for their independent city. The Āl-Sabāhs had already known that from the early days of Shaikh 'Abd Allāh ibn Sabāh when similar, but less ferocious Wahhābī attacks were staged in the 1790's.[15] The battle of al-Jahra, whose memory is still alive in the hearts and minds of the Kuwaitīs, strengthened the bonds among the various Kuwaitī families and also the city's ties with the tribal forces which fought in line with Sālim and his soldiers.

As far as its effects on the Gulf region and the different alliances concerned, the Ikhwān's attack of October 1920 put the Anglo-Kuwaitī agreement of 1899 to a test.[16] Britain found itself obliged to abide by the terms of the agreement; when Faisal al-Duwaish seemed determined on capturing the Red Fort, British planes stationed in the neighbourhood of Basra dropped notices on the Wahhābī encampments, warning them against pursuing their agression against the forces of Kuwait.[17] British warships anchored in Kuwait Bay in plain sight of the Ikhwān and some of their marines landed in Kuwait City. A few cannon balls were enough to warn them that the British wanted them to withdraw. Thus ended the battle of al-Jahra with the Ikhwān's retreat and the British carrying out the promises made to Mubārak in 1899. But the territorial dispute over

Photographs of Kuwait taken by Foreign Resident between 1913–1930.

A view of the city of Kuwait, 1914. (Author's collection)

A view of the wall and some houses, 1914. (Author's collection)

A view of two gates of the city of Kuwait, c.1920. (Author's collection)

*Kuwait city gate with
defenders, 1920 war.
(Author's collection)*

*A mosque in old Kuwait,
c.1915. (Author's collection)*

A coffee shop in the old sūq (market), c. 1915. (Author's collection)

The first tennis court in progress, Kuwait's Political Agency, c. 1926. (Author's collection)

Water carriers in old Kuwait,
c.1916. (Author's collection)

Drinking coffee in the bazar,
c.1916. (Author's collection)

A festive scene, Kuwait,
c.1921. (Author's collection)

Schoolboy hoisting the flag of
Kuwait, c. 1921. (Author's
collection)

*Launching of a new Kuwaiti
dhow at the Kuwait Bay,
c.1912. (Author's collection)*

*The Amir's car and
bodyguard, Kuwait, 1920's.
(Author's collection)*

Major More, wife and son, Kuwait, c.1928. (Author's collection)

Landing in Arabia, c.1910. (Author's collection)

*The first lady doctor in
Kuwait and daughter.
(Author's collection)*

*Two shaikhs of Kuwait.
(Author's collection)*

Money changer. (Author's collection)

Kuwait. (Van Ess collection, MEC Oxford)

City gate, Kuwait, 1928. (Provenance unknown, MEC Oxford)

the boundaries in the region was not quickly settled. It wasn't until two years later that the matter was brought up for discussion at the 'Uqair Conference of 1922, presided over by Sir Percy Cox, British High Commissioner in 'Irāq and a close friend of 'Abd al-'Azīz Āl-Su'ūd. This conference will be discussed later along with the history of Kuwait during the rule of Shaikh Ahmad al-Jābir al-Sabāh.[18]

Relations between Kuwait and Najd during the rule of Sālim did not return to normal or even improve as a result of the Ikhwān's withdrawal. Yet some attempts in that direction were taking place. Perhaps the most important of these was the mediation of Kāsib, son of Shaikh Khaz'al of al-Muhammara, who reached Riyād, accompanied by Ahmad al-Jābir Āl-Sabāh early in March of 1921. The mediators had an audience with 'Abd al-'Azīz soon after their arrival, not knowing that Shaikh Sālim had passed away on the 22nd of February. On receiving the news of the death of Sālim, 'Abd al-Azīz told Ahmad al-Jābir that the problems they were coming to discuss with him did not exist any longer, having become a dead issue upon the demise of Sālim. Shaikh Ahmad - who was charged with the defence of Kuwait town while his uncle Sālim was fighting the Ikhwān at al-Jahra - returned to Kuwait from Riyād to become the tenth ruler of the Āl-Sabāh family.

This deterioration in Kuwaitī-Najdī relations during the reign of Shaikh Sālim may perplex the student of the history of Eastern Arabia in modern times, especially after the noticeable goodwill which marked the twenty years of Mubārak's shaikhship in Kuwait. Was the British policy, in a sense, partially responsible for this breakdown? Were the British trying to teach Sālim a harsh lesson because of his bias towards the Ottomans in the early years of his rule? A similar event in the history of Eastern Arabia occurred when the British Resident in the Gulf, Captain Hennell, warned 'Abd Allāh ibn Ahmad Āl-Khalīfa, Shaikh of Bahrain, not to sign a treaty with Khurshid Pasha, the Egyptian Commander in Eastern Arabia. 'Abd Allāh ibn Ahmad, against their advice, endorsed the treaty with the Egyptians in May 1839 and consequently lost his shaikhship to his nephew, Muhammad Āl-Khalīfa, a few years later. The British were very instrumental in the removal of 'Abd Allāh from the seat of authority in the Island of Bahrain. The question to be answered in Sālim's instance is: Why was Sālim not removed from office? Although there may be more than one answer to this question, the clearest and most obvious is that the 1899 agreement with Kuwait excluded the British from interfering in Kuwait's internal affairs, the Shaikhship being definitely one of them. The British policy in the region during the early years of the twentieth century seems to have been inclined towards supporting the strong rulers against the weak. If it is argued that this fact is not true, it becomes difficult to explain how the British backed 'Abd al-'Azīz's demands when they were directed towards weaker rulers. This matter will be taken up in the section dealing with the role of the British representatives who attended the 'Uqair Conference in 1922, during Ahmad al-Jābir's rule.

18. See below, pp. 147 and 153.

Shaikh Ahmad Al-Jābir 1921–1950

Problems of the Borders

In order to understand how the British functioned in solving the problems of the borders which separated 'Irāq, Kuwait and Najd, it becomes necessary to examine British relations with each of these countries.

The British gained control of 'Irāq as a mandate after the end of the war in 1918 and managed to make Faisal, son of King Husain of the Hijāz, the king of 'Irāq. The 1899 Exclusive Agreement between the British and Mubārak gave the British a free hand in managing the foreign affairs of Kuwait. In Najd, 'Abd al-'Azīz Āl-Su'ūd had been a recipient of British financial aid since he allied himself with them against the Ottomans. The British were also furnishing military supplies for his army. It is evident that the British were definitely enjoying a provileged position in these three countries at the time when Sir Percy Cox was working on a matter of utmost importance to the British i.e., the settlement of differences over mutual borders. A final solution of the problem would give each of these countries internationally recognized borders which would make it possible for them to sign agreements concerning oil exploration. This was an urgent matter for companies which were waiting to sign contracts with 'Irāq for the oil-rich Mūsil area in northern 'Irāq.,[19] Indeed the establishment of well-defined borders was more important to the British than to the people involved.

To draw these borderlines was not an easy task. They would separate entities which, in the main, formed one geographic unit under the Ottoman rule until 1918, and also would make it difficult for nomadic tribes to move between pastures lying across borders that had never existed before in the history of the Arabian Peninsula.

Mention has already been made of the 1913 agreement between the British and the Ottomans on a map that marked the borders of 'Irāq, Kuwait and Najd. According to that agreement, Kuwait's borders in the south extended to *Jabal* Munīfa, about 160 miles south of its present borders with Sa'udi Arabia. It should be remembered that this agreement was reached when Kuwait was governed by Shaikh Mubārak Āl-Sabāh, the strongest ruler in the Arabian Peninsula at the time. It seems unlikely that 'Abd al-'Azīz Āl-Su'ūd was then able to offend Mubārak, his benefactor. The situation however, was not the same when Sir Percy Cox called 'Irāq, Kuwait and Najd together for a conference to be held at 'Uqair, the seaport of al-Hasā.

The 'Uqair Conference (1922)

This conference could be considered a continuation of an earlier meeting which was held in May 1922, at Muhammara, the capital of Shaikh Khaz'al's Ka'b territory on the Persian southern border with 'Irāq. That meeting had been called to discuss the borders between the territories of the Sultan of Najd, 'Abd al-'Azīz, and 'Irāq.

19. See Dickson, *Kuwait and her Neighbours*, Chapter XI, "The Demarcation of the Frontiers, 1921-1923", pp. 262 ff.

Shaikh Faisal's visit to England, 1919. The voyage down the Arabian Gulf

Humphrey Bowman, Shaikh Ahmad Al- Jābir and another Shaikh. (Bowman collection, MEC Oxford)

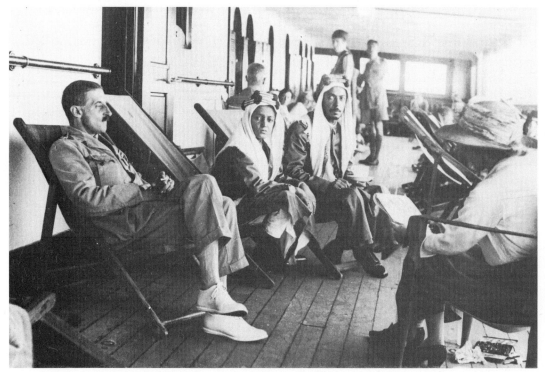

H. E. Bowman, Shaikh Faisal, Quseibi and Miss Altham sketching Faisal on board H.M. Transport 'Kigoma', September 1919. (Bowman collection, MEC Oxford)

Left: Shaikh Ahmad Al-Jābir Koweit. Taken aboard H.M.T. 'Kigoma', September 1919. (Bowman collection, MEC Oxford)

Right: Shaikh Fahad of Kuwait, 1919. (Provenance unknown, MEC Oxford)

Coming ashore at Kuwait (Bowman collection, MEC Oxford)

Entrance to the fort, Musqat. (Bowman collection, MEC Oxford)

Faisal, Sultan of Musqat, Howarth (Consul at Musqat) and Ahmed Athniyan. (Bowman collection, MEC Oxford)

Group at Musqat Palace. (Bowman collection, MEC Oxford)

Musqat: Faisal and suite. (Bowman collection, MEC Oxford)

Qasaibi, Howarth, Faisal, Ahmed Athniyan, Bowman, Sultan, Ahmad Al-Jābir at Musqat. (Bowman collection, MEC Oxford)

Al-Muhammara accord which was signed on May 5, 1922, regulated the 'Iraqī-Najdī borders and adopted the 1913 agreement for the borders of Kuwait with the Sultanate of Najd. Though 'Abd al-'Azīz had accepted the Muhammara accord at first, he felt after he had returned to Riyād that the terms of the accord were in reality unfair. 'Irāq, in his view, gained by that agreement lands that had never before belonged to it. He also felt that Kuwait's southern borders with al-Hasā needed some modifications. On the basis of these misgivings, he rejected the Muhammara accord. The stage was then set for another meeting to be held later in the year.

When Sir Percy Cox, British High Commissioner in 'Irāq, learned how deeply incensed his friend 'Abd al-'Azīz was, he decided to ask 'Irāq, Kuwait and Najd to meet at al-'Uqair in al-Hasā. Colonel Dickson, the British representative in Bahrain was instructed to contact 'Abd al-'Azīz Āl-Su'ūd and ask him to meet with Cox and the other representatives at that port.[20] Kuwait was represented by Major More, the British Political Agent. Though the invitations for that conference were sent in September 1922, the sessions were not held until later in November of the same year. The objectives, as set by Cox, were varied. As far as 'Irāq was concerned, clear borders would mean, as previously stated, the speeding up of international recognition of an independent, or semi-independent status, which would allow it to sign international agreements. Najd, he hoped, would, as a result of the demarcation of its borders, stop tribal raids into 'Irāq, Jordan and Kuwait territories. Kuwait was viewed as a buffer state, preventing friction between 'Irāq to its north and Su'ūdī territories in the south.

Since Sir Percy Cox was the coordinator, initiator of, and dominant figure in the 'Uqair Conference, the results which it was to bear came as no surprise. These had to be in line with what Great Britain expected the region to look like following the end of World War One thus adhering to previous British policy in the Gulf region. Such a policy aimed at establishing the kind of peace which the British had favoured since the destruction of Rās al-Khayma and Qāsimī ports which were considered pirates' nests.[21] The British were intent on seeing the rise of a strong Arab power which would ally itself with them. The result of such policy, as far as Kuwait was concerned, was to allow 'Abd al-'Azīz, the strong, to gain territory at the expense of the then weak country, Kuwait, despite the fact that Shaikh Ahmad al-Jābir Āl-Sabāh had maintained friendly relations with the British ever since assuming the office of the ruler of Kuwait in 1921.

'Abd al-'Azīz resented his territorial losses to 'Irāq which the Muhammara accord alloted it. Thus, when the agreement of 'Uqair was signed by the respective representatives of the countries concerned on December 2, 1922, Kuwait lost to the Su'ūdī Sultanate of Najd, lands from its southern territories that extended 160 miles beyond its present borders. The same agreement tried to resolve the grievances of the nomadic tribes by creating two neutral zones, one between Kuwait and

20. *ibid.*

21. In its war against the Qawasim in 1819.

Shaikh 'Abd Allāh Al-Salim 1950–1965

al-Hasā (Su'ūdī territory) and the other between Najd and 'Irāq in the north, thereby allowing tribes free access into those neutral zones for grazing.

Ahmad al-Jābir's Reaction to the 'Uqair Agreement[22]

When Sir Percy Cox presented the agreement to Shaikh Ahmad al-Jābir, after explaining its terms to him, Shaikh Ahmad hesitated to sign an agreement that robbed Kuwait of almost two-thirds of its territory which was to be handed over to 'Abd al-'Azīz Āl-Su'ūd. On the other hand, Kuwait's borders with 'Irāq remained as they stood before the agreement. Shaikh Ahmad asked Sir Percy Cox to explain to him why he had agreed to the Najdī territorial gains. Sir Percy's painfully frank reply was that it was because 'Abd al-'Azīz was strong and Kuwait was weak and unable to withstand serious Najdī attacks which may end by the occupation of all the country. Sir Percy added that to compensate for the loss in the south, the British would guarantee Kuwait's borders with 'Irāq, as promised to Mubārak when he joined the British against the Ottomans after the start of the First World War. Needless to say that while Ahmad al-Jābir signed this agreement he was at the same time denouncing it. It is also related that Ahmad al-Jābir confronted Sir Percy with the possibility that he might become as powerful as his grandfather, Mubārak; would the British then prevent him from using force to regain his lost territories? Sir Percy assured him that he could do this and that Britain would not stand in the way. Contemporary sources add that Ahmad al-Jābir never forgave Britain for the anguish he suffered because of the 'Uqair agreement.

The question which the reader will raise is: Did the 'Uqair agreement contribute to the spread of peace and tranquility? The answer must be in the negative, for no sooner had the agreement been signed than 'Abd al-'Azīz initiated an economic war against Kuwait, a campaign which began in 1923 and continued until 1937.

Economic War

This war between Najd and Kuwait started as a result of the demands made by 'Abd al-'Azīz upon Shaikh Ahmad to collect taxes from Najdī bedouins *(al-Sābila)* [23] who would purchase their food and clothing at the Kuwait market certain seasons each year and return the year after to pay for what they had bought not in cash but in sheep or camels. 'Abd al-'Azīz claimed that this type of trade robbed his treasury of a huge amount of income. It was looked upon as a kind of tax evasion. Shaikh Ahmad refused to collect these requested dues saying that he was not a governor of a province in Najd. He rejected another suggestion made by 'Abdul-'Azīz aimed at placing in Kuwait a Najdī agent to collect dues from the Najdī bedouins. These nomadic tribes were forced to shop elsewhere and the loss suffered by Kuwaitī merchants as a result was very

22. See Dickson, *Kuwait and her Neighbours*, pp. 278-280.

23. For *al-Sābila* see al-Qinā'ī, pp. 91-92; see also Hafiz Wahba, *Jazīrat al-'Arab fil Qarn al-'Ishrīn*, pp. 87-88. See also Dickson, *Kuwait and her Neighbours*, pp. 331-332, where he comments on the end of the economic war between Kuwait and 'Abd al-'Azīz ibn Su'ūd.

24. See *Kuwait and her Neighbours*, pp. 323-328.

substantial, especially since this situation persisted for fourteen years. During this period Kuwait, the main depot for goods imported into that part of Najd, was forced to stop supplying northern Najd with its requirements of food, clothing and other commodities.

It must be recalled in the context of the deterioration in relations between Najd and Kuwait that the Ikhwān raids on Kuwaitī territories did not cease after the episode of the siege of al-Jahra in 1920, but persisted even after the ratification of the 'Uqair agreement in 1922. Faisal al-Duwaish was still in command of the Ikhwān, and remained in that position until 1930 when King 'Abd al-'Azīz Āl-Su'ūd found out that al-Duwaish was by then defying his own authority over his subjects. In that year, 'Abd al-Azīz's forces, equipped with superior arms and tanks which the British had supplied at an earlier date, marched against al-Duwaish and the Ikhwān who were encamped in the vicinity of Kuwait and annihilated their forces. Faisal al-Duwaish and other Ikhwān leaders entered Kuwait and surrendered themselves to the British authorities who were keeping a watchful eye on the battle from Kuwait and southern 'Irāq. The British later handed Faisal al-Duwaish and his colleagues to 'Abd al'Azīz who, after an initially warm reception, put them in jail where they spent the remaining years of their lives.[24]

Internal Affairs, Unrest and Change

The lean years of the economic war which ended in 1937 were followed the next year by an event which promised Kuwait economic prosperity that was urgently needed. In February 1938, oil was found in commercial quantities and the prospects of an economic boom were not far off. However, the same year witnessed signs of internal unrest, and a year later the world was involved in World War II. But before discussing the effects of these events on Kuwait's economic and political future, let us see how Kuwait fared with its neighbours.

The third and fourth decades of the twentieth century were years of economic and political hardships. We have already seen how the Najdī economic war had caused Kuwait's economy to suffer. But this was not the only reason for the economic stagnation in the markets of Kuwait. Another equally important factor helped to worsen the situation and that was the Japanese cultured pearl industry. Natural pearls were a major source of income for Kuwait and other eastern Arabian shaikhdoms. In addition, the world depression of the early 1930's added to Kuwait's financial troubles.

All these factors led the merchants and other sectors of the Kuwaitī population to blame the government for its inability to offer solutions which would reactivate commercial life. Their cries went unheeded for some time. Finally, they asked for the democratization of the government by allowing elected officials to share with the ruler the running of Kuwait's affairs. In the beginning, Ahmad hesitated granting the request because he discovered that these protests were not spontaneous but were inspired by a neighbouring country. When the British Political Agent, Colonel De Gaury, intervened and proposed that the ruler democratize his government after the Western democratic pattern, the Shaikh refused to listen to De Gaury and reminded him that the internal affairs of Kuwait were his own, and not the British, responsibility. This internal movement of political dissent is referred to as *Harakat al-Majlis* (the council).

However, a Legistlative Council was set up so that the ruler might seek its members' advice in running the affairs of the country. This Council, which was established on June 24, 1938, was not in existence very long for on the 21st of December in the same year it was dissolved. Nevertheless, it is important to note that it was one of the earliest councils of its kind to exist in any Arab country. It was a progressive council in a traditional country ruled by a conservative, yet enlightened ruler.

Kuwait did not wait long before another Council, headed by Shaikh 'Abd Allāh al-Sālim, was established on March 14, 1939. Other members of the Council were four Shaikhs from the Āl-Sabāh family and nine Kuwaitī notables. This Consultative Council, as it was called, replaced the previous Council, but was unable to solve the problems of political unrest which were caused by external instigation coming from Kuwait's neighbour in the north, 'Iraq.[25]

Oil and Prosperity

Perhaps what played a major role in settling the question of political unrest was the discovery of oil, the effects of which were not felt immediately since production was delayed until the end of the Second World War in 1945. The story of oil exploration in Kuwait is beyond the scope of the present work, but it has been well presented in many books written in European as well as other languages.[26] The effects of oil production on Kuwait's political stability, economic prosperity and future development should be emphasized at this point.

On the 30th of June, 1946, the year after the Second World War had ended, Shaikh Ahmad al-Jābir turned the oil tap on and from that moment began an era of change and development in Kuwait. The country started its gradual transformation from an advanced medieval shaikhdom to a sophisticated modern State. It is related that Shaikh Ahmad al-Jābir was so eager for change and development that he spent the first payment, handed to him by the oil companies before the discovery of oil, to advance education for women.[27] It must also be stated that the first Kuwaitī income from its oil, in its first year of production was L280,000. That amount quickly escalated and by the end of Shaikh Ahmad's rule in 1950, the amount reached L4,000,000. This comparatively huge income helped Ahmad al-Jābir continue, on a larger scale, his plans for the development of health and educational services in the country. Shaikh Ahmad al-Jābir entrusted his cousin, Shaikh 'Abd Allāh al-Sālim, with the supervision and execution of these ambitious plans. Shaikh 'Abd Allāh had already

25. See Freeth and Winstone, *Kuwait, Prospect and Reality*, pp. 118-121. See also in *I.O.R.* documents for the period 1938-1940, under *Political Agency Kuwait R/15/2054/20 I and 4/20 II.*

26. For a specialist study see Chisholm's *The First Kuwait Oil Concession, a Record of the Negotiations for the 1934 Agreement*, London, 1975.

27. This is the impression I concluded from a lengthy interview I carried out with Mrs. Van Blarcom (formerly Miss Mary van Pelt) who now resides in Carolina Village near Hendersonville, North Carolina. She went to Kuwait in 1919 when she was serving as the principal matron of both the men and women American Mission hospitals in Kuwait, until her return to the United States in 1941. The ruling family as well as many rich Kuwaitī merchants were very friendly with the members of the Medical Mission. Mrs. Mary van Blarcom is now (1979) eighty-eight years old, and enjoys good health. She is one of a dozen Arabian American Mission whom I have been interviewing since 1977. One of the most informative among those members of the American Arabian Mission is Miss Cornelia Dalenberg or Sharifa Dalenberg, as she liked to be called. She worked as a nurse in Bahrain and Masqat from 1921 to 1961. She is now eighty-six years old.

served as president of the Consultative Council. But before an account of 'Abd Allāh al-Sālim's rule is given, a summary of Ahmad al-Jābir's management of Kuwait's internal affairs and external pressures, may be in order.

When Ahmad al-Jābir assumed the office of the ruler in 1921, Kuwait was still suffering from the aftermath of the siege of al-Jahra by the Ikhwān. A year after that date, the 'Uqair Conference deprived Kuwait of about two-thirds of its territory which was given to 'Abd al-'Azīz Āl-Su'ūd in December 1922. In the following year, 'Abd al-'Azīz declared an economic war on Kuwait which lasted for fourteen years. These adversities shook the country's economic stability from its foundations and brought about much unrest. The Council's moves signalled the start of political chaos which was instigated by Kuwait's northern neighbour, 'Irāq. To add to Ahmad's financial problems, the Japanese began to market their cheap cultured pearls which had disastrous effects on the sale of natural Gulf pearls. The early years of the 1930's also witnessed the world financial depression. All in all, these difficulties were bound to drive any government into bankruptcy. Kuwait, however, managed to escape, not only because oil was discovered there late in the 1930's, but also because of the wisdom of the man in command.

Shaikh Ahmad al-Jābir found solutions for these pressing internal and external troubles. When the oil tap was turned on, in his address to his people he referred to Kuwait as a State and not as a shaikhdom, a sign of the things that were to come in the near future in the reign of his successor, 'Abd Allāh al-Sālim. If Kuwait was not ready for modern democratic rule under Ahmad al-Jābir, the constitution [*Majlis*] movement took the shape of a National Assembly under 'Abd Allāh al-Sālim, whose rule was in essence a continuation of that of his predecessor.

'Abd Allāh al-Sālim Āl-Sabāh (1950-1965)

'Abd Allāh al-Sālim's rule began at a time when Kuwait's income from oil was on the increase. For those who lived in Kuwait during the 1950's, change and development were two continuing noticeable processes. Perhaps the greatness of 'Abd Allāh al-Sālim lies in a modesty which did not betray the great mind that was hidden behind it. For 'Abd Allāh was the architect of modern Kuwait. Shaikh Ahmad al-Jābir's development plans in the fields of education, health, water desalination, generation of electricity, and construction were enthusiastically pursued. Progress was made in two fields: material and human.

In the field of education, numerous schools were built to meet the demands of the increasing numbers of students. The government managed to recruit highly qualified teachers from many Arab countries. Health services were free for residents of Kuwait, foreign or native. Even medicines were dispensed to patients free of charge. The construction of modern roads started in the early fifties met the needs of modern transportation.

'Abd Allāh al-Sālim, as already mentioned, was assuming certain administrative responsibilities allocated to him by Shaikh Ahmad. He was nominated as president of the Consultative Council in 1939 and also placed in charge of the treasury. Apparently, Ahmad and 'Abd Allāh were in complete accord on most internal and external affairs.

It came as no surprise, therefore, that 'Abd Allāh was very knowledgeable about Kuwait's relations with its neighbours. His policy towards them was based on mutual respect. King Su'ūd, who succeeded his father, 'Abd 'Azīz, paid a visit to Kuwait in 1954. 'Abd Allāh also tried to establish cordial relations with 'Irāq. His alliance with the British continued to be a strong one even after Kuwait's independence was declared in June 1961. The 1899 agreement was replaced by a treaty of mutual cooperation and friendship. Kuwait's image on the international scene was enhanced when it joined the United Nations and became an active participant in global politics.

When Kuwait's income from oil production increased, Shaikh 'Abd Allāh expanded the spending of Kuwait's money to provide assistance in the form of medical and educational programmes to the impoverished Arabian Gulf shaikhdoms.

The fifteen years of 'Abd Allāh's leadership would require more than a few pages in a book on the history of Kuwait. The nation witnessed a spectacular state of development and change, both human and material. To accord it the justice due, a study of the extent of this extraordinary transformation would necessitate a volume in itself.

APPENDIX   I

THE AFFAIR OF M. BOREL DE BOURGES ([1])

In consequence of intelligence received from Grain of the arrival there of a French Officer having in charge a packet of importance for Pondicherry, it was determined by your Honours Factors at Bussora to endeavour to get possession of it, a measure which appeared to them the more necessary from an unguarded declaration made at Grain by the officer in question that war was absolutely declared between France and England.

I was in consequence, ordered immediately to repair to Grain to use my utmost endeavours towards getting possession not only of the packet but of the bearer also. I departed from Bussora the 1st at night on board your Honours Cruizer the Eagle; and finding the wind unfavourable and a great probability of being detained so long perhaps as to afford an opportunity to the bearer of the packet to escape to Muscat, I procured a boat in the river which I was convinced would convey me to Grain by some days sooner than I could expect to reach it in the Eagle whose presence too I judged might alarm the Prey I had in view and give him an opportunity, if not of avoiding me entirely, at least of destroying his packet. I therefore left the Eagle in the river, and in about twenty hours arrived at Grain at 10 o'clock at night; I immediately proceeded to the Sheik and having gained him to my interest so far as not to interfere in the business I had in hand, I proceeded

---

[1] Abraham to the C. of D., Grain, 7.xi.1778, *F.R.P.P.G.*, Vol. 17

directly to the house where the messenger lodged, and informed him who I was, seized him together with his packet, and conveyed him instantly on board my boat — this was all effected without the least disturbance.

I arrived on board the Eagle in about twelve hours, where having examined the packet, I find it contains sundry advices in cypher from Monsieur de Sartine, Minister for the Marine Department in France directed to Monsieur de Bellecombe, Commander-in-Chief at Pondicherry, and to Monsieur de Briancourt, the French Consul at Surat, together with a declaration of War between France and England, and sundry private letters from all which I can only gather that the bearer of the packet is Captain Borel du Bourg, that the advices he bears are of the utmost consequence, and that he is directed to fix a Resident at Muscat in order to convey all French packets with the utmost expedition by way of Aleppo, and that, the King of France having acknowledged the Independency of the United States of America, all vessels belonging to them are to be received into the port belonging to the King of France and to be paid the same honors as are paid to the United States of Holland. From a Journal of Captain du Bourg, I find he left Marseilles the 14 of August, and arrived here from Aleppo in 21 days.

Before I left Bussora, it was determined should I find the packet in question to be of any consequence immediately to despatch it to India by the Eagle. The Declaration of War alone therefore I have judged to be of sufficient consequence to warrant her despatch. I have in consequence ordered Captain Sheriff, the Commander, immediately to proceed to Bombay without touching at Bushire or Muscat and to deliver Monsieur du Bourg together with his packet to the Honorable the Governor and Council.

A letter from William Digges Latouche (Basra Fact.)
to Mr. Manesty (Basra Fact.) ([1])

There are several other Powers (besides the Banī Ka'b) with
whom it is the Company's Interest to continue on friendly Terms—
with the Bunderick, the Grain People, and other Tribes of Arabs
on the Persian and Arabian Coasts, who have it in their Power to
annoy our Trade — with the shaiks of the Montificks, of the
Benechalids, of the Anisas, of the Gheesaals for the Security of the
Company's Dispatches, of the English Trade, and of English
Travellers passing between Bussora, Aleppo and Bagdat.

Timely Presents are often of great Use in preserving this good
Understanding. Those on the changes of the Mussalems here are
fixed, and should not be increased though Attempts under various
Pretences have been, and will be probably made for that Purpose.
The Others must be regulated by your own Prudence and according
to Circumstances — they should be made with Caution. If they
are too frequent and too large they will increase Expectations of
future Ones. If on the other hand they do not in some Measure
answer the Expectation of the Person to whom they are given, the
giving them will be worse than not giving any. They are too often
in this country considered as a kind of Tribute and therefore as
a Right. When I have found this to be the Case, I have deferred
them until they appeared as made from my own Inclination, and
rather as a Return for Favours received, than as given through
for or in Expectation of future Services.

Baṣra 6th Nov. 1784   Signed Latouche

---

[1] *F.R.P.P.G.*, Vol. 18, dispatch No. 1299.

The   Capture of Baḥrain by the 'Utūb
A letter from Mr. Latouche (Baṣra Resid.)
to the Court of Dir., London, dated 4th Nov., 1782. ([1])

The Zebara, and the Grain People, have lately taken and plundered Bahreen, and have likewise seized at the Entrance of this River, several Boats belonging to Bushire and Bunderick. Shaik Nassir of Bushire, in return is collecting a Marine, as well as a Military Force, at Bushire, Bunderick, and other Persian Ports — he gives out that he intends to revenge these Hostilities by attacking Zebarra, and has wrote for a Supply of Money to Aly Morat Caum at Isphahan. Notwithstanding this show of vigor, however, it is said, that he has lately sent to Grain to request a Peace, but that the Shaik had refused to grant it, unless Shaik Nassir pays him half the Revenues of Bahreen, and a large Annual Tribute also for Bushire.

It is not many years since Grain, was obliged to pay a large tribute to the Chaub, and that the name of Zebarra , was scarcely known. On the Persians attacking Bussora, one of the Shaiks of Grain, retired to Zebarra, with many of the principal People. Some of the Bussora Merchants also retired thither. A great Part of the Pearl and India Trade, by this means entered there, and at Grain, during the Time that the Persians were in possession of Bussora, and those Places have increased so much in Strength and Consequence, that they have for some time past set the Chaub at defiance, have gained very considerable Advantages against him, and now under no Apprehensions from the Force, which Shaik Nassir threatens to collect against them.

Baṣra 4th Nov. 1782   Signed Latouche

----

1   *F. R. P.P.G.*, Vol. 17, dispatch No. 1230.

Translate of a Letter from the Resident to
Abdulla ibn Subbah Shaik of Grain dated the
17th April 1789 ([1])

I am induced by the Consideration of the Friendship which has long subsisted between us, to write to You in the present Hour.

I have lately paid a Visit to the Bacha of Bagdat in his Camp. In the Course of our Conversations the Bacha mentioned Your Name. He said that an ancient Friendship had subsisted between the People of Grain and of Bussora, he expressed great Surprise and anger at Your Conduct in giving Protection to People, who had been in Rebellion against him, and who had fled to avoid the Punishment due to their Guilt, he said that unless You delivered them up to him, or ordered them to quit the Town of Grain, they should consider You, as his Enemy, and proceed on an Expedition against You. He said that he would march with his Army to Grain and order his Fleet, to repair thither to cooperate with it. He said that he would write a letter to the Governor of Bombay, requesting the early Assistance of a Marine force and he desired that I would also write a Letter to the Governor of Bombay to the same Purport.

Friendship has urged me thus to make known to you the Sentiments of the Bacha of Bagdat.

Translate of a Letter from Shaik Abdulla ibn Sabbah
to the Resident received the 30th April 1789.

After Compliments,

I have received Your Letter and understand its Contents. You

---

[1]   This letter with its heading and the following one come from Volume 18 of the Factory Records, Persia and Persian Gulf. Their serial number in that volume is 1532.

mention that a friendship has always subsisted between the English and myself, I pray God, it may continue so to the End of time.

I am obliged to You for the Information You have given me in Regard to the Intentions of Soliman Bacha, whom I am sorry to observe is dispeased at my Conduct towards Mustapha Aga.

The Town of Grain belongs to the Bacha, the Inhabitants of it are his Servants but You Yourself thank God are well enough acquainted with our Customs, to know, that if any Person whatsoever falls upon Us for Protection we cannot refuse to afford it to him and that after having afforded it, it is the extreme of Infamy to desert him or to deliver him into the hands of his Enemies.

You know the Bacha knows, the whole World knows that I receive no Advantage from Mustapha Aga's Residence at Grain but to turn him out is wrong, to deliver him up is Infamy.

I depend upon Your Friendship to stop this Matter to the Bacha in its proper Light.

May Your Years be long and happy

Bussora the 29th June 1789.

True Translates

(signed) Samuel Manesty

Translation of a contract with the Shaik Suliman for an escort of Arabs across the Great Desert from Aleppo to Bassora. (¹)

"THIS writing is to certify, that we the under-written of the tribe of Arabs Nigadi, have for our own free will agreed to accompany and conduct the bearer of this contract, Colonel Capper, an Englishman, and those of his company: and that we oblige ourselves to take with us seventy guards of the tribes of Arabs Nigadi, and Agalli and Benni Khaled, who are all to be armed with muskets; we the under-written are included in the number, excepting Shaik Haggy Suliman Eben Adeyah. — And we do promise also to carry with us nine refeeks with their muskets, two of whom of the two different tribes called Edgelass, two of the two tribes Il Fedaan, one of the tribe of Welled Aly, one of the tribe of Benni Waheb, one of the tribe of Lacruti, one of the tribe of Baigee, and one of the tribe of Sarhaani, making in all nine refeeks, as above-mentioned.

AND it is agreed, that we the underwritten are to bring with us our own provisions, and the provisions for the guards and refeeks above-mentioned, and the same provisions are to be loaded upon our camels, the hire of which camels is to be paid by us; and we likewise agree to buy ourselves thirteen rotolas of gunpower, and twenty-six rotolas of balls, the cost of all the aforesaid things are to be paid by us, and not by Colonel Capper.

AND we also oblige ourselves to provide for him and his people nineteen camels, for the use of himself and his company, to carry their tents and baggage, water and provisions for themselves and for their horses, beside those nineteen camels above-mentioned; we also oblige ourselves to provide them two other strong camels to carry the mohafa, in order that they may change every day one camel, and to provide a person to lead the camel that carries the mohafa from Aleppo to Graine, and moreover we will appoint him a person to take care of his horses.

WE the underwritten do promise Colonel Capper, by our own free will and consent, and oblige ourselves to pay all kafars and giawayez (that is to say duties) to all the Arabs, and to the Shaik Tamur, the Shaik Tiveini, and all the Shaik of the tribe of Beni Khaled, and to all other tribes of Arabs whatever; and we make ourselves responsible for all what is above-written, and further when we approach the tribe of Arabs called Il Aslam, and

---

¹ CAPPER, *Observations on the Passage to India*, pp. 55-58.

Shammar and any other tribes, we oblige ourselves to take from them a refeek to walk with us till we have passed their confines.

WE agree to carry no goods, or even letters from any other person or persons, excepting the goods from Khwaja Rubens, which are thirty-one loads, for the hire of the said goods from Khwaja Rubens we have received in full, that is, the hire, the inamalumi, the refeeks, the giawayez, figmaniah, and all other expences to Graine; we have received of him in full, according to the receipt in the hands of the said Khwaja Rubens: moreover we have agreed with our free will to provide for the said thirty-one loads, for every load of camels, in order to keep up with the above-mentioned Colonel Capper, and never separate from his company till our arrival at Graine; and we also oblige ourselves to pay the dolleels (scouts) the maadeb, the birakdar, and the chaous (officers of the guards) all the said persons we are to pay ourselves, and not Colonel Capper. We have agreed also with our free will, with the said Colonel Capper, to carry him and his company safe in thirty-six days to Graine, from the day we depart from the village of Nayreb; but in case the said Colonel Capper should be desirous of staying to rest a day or more the said delay is not to be reckoned in the aforesaid thirty-six days. And we the underwritten also engage three days before our arrival at Graine, to dispatch a messenger from our parts with Colonel Capper's letter to the agent of the British nation in Graine. And by this instrument it is stipulated and agreed between the said Colonel Capper and us the underwritten persons, that he pays us for all the services above-mentioned dollars nine hundred forty-one and one fourth in Aleppo, which sum we have received in full; besides which the said Colonel Capper does oblige himself to give us on the road dollars five hundred; and moreover at our safe arrival at Graine, on our having fulfilled this our agreement with him, he the said Colonel Capper obliges himself to pay us dollars eight hundred rumi, and in case we should fail in performing any part of our agreement with him, we then are to forfeit the last-mentioned eight hundred dollars, and all we the underwritten are responsible one for the other, for the performance of the promises as above agreed between the contracting parties. In witness whereof, we have signed with our fingers this the sixteenth day of the moon called Shewal, in the year of the Hegira, one thousand one hundred and ninety-two.

Suliman Ebben Adeyah — Mohamed il Bisshir — Ally Ebben Faddil — Haggy Isa Ebben Hameidan — Nasseh Ebn Resheidan

— Suliman Ebben Gaddib — Mohamed Ebn Nidghem — Suliman Ebben Naaisay.

The witnesses to the agreement are:

Il Haggi Omar Ulleed — Ismael Estracy — Il Haggi Mahomed Firous — Il Haggi Ibrahim Ulbed — Il Haggi Mahomed Emin il Takrity — Il Haggi Fathu Ebn il Haggu Usuph Maadaraloy — Ismael Ebben Achmed Tecrity.

APPENDIX   II

English and Arabic Texts of the General Treaty of Peace, 1820

General Treaty with the Arab Tribes of the Persian Gulf, 1820 [from C. U. Aitchison, <u>A Collection of Treaties, Engagements and Sanads relating to India and Neighbouring Countries</u>, XI, 245-49]

In the name of God, the merciful, the compassionate!

Praise be to God, who hath ordained peace to be a blessing to his creatures. There is established a lasting peace between the British Government and the Arab tribes, who are parties to this contract, on the following conditions:--

<u>Article 1</u>.   There shall be a cessation of plunder and piracy by land and sea on the part of the Arabs, who are parties to this contract, for ever.

<u>Article 2</u>.   If any individual of the people of the Arabs contracting shall attack any that pass by land or sea of any nation whatsoever, in the way of plunder and piracy and not of acknowledged war, he shall be accounted an enemy of all mankind and shall be held to have forfeited both life and goods. An acknowledged war is that which is proclaimed, avowed, and ordered by government against government; and the killing of men and taking of goods without proclamation, avowal, and the order of a government, is plunder and piracy.

<u>Article 3</u>.   The friendly (literally the pacificated) Arabs shall carry by land and sea a red flag, with or without letters in it, at their

option, and this shall be in a border of white, the breadth of the white in the border being equal to the breadth of the red, as represented in the margin (the whole forming the flag known in the British Navy by the title of white pierced red), this shall be the flag of the friendly Arabs, and they shall use it and no other.

<u>Article 4</u>.   The pacificated tribes shall all of them continue in their former relations, with the exception that they shall be at peace with the British Government, and shall not fight with each other, and the flag shall be a symbol of this only and of nothing further.

<u>Article 5</u>.   The vessels of the friendly Arabs shall all of them have in their possession a paper (Register) signed with the signature of their Chief, in which shall be the name of the vessel, its length, its breadth, and how many Karahs it holds. And they shall also have in their possession another writing (Port Clearance) signed with the signature of their Chief, in which shall be the name of the owner, the name of the Nacodah, the number of men, the number of arms, from whence sailed, at what time, and

to what port bound. And if a British or other vessel meet them, they shall produce the Register and the clearance.

Article 6.   The friendly Arabs, if they choose, shall send an envoy to the British Residency in the Persian Gulf with the necessary accompaniments, and he shall remain there for the transaction of their business with the Residency; and the British Government, if it chooses, shall send an envoy also to them in like manner; and the envoy shall add his signature to the signature of the Chief in the paper (Register) of their vessels, which contains the length of the vessel, its breadth, and tonnage the signature of the envoy to be renewed every year. Also all such envoy shall be at the expense of their own party.

Article 7.   If any tribe, or others, shall not desist from plunder and piracy, the friendly Arabs shall act against them according to their ability and circumstances, and an arrangement for this purpose shall take place between the friendly Arabs and the British at the time when such plunder and piracy shall occur.

Article 8.   The putting men to death after they have given up their arms is an act of piracy and not of acknowledged war; and if any, tribe shall put to death any persons, either Muhammadans or others, after they have given up their arms, such tribe shall be held to have broken the peace; and the friendly Arabs shall act against them in conjunction with the British, and God willing, the war against them shall not cease until the surrender of those who performed the act and of those who ordered it.

Article 9.   The carrying off of slaves, men, women, or children from the coasts of Africa or elsewhere, and the transporting them in vessels, is plunder and piracy, and the firendly Arabs shall do nothing of this nature.

Article 10.   The vessels of the friendly Arabs, bearing their flag above described, shall enter into all the British ports and into the ports of the allies of the British so far as they shall be able to effect it; and they shall buy and sell therein, and if any shall attack them the British Government shall take notice of it.

Article 11.   These conditions aforesaid shall be common to all tribes and persons, who shall hereafter adhere thereto in the same manner as to those who adhere to them at the time present. End of the Articles.

Issued at Ras-ool-Kheimah, in triplicate, at midday, on Saturday, the twenty-second of the month of Rabee-ul-Awul, in the year of the Hegira one thousand two hundred and thirty-five, corresponding to the eighth of January one thousand eight hundred and twenty, and signed by the contracting parties at the places and times under written.

Signed at Ras-ool-Kheimah at the time of issue by

W. Grant Keir, Major General.

Hassan bin Rahmah, Sheikh of Hatt and Falna,
                      formerly of Ras-ool-Kheimah.

Rajib bin Ahmed, Sheikh of Jourat al Kamra
                      [Jazīrat al-Ḥamra]

(An exact translation.)

J. [T.] P. Thompson, Captain, 17th Light Dragoons,
                      and Interpreter.

Signed at Ras-ool-Kheimah on Tuesday, the twenty-fifth of the month of
Rabee-ul-Awul, in the year of the Hegira one thousand two hundred and
thirty-five, corresponding to the eleventh of January 1820.

> Shakbout, Sheikh of Aboo Dhebbee.

Signed at Ras-ool-Kheimah at midday, on Saturday, the twenty-ninth of
the month of Rabee-ul-Awul, in the year of the Hegira one thousand two
hundred and thirty-five, corresponding to the fifteenth of January 1820.

> Hussun bin Ali, Sheikh of Zyah [Ḍāya].

> The seal is Captain Thompson's, as Sheikh Hassun bin
> Ali had not a seal at the time of signature.

Copy of the general Treaty with the friendly (literally the "pacificated")
Arabs, with the signatures attached to it, up to the fifteenth day of
January 1820 inclusive. Given under my hand and seal.

> W. Grant Keir, Major-General.

> J. [T.] P. Thompson, Captain, 17th Light Dragoons,
>   and Interpreter.

Ratified by the Governor-General in Council [at Calcutta] on 2nd April
1820.

Signed for Mahomed ibn Haza bin Zaal, Sheikh of Debay, a minor, at
Shargah on Friday, the twelfth of the month of Rubee-oos-Sanee, in the
year of the Hegira one thousand two hundred and thirty-five, corresponding
to the twenty-eighth of January 1820.

> Saeed bin Syf, Uncle of Sheikh Mahomed.

Signed at Shargah at mid-day, on Frieday, the nineteenth of the month of
Rubee-oos-Sanee, in the year of the Hegira one thousand two hundred and
thiery-five, corresponding to the fourth of February 1820.

> Sultan bin Suggur, Chief of Shargah.

Signed at Shargah by the Vakeel on the part of the Sheikhs Suleman
bin Ahmed and Abdulla bin Ahmed, in his quality of Vakeel to the Sheikhs
aforesaid, on Saturday, the twentieth of the month of Rubee-oos-Sanee in
the year of the Hegira one thousand two hundred and thirty-five,
corresponding to the 5th of February 1820.

> Syud Abdool Jabel bin Syud Yas, Vakeel of Sheikh
> Suleman bin Ahmed and Sheikh Abdoola bin Ahmed of
> the family of Khalifa, Sheikhs of Bahrein.

Signed and accepted by Suleman bin Ahmed, of the house of Khalifa, at
Bahrein on the ninth of Jemadee-ool-Awul, in the year of the Hegira one
thousand two hundred and thirty-five, corresponding to the twenty-third
of February 1820.

Signed at Faleia, at noon on Wednesday, the twenty-ninth of the month of
Jemadee-ool Awul, in the year of the Hegira one thousand two hundred and
thirty-five, corresponding to the fifteenth of March 1820.

> Rashed bin Hamid, Chief of Ejman.

Signed at Faleia, at noon on Wednesday, the twenty-ninth of the month of Jemadee-ool-Awul in the year of the Hegira one thousand two hundred and thirty-five, corresponding to the fifteenth of March 1820.

Abdoola bin Rashid, Chief of Umm-ool-Keiweyn.

W. Grant Keir, Major-General.

******

The following appears as a footnote in H. Moyse-Bartlett, The Pirates of Trucial Oman, p. 110:

Note on the Arabic version of the treaty [of 1820] by Mr. T. M. Johnstone: In general, the text of the treaty is ungrammatical and not Arabic in idiom. Thompson appears to have written it with the help of a Gulf Arab who probably knew no English, for a large number of colloquial words and forms appears in the text. The fact that it is a translation is obvious; the English text is occasionally abridged, and the document is not easy to understand from the Arabic alone. From a practical viewpoint the most important criticism is the fact that prohibitions ("shall not") and commands ("shall") are translated by simple indicatives, i.e., the equivalent of future tenses. This may have been intentional as conveying the appearance of mutual agreement ("will not") rather than force, but it is possible that the meaning of such clauses as that relating to the slave trade may have been misunderstood by the Arabs.

Reproduced from Treaties and engagements in force on lst January 1906
between the British Government and the Trucial Chiefs of the Arab Coast...
(Calcutta: Superintendent of Government Printing, India, 1919).

معاهدة العمومية مع الاتزام العرب في خليج فارس في سنة ١٨٢٠ ع

بسم الله الرحمن الرحيم

الحمد لله الذي جعل الصلح خيراً لانام وبعد لله صار الصلح الدائم بين دولة سركار الانكريز وبين الطرايف العربية المشروطين على هذه الشروط .

الشرط الأول ــ لي يزال النهب و الغارات في البر والبحر من طرف العرب المشروطين في كل الأزمنه .

الشرط الثاني ــ لي تعرض لحد من قوم العرب المشروطين على المشروطين في البر والبحر من كانه الناس بالنهب و الغارات به وحرب معروف فهو عدو للناس فليس له الأ مان على حاله و ما له والعرب المعروف هو الذي مثلاً به مبين مأمورين من دولة الى دولة و قتل الناس و اخذ المال بغير مقاتلة وتقبين و امر دولة لمو النهب و الغارات .

الشرط الثالث ــ لي العرب المصالحين لهم في البر والبحر منكم ...

الشرط الرابع ــ لي الطرايف المصالحين كلهم على حالة الأول أن قيم صار الصلح بينهم و بين دولة سركار الانكريز ولي لا يحرب بعدم بعضاً والعلم هو الشاهد على ذلك نقط وليس هو شاهد على غيرو .

الشرط الخامس ــ لي مركب العرب المصالحين كلهم بايديهم ارطاس مرشن لنط اميرهم فيه اسم ...

الشرط السادس ــ لي العرب المصالحين ان كل مرادهم يرسلو رسولاً الى سركار الانكريز في بحرالفارس ...

الشرط السابع ــ لي في كل طايفة لو نهر هم البزاري من اللهب و الغارات للعرب المصالحين يقومص عليهم ...

الشرط الثامن ــ لي نتل الناس بعد تسلم السلح لهو من الغارات و ا من العرب

الحميف و لي كل طايفة يقتل الناس مسلمون لو فيره وبعد تسليم السلح فهو قد اتلاف الصلح لان العرب المصالحين مع الانكريز يقومص عليهم ولي يزال الله تعالى ...

الشرط التاسع ــ لي لهو الرقيق الرجال و النسا ...

الشرط العاشر ــ لي مراكب العرب المصالحين العاملة تسلمهم الذكور بدخلي في كل بنادر دولة سركار الانكريز و لي بلاندر رايتهم على للدرم يختارون و يبيعون فيها و ان كان احد تعرض لهم فذلك على سركار الانكريز .

الشرط حادي عشر ــ لي هذا الشرط المذكورا فهي على جميع الطرايف ...

خط أمردار بيده وخاتمه

(Sd.) W. GRANT KEIR,
Major-General.

APPENDIX   III

Secret Department   **H.C. Sloop of war code**
                                     Koweit or Grane Harbour 24 April,
                                     1841.

To The Honorable The Secret Committee
of the Honorable the Court of Directors
of the East India Company.

Honorable Sirs,

      My last letter to the address of your Honorable Committee in this department was dated the 5th instant.

2. On the 17th of this month, I had the honor to receive your dispatch No. 709 under date the 23rd Feb. last, directing me to inquire and report upon the suitableness of Grane for a station, if we should remove from Karrak, and if suitable how it might be aquired.

3. At the time of the receipt of the letter now acknowledged, I had made the requisite arrangements for proceeding on a tour of the Arabian Coast for the purpose of taking measures to renew the annual maritime Truce prior to the commencement of the Pearl Fishery. I therefore considered it expedient to proceed to this port in the first instance, inorder, that I might be better enabled to report upon the subject to which my attention has been directed by your honorable Committee.

4. My own opinion has always been, that many and serious objections exist to the location of an establishment upon the main land, or any place which could not be effectively protected by our naval means, if necessary. Without however referring to this objection, the result of a careful examination of the Town of Grane, and its vicinity, is, that although not unsuitable for a naval station, and Coal Depot, it is, on account of the scarcity and badness of the fresh water on the spot, and in its neighbourhood, as well as for other reasons, hereafter adverted to, altogether unfitted for military occupation.

5. The principal point in favor of Grane, is its Harbour, which is certainly an exceedingly fine one, capable of holding the navy of Great Britain, but so far as my observation goes, it possesses no other advantage. The country around is a salt and sandy desert, of the most barren and unhospitable description, with not a tree or shrub visible, as far as the eye can reach, excepting a few bushes which mark the wells. From the taste and quality of the water, I feel almost certain that it would not agree with the constituations of either Europeans, or Indians, and that the latter especially, would from drinking it, be liable to the attack of a dangerous disease called the Bereherse.

6. In respect however to a naval station, and Coal Depot, the above objection would not exist to anything like the same extent, as in the case of a military port. The vessels of war can always water at places on the coast where this essential necessary is procurable of a better and purer quality than at Grane. I have reasons however to think, that our location in his neighbourhood would be received by Shaikh Jabir with much dissatisfaction : the information I received from those who had the best means of knowing his sentiments leads me to believe, that although the proposition to form an establishment within his territories would be exceedingly unpalatable to him, still his Town, Commerce, and means of subsistence, are so wholly in our power, by means of our Naval Force, that he would not dare to return a direct refusal, or offer open opposition to it.

7. I trust sincerely that the course of events may not compel us to remove from a place so suitable to our views, and so rapidly improving in population and prosperity, as Karrak. Should however such a contingency arise, it would probably become necessary to change the location of our Coal Depot from that Island to some other place, in which case, I am inclined to the opinion, that excepting Bushire, no other Port in the Northern part of this Gulf would be found better adapted for the purpose in question than Grane.

8. This Town presents a singular instance of commercial prosperity, although wanting in almost every advantage, excepting its magnificent Harbour. Its population is large, as it can produce about six thousand men capable of bearing arms, which at a moderate average would make the total number of inhabitants nearly twenty five thousand individuals. They possess thirty one Buglas and Bateels, from one hundred and fifty to three hundred Tons burthen, which trade constantly with India. Fifty smaller vessels are employed in the coasting commerce of the Gulf, and about three hundred and fifty boats engaged in fishing and on the Pearl Banks. The energy and courage of the people, who are closely united, and free from feuds and factions, render them respected and feared by all the other Maritime Tribes, and as

in fact, they are as prompt to resent insult or aggression toward themselves as they are cautious in refraining from injury or arrogance towards their peaceable neighbours, piracy upon a Grane boat is of rare occurrence. The government of Shaikh Jabir is of a truly mild and paternal character. Both himself and his Sons are perhaps among the worst dressed and most ill lodged residents in the place. Excepting a small duty levied upon the sales and purchases of the Bedouins who resort to his Town, the Sheik collects no taxes or customs, the port being entirely a free one. nearly all the small revenue realized by him, not perhaps exceeding 3000 Dollars yearly. together with the profits derived from his trading vessels are expended in keeping up a sort of public label of a plentiful but coarse description to which every one appears to be welcome. This liberality together with the utter absence of all pretension of outward superiority, renders Shaikh Jabir and his Son Soobah, (to whom the management of affairs has been made over by his father) most popular among his subjects, who are consequently devoted to them in an unusual degree, and ready to place at their disposal, both person and property, when called upon to do so.

9. These remarks may perhaps appear somewhat irrelevant to the subject of this letter, but from the peculiar nature of the state of society, and government of Grane, your Honorable Committee will be better able to understand the reluctance with which a chief holding himself so much above the common motives of interest, would view the introduction of a foreign power, which according to the rooted belief entertained by these people, would probably sooner or later dispossess him and his Son of the power and influence they now enjoy Moreover in respect to forming a military station at Grane, it will not escape the notice of your Honorable Committee, that great risks of collision would exist, lending perhaps to serious and even fatal results, were our Troops located among, or in the immediate neighbourhood of an independent and bold population like the inhabitants of this port. The Walls and Towers of the Town, are in a state of delapidation and ruin, consequently there does not exist a single place which without undergoing extensive repairs, could be made available as a defence or military post. For these reasons, in addition to the more weighty consideration regarding the bad quality of the water, referred to in the 4th para of this letter, I must repeat my conviction that Grane is quite unsuitable for a Military Station.

I have the honor to be
Honorable Sirs
Your most obedient
humble Servant
S. HENNELL,
Resident Persian Gulf

APPENDIX   IV

TREATIES AND UNDERTAKINGS

IN FORCE BETWEEN

THE BRITISH GOVERNMENT

AND

THE RULERS OF KUWAIT

1841—1913.

المعاهدات و المقاولات الجارية

فيمابين

حاكم الكويت و الدولة البهية القيصرية الانكليس

ه ١٣٣١ — ١٢٥٧

ء ١٩١٣ — ١٨٤١

Treaties and Undertakings in force between the British Government and the Rulers of Kuwait, 1841—1913.

Serial No.	Title.	Date.
1	Adherence to Maritime Truce . . .	1841.
2	Agreement of 1899*	23rd January 1899.
3 (a) 3 (b) 3 (c)	Arms Traffic Agreement of 1900* and 2 proclamations.	24th May 1900.
4	Post Office Agreement of 1904 * . . .	28th February 1904.
5 (a) 5 (b)	Bandar Shwaikh lease (two documents) . .	15th October 1907.
6 (a) 6 (b)	Pearl Fisheries Agreement of 1911 (2 letters) .	29th July 1911.
7	Wireless Telegraph Agreement of 1912 . .	26th July 1912.
8 (a) 8 (b)	Kuwait Oil Agreement of 1913 (2 letters). .	27th October 1913.

* Translations communicated to Porte on October 24th, 1911.

Treaties and Undertakings in force between the British Government and the Rulers of Kuwait, 1841—1913.

[Note.—In the event of doubt hereafter arising as to the precise interpretation of any portion of the English or Arabic text of one or other of the Treaty stipulations, the English text shall be considered decisive.]

No. 1.

ADHERENCE OF SHAIKH OF KUWAIT TO MARITIME TRUCE FOR ONE YEAR, 1841.

IN THE NAME OF GOD.

The purport of these lines is this that I, Subah bin Jaber, acting on behalf of my father Jaber bin Abdullah-es-Subah, Ruler of Kuwait, have agreed to and accepted, on behalf of myself, my subjects and my dependents, the engagement which has been concluded by His Honour Captain Hennell, the Resident in the Persian Gulf, with the Trucial Arab Shaikhs for the maintenance of truce and peace against the exercise of aggression at sea, and that I shall have no war and fight at sea with any of the Arab Shaikhs who are subscribers to the peace and truce with the exalted British Government and that I shall check my subjects and dependents from committing acts of aggression on the other Trucial tribes at sea. Should, God forbid, any one commit an act of aggression on my subjects and dependents at sea, I will not proceed immediately to retaliate but will inform the aforesaid Resident, so that he may proceed to carry out the necessary punishment and retaliation after enquiring into the matter. I have undertaken for His Honour to observe the above from the date of writing, *viz.*, the 1st Rabi I 1257 = (24th April 1841) until the period of one full year.

And God is the best of witnesses.

(L. S.)   SUBAH BIN JABER.

No. 2.

AGREEMENT OF 23ʀᴅ JANUARY 1899 WITH RULER OF KUWAIT.

(Translation.)

Praise be to God alone (*lit.* in the name of God Almighty) ("Bissim Illah Ta'alah Shanuho ").

The object of writing this lawful and honourable bond is, that it is hereby covenanted and agreed between Lieutenant-Colonel Malcolm John Meade, I.S.C., Her Britannic Majesty's Political Resident, on behalf of the British Government, on the one part, and Shaikh Mubarak-bin-Shaikh Subah, Shaikh of Kuwait, on the other part; that the said Shaikh Mubarak-bin-Shaikh Subah, of his own free will and desire, does hereby pledge and bind himself, his heirs and successors, not to receive the agent or representative of any Power or Government at Kuwait, or at any other place within the limits of his territory, without the previous sanction of the British Government; and he further binds himself, his heirs and successors, not to cede, sell, lease, mortgage, or give for occupation or for any other purpose, any portion of his territory to the Government or subjects of any other power without the previous consent of Her Majesty's Government for these purposes. This engagement also to extend to any portion of the territory of the said Shaikh Mubarak which may now be in possession of the subjects of any other Government.

In token of the conclusion of this lawful and honourable bond, Lieutenant-Colonel Malcolm John Meade, I.S.C., Her Britannic Majesty's Political Resident in the Persian Gulf, and Shaikh Mubarak-bin-Shaikh Subah, the former on behalf of the British Government, and the latter on behalf of himself, his heirs and successors, do each, in the presence of witnesses, affix their signatures, on this the 10th day of Ramazan, 1316, corresponding with the 23rd day of January 1899.

(Sd.) M. J. MEADE, *Lieut.-Col.,*
Political Resident in the Persian Gulf.

(L. S.) (Sd.) MUBARAK-AL-SUBAH.

Witnesses:
    (Sd.) E. WICKHAM HORE, *Captain, I.M.S.*
    (Sd.) J. CALCOTT GASKIN.
  (L. S.) MUHAMMAD RAHIM-BIN-ABDUL NEBI SAFFER.

(Sd.) CURZON ᴏꜰ KEDLESTON,
Viceroy and Governor-General of India.

Ratified by His Excellency the Viceroy and Governor-General of India at Fort William on the 16th day of February 1899.

| Seal. |

(Sd.) W. J. CUNINGHAM,
Secretary to the Government of India in the
Foreign Department.

AGREEMENT BY THE SHAIKH OF
KUWAIT REGARDING THE NON-RECEPTION OF FOR-
EIGN REPRESENTATIVES AND THE NON-CESSION
OF TERRITORY TO FOREIGN POWERS OR SUBJECTS,
23RD JANUARY 1899.

The object of writing this lawful and honourable bond is that
it is hereby covenanted and agreed between Lieutenant-Colonel Malcolm
John Meade, I.S.C., Her Britannic Majesty's Political Resident, on
behalf of the British Government on the one part, and Sheikh Mubarak-
bin-Sheikh Subah, Sheikh of Koweit, on the other part, that the said
Sheikh Mubarak-bin-Sheikh Subah of his own free will and desire does
hereby pledge and bind himself, his heirs and successors not to receive
the Agent or Representative of any Power or Government at Koweit, or
at any other place within the limits of his territory, without the previous
sanction of the British Government; and he further binds himself, his
heirs and successors not to cede, sell, lease, mortgage, or give for occupation or for any other purpose any portion of his territory to the Government or subjects of any other Power without the previous consent of
Her Majesty's Government for these purposes. This engagement also to
extend to any portion of the territory of the said Sheikh Mubarak, which
may now be in the possession of the subjects of any other Government.

In token of the conclusion of this lawful and honourable bond,
Lieutenant-Colonel Malcolm John Meade, I.S.C., Her Britannic
Majesty's Political Resident in the Persian Gulf, and Sheikh Mubarak-
bin-Sheikh Subah, the former on behalf of the British Government and
the latter on behalf of himself, his heirs and successors do each, in the
presence of witnesses, affix their signatures on this, the tenth day of
Ramazan 1316, corresponding with the twenty-third day of January
1899.

(Sd.) M. J. MEADE,   MUBARAK-AL-SUBAH.
Political Resident in the
Persian Gulf.   (L.S.)

Witnesses.

(Sd.) E. WICKHAM HORE,   MUHAMMAD RAHIM BIN
Captain, I.M.S.   ABDUL NEBI SAFFER.
(Sd.) J. CALCOTT GASKIN.   (L.S.)

Letter accompanying the execution of the above Agreement.

Dated the 23rd January 1899.

From—LIEUTENANT-COLONEL M. J. MEADE, Political Resident in the Persian Gulf,

To—SHEIKH MUBARAK-BIN-SUBAH, Sheikh of Koweit.

After compliments.—In view of the signing to-day of the agreement, so happily concluded between you, Sheikh Mubarak-bin-Subah, on behalf of yourself, your heirs and successors, on the one part, and myself, on behalf of Her Britannic Majesty's Government, I now assure you, as Sheikh of Koweit, of the good offices of the British Government towards you, your heirs and successors as long as you, your heirs and successors scrupulously and faithfully observe the conditions of the said bond.

The three copies of the bond will be sent to India to be ratified by His Excellency Lord Curzon of Kedleston, Her Imperial Majesty's Viceroy and Governor-General in Council, and, on their return, one copy, duly ratified, will be conveyed to you, when I will take measures to send you, as agreed, a sum of Rs. 15,000 from the Bushire Treasury. A most important condition of the execution of this agreement is that it is to be kept absolutely secret, and not divulged or made public in any way without the previous consent of the British Government.

No. 3 (*a*).

UNDERTAKING OF RULER OF KUWAIT REGARDING THE ARMS TRAFFIC, 1900.

I agree absolutely to prohibit the importation of arms into Kuwait or exportation therefrom and to enforce this I have issued a notification and proclamation to all concerned.

Dated this 24th Muharram 1318 (=24th May 1900).

(L. S.) MUBARAK-BIN-SUBAH.

No. 3 (*b*).

NOTIFICATION BY SHAIKH MUBARAK-BIN-SUBAH, CHIEF OF KUWAIT.

Be it known to all who see this that British and Persian vessels of war have permission to search vessels carrying their and our flags in Kuwait territorial waters and to confiscate all arms and ammunition in them if these arms and ammunition are intended for Indian or Persian or Kuwait ports. Kuwait vessels found in Indian and Persian waters by British and Persian vessels of war suspected to contain arms and ammunition for Indian, Persian and Kuwait ports are liable to be searched by the said vessels and all such arms and ammunition found in them will be confiscated.

Dated this 24th Muharram 1318 (=24th May 1900).

(L. S.) MUBARAK-BIN-SUBAH.

No. 3 (*c*).

NOTIFICATION BY SHAIKH MUBARAK-BIN-SUBAH, SHAIKH OF KUWAIT.

Be it known to all who see this that whereas it has become known to us that the traffic in arms in British India and Persia, is prohibited, we have therefore decided to do all that lies in our power to assist the British and Persian Governments in putting a stop to this illegal traffic, and we hereby declare that from the date of this notification the importation of arms and ammunition into Kuwait and the territory under my control, and the exportation of the same are absolutely prohibited. All arms and ammunition imported into any part of Kuwait territory or exported therefrom will in future be seized and confiscated.

Dated this 24th Muharram 1318 (= 24th May 1900).

(L. S.) MUBARAK-BIN-SUBAH.

No. 4.

POSTAL AGREEMENT OF FEBRUARY 28TH, 1904, WITH THE SHAIKH OF KUWAIT.

(Translation.)

As the British Government has agreed, in accordance with my desire and for the benefit of traders, to establish a Post Office at Kuwait, I, on my part, agree not to allow the establishment of a Post Office here by any other Government.

I accordingly write this undertaking on behalf of myself and my successors.

(L. S.)   MUBARAK-US-SUBAH.

Kuwait, dated 11th Zil Haj 1321 (= February 28th, 1904).

LEASE AND ACCEPTANCE OF LEASE OF LAND AT BANDER SHWAIKH, 1907.

No. 5 (a).

Translation of lease of the Shwaikh lands.

IN THE NAME OF GOD, THE EXALTED!

This agreement is from me, Shaikh Mubarak-us-Subah, ruler of Kuwait, on behalf of myself and on behalf of my heirs after me, to Major S. G. Knox, Political Agent of the precious Imperial English Government in Kuwait, on behalf of the precious Imperial English Government. The reason of writing this paper is that I, Shaikh Mubarak-us-Subah, the ruler of Kuwait, have, on behalf of myself and on behalf of my heirs after me, leased in perpetuity to the precious Imperial English Government the land, of which the boundaries are detailed below and south of Bander Shwaikh :—

Firstly.—The boundary of the land on the north-west shall be 7,500 cubits in length in a straight line and situated in it the coal-house which I, Shaikh Mubarak-us-Subah, have constructed in these days in the aforesaid land and the straight line shall march, as far as possible, corresponding with sea-line but, apart from these two conditions, it shall be lawful to Major S. G. Knox, Political Agent, Kuwait, or to any other person, duly authorised on behalf of the precious Imperial English Government, to draw this direct north-western boundary at their choice and pleasure, and such boundary shall be accepted by me, Shaikh Mubarak-us-Subah, ruler of Kuwait, on behalf of myself and on behalf of my heirs after me.

" And secondly (as to) the eastern side and the western side, the length of each side (shall be) six hundred cubits, and the southern side seven thousand and five hundred cubits, and the whole land (shall be) rectangular; and from this land, there shall come from it to me, Shaikh Mubarak-us-Subah, ruler of Kuwait, and to my heirs after me, a piece from the north side on which shall be the coal-house abovementioned; on the four sides the length of each side shall be three hundred cubits, the whole amounting to a thousand and two hundred cubits, exclusive of the measurement of the house and (the space) opposite this piece, on the north, shall be to me, Shaikh Mubarak-us-Subah, ruler of Kuwait, and to my heirs after me."

Secondly.—The rent of the land aforesaid shall be counted at R4 per cubit yearly which shall flow from the day that this paper, duly agreed, signed and sealed, shall pass between the hands of the two parties and the rent shall be paid yearly in advance.

Thirdly.—In explanation of the preceding paragraph, the aforesaid lands are embraced by one line, the length of which is 16,200 cubits. Exclusive of the dimensions of the plot of ground of 1,200 cubits, reserved by this agreement to me, Shaikh Mubarak-us-Subah, ruler of Kuwait, and to my heirs after me, the remainder is 15,000 cubits and the rent of the land, according to this line, amounts to R60,000, which shall be paid yearly in advance to me, Shaikh Mubarak-us-Subah, ruler of Kuwait, and to my heirs after me, as long as the precious Imperial English Government desires the lands aforesaid. But it is clearly understood and agreed upon between me, Shaikh Mubarak-us-Subah, ruler of Kuwait, on behalf of myself and on behalf of my heirs after me, and Major S. G. Knox, Political Agent of the precious Imperial English Government in Kuwait, on behalf of the precious Imperial English Government, that should the precious Imperial English Government no longer desire to lease the lands aforesaid, they have the right to inform me, Shaikh Mubarak-us-Subah, or my heirs after me, of their decision at any time they wish and that, after such intimation, the rent ceases, and the land will return to me, Shaikh Mubarak-us-Subah, or to my heirs after me, but, if the Government should have any desire in land, other than the lands of Shwaikh, as the lands enumerated in the sixth paragraph below, it will be by way of rent by consent with me, Shaikh Mubarak-us-Subah, or my heirs after me.

Fourthly.—There is included in the aforesaid rent, without other rent or demand of any kind, the right to all land above ground or under sea between the two sides, the east and the west, produced in the north-west direction to three fathoms of sea-water at the time of the lowest tide opposite to the north-west boundary, and it is lawful for the precious Imperial English Government to build and construct between the aforesaid limits any building of any kind, coal-sheds, harbour-works, *etcetera.*

And, also, it is lawful for the aforesaid English Government to put down buoys and do all works needful for the ease of the ships from the open sea to the Bander Shwaikh such as, *inter alia,* the construction of lighthouses and beacon in Kuwait territory, as may at any time be found to be necessary.

And, also, it is lawful for the aforesaid English Government that they should lease the lands in part or in whole for a fixed term of years or in perpetuity to English subjects or to the subjects of British India—I mean the people of India—or to the subjects of me, Shaikh Mubarak-us-Subah, ruler of Kuwait—I mean the people of Kuwait, at their perfect will and desire.

Fifthly.—And, further, in consideration of the rent detailed, I, Shaikh Mubarak-us-Subah, ruler of Kuwait, on behalf of myself and on behalf of my heirs after me, confirm my former promise that, neither I, nor my heirs after me, will grant, sell or lease to a Foreign Government, and in this is included the Ottoman Government, nor to the subjects of any foreign Government, any of our land within Kuwait boundaries, or around it, without the permission of the precious Imperial English Government.

Sixthly.—And, also, I, Shaikh Mubarak-us-Subah, ruler of Kuwait, on behalf of myself and on behalf of my heirs after me, am bound in this paper that we will give to the precious Imperial English Government the right of pre-emption in sale or lease of the lands detailed below :—

Firstly.—The lands which lie adjacent to the lands leased at a distance of 2,000 cubits in any direction from the nearest boundary of the leased lands, but to my subjects, the people of Kuwait to them shall be a right of pre-emption, stronger and prior to that of the English Government in this special land.

Secondly.—The entire island of Shwaikh and its surrounding foreshore: only the fishing nets are to me, Shaikh Mubarak-us-Subah.

Thirdly.—The entire island of Warba, situated near the Khor Abdulla, and its surrounding foreshore.

Fourthly.—All the lands and the foreshore in the direction of Ras Kathama to a distance of two sea-miles, I mean 8,000 cubits, in any direction from Rash Kathama: if the precious Imperial English Government should have any desire in the aforesaid place, I mean, Kathama, then it will be on lease, separate from the lands of Shwaikh, at a rent that shall please me, Shaikh Mubarak-us-Subah, ruler of Kuwait, or my heirs after me, and there shall be to me, Shaikh Mubarak-us-Subah, ruler of Kuwait, and to my heirs after me, a house near the house of the precious Imperial English Government, should the aforesaid Government desire the lands and the house which shall be to me, Shaikh Mubarak-us-Subah, ruler of Kuwait, and to my heirs after me, shall be a square, each side of which shall be 300 cubits long, the total 1,200 cubits long and to the subjects of me, Shaikh Mubarak-us-Subah, ruler of Kuwait, the land which does not oppose the desire of the aforesaid English Government and, if it should be necessary, I, Shaikh Mubarak-us-Subah, ruler of Kuwait, and my heirs after me will leave to the aforesaid English Government a road to the sea, within our limits, the breadth of which shall not be less than ten cubits.

Seventhly.—In explanation of the preceding paragraph, whenever anysoever may come and desire to buy or to take on lease the lands, detailed in the sixth paragraph above, either in part or the whole, every time before that I, Shaikh Mubarak-us-Subah, ruler of Kuwait, or my heirs after me, accept the offer of the buyer or the lessee, it behoves and it is incumbent on me, Shaikh Mubarak-us-Subah, ruler of Kuwait, and my heirs after me, that we should inform the Agent of the English Government in Kuwait, or the Consul-General of the precious Imperial English Government in Bushire, and that we should give to the aforesaid friend a full opportunity, not less than 3 months, that he may consult higher authority and decide whether the precious Imperial English Government wishes to buy or to take on lease the aforesaid lands or no.

Eighthly.—If the opinion of the aforesaid English Government is fixed on the purchase of the land sought for in accordance with the offer and conditions of the purchaser or the lessee, the offer of the aforesaid English Government will be accepted without further talk or demand, and the demanded lands will be sold or leased to the aforesaid English Government on these conditions.

Ninthly.—And it is clearly understood and agreed upon between the two parties and Major S. G. Knox, Political Agent of the precious Imperial English Government, on behalf of the precious Imperial English Government, is duly authorised to promise and does promise that the town of Kuwait and its boundaries likewise belong to me, Shaikh Mubarak-us-Subah, ruler of Kuwait, and to my heirs after me, and that all my, Shaikh Mubarak's, arrangements at the present day shall remain in the hands of me, Shaikh Mubarak-us-Subah, ruler of Kuwait, and to my heirs after me and that, in the matter of the Shwaikh lands and of the lands which the aforesaid English Government may hereafter rent from me, Shaikh Mubarak-us-Subah, or from my heirs after me, the aforesaid English Government will not take customs on anything in all the lands which they may rent or in which they may dwell within the limits of Kuwait.

Tenthly.—In consideration of the above promise, I, Shaikh Mubarak-us-Subah, ruler of Kuwait, on behalf of myself and on behalf of my heirs after me, hereby promise that we will not collect customs dues on goods imported or exported by the subjects of the aforesaid English Government—I mean English subjects and people of India and other than them of the subjects of the aforesaid English Government—at a rate in excess of 4 *per centum* per invoice value of goods at the port of export. Should, however, I, Shaikh Mubarak-us-Subah, ruler of Kuwait, or my heirs after me, at any time find it necessary to increase the rate of customs beyond 4 *per centum ad valorem*, I hereby promise, on behalf of myself and on behalf of my heirs after me, that such an increase shall be levied on the subjects of the aforesaid English Government only after the consent of the precious Imperial English Government has been duly asked for and obtained to such increase.

Eleventhly.—And, further, I, Shaikh Mubarak-us-Subah, ruler of Kuwait, on behalf of myself and on behalf of my heirs after me, promise that the rate levied on goods imported or exported by the subjects of the aforesaid English Government to or from Kuwait territory shall not exceed the rate levied on goods imported or exported by my subjects—I mean the people of Kuwait—to or from Kuwait territories.

Twelfthly.—It is further clearly understood that I, Shaikh Mubarak-us-Subah, ruler of Kuwait, have accepted this rent especially from the precious Imperial English Government and that, as for others than it, I, Shaikh Mubarak-us-Subah, would not accept from among all the powers: though they should give me more than this rent, I, Shaikh Mubarak-us-Subah, would not allow them to possess authority in my dominions and, as for the precious Imperial English Government, I am grateful to them and their generosity is upon me and I will not consent that a Power, other than them, shall interfere, though they give me more than this rent, and I hope for the permanence of the care of the precious Imperial English Government, and its kindness on me and on my heirs after me, and the precious Imperial English Government has honoured Major S. G. Knox, Political Agent of the precious Imperial English Government in Kuwait, with the special permission that he may assure me, Shaikh Mubarak-us-Subah, ruler of Kuwait, on behalf of the precious Imperial English Government, that the aforesaid English Government does not wish to interfere in the affairs of Kuwait except for the profit of the people of Kuwait and the increase of trade and knowledge and friendship between the English Government and the people of Kuwait and, as regards me, Shaikh Mubarak-us-Subah, and my heirs after me, the desire of the precious Imperial English Government is that the friendship between the precious Imperial English Government and the Shaikh of Kuwait may be perpetual.

And, finally, I, Shaikh Mubarak-us-Subah, at the express wish of the precious Imperial English Government hereby promise that this agreement shall be kept absolutely secret, until such time as the precious Imperial English Government gives permission for its disclosure. And I, Shaikh Mubarak-us-Subah, ruler of Kuwait, on behalf of myself and on behalf of my heirs after me, have accepted each and all of the terms set forth in this agreement, and, therefore, I have set my seal this eighth day of Ramthan, 1325 H., corresponding to this fifteenth day of October, 1907 A.D., and to what I say God is the best witness and protector.

Seal of Shaikh Mubarak-us-Subah.   Seal of Sheikh Jabir.

———

No. 5 (*b*).

Translation of acceptance of lease of Shwaikh lands.

IN THE NAME OF GOD, THE EXALTED!

This agreement is from me, Major S. G. Knox, Political Agent of the precious Imperial English Government in Kuwait, on behalf of the precious Imperial English Government, to Shaikh Mubarak-us-Subah, ruler of Kuwait, on behalf of himself and his heirs after him. The reason of writing this paper is that I, Major S. G. Knox, Political Agent of the precious Imperial English Government, on behalf of the precious Imperial English Government, have, subject to the important provision contained in paragraph 3 below, taken on lease in perpetuity from Shaikh Mubarak-us-Subah, ruler of Kuwait, on behalf of himself and his heirs, the land of which the boundaries are detailed below and south of Bander Shwaikh :—

Firstly.—The boundary of the land on the north-west shall be 7,500 cubits in length in a straight line and situated in it the coal-house which Shaikh Mubarak-us-Subah has constructed in these days in the aforesaid land and the straight line shall march, as far as possible, corresponding with the sea-line, but, apart from these two conditions, it shall be lawful to me, or to any other person, duly authorised on behalf of the precious Imperial English Government, to draw this direct north-western boundary at our choice and pleasure, and such boundary shall be accepted by Shaikh Mubarak-us-Subah, ruler of Kuwait, on behalf of himself and on behalf of his heirs after him.

" And secondly, (as to) the eastern side and the western side, the length of each side (shall be) six hundred cubits, and the southern side seven thousand and five hundred cubits, and the whole land (shall be) rectangular; and from this land, there shall come from it to Shaikh Mubarak-us-Subah, ruler of Kuwait, and to his heirs after him, a piece from the north side, on which shall be the coal-house above-mentioned; on the four sides the length of each side shall be three hundred cubits, the whole amounting to a thousand and two hundred cubits, exclusive of the measurement of the house, and (the space) opposite this piece, on the north, shall be to Shaikh Mubarak-us-Subah, ruler of Kuwait, and to his heirs after him."

Secondly.—The rent of the land aforesaid shall be counted at R4 per cubit yearly which shall flow from the day that this paper, duly agreed, signed, and sealed, shall pass between the hands of the two parties and the rent shall be paid yearly in advance.

Thirdly.—In explanation of the preceding paragraph, the aforesaid lands are embraced by one line, the length of which is 16,200 cubits. Exclusive of the dimensions of the plot of ground of 1,200 cubits, reserved by this agreement to Shaikh Mubarak-us-Subah, ruler of Kuwait, and to his heirs after him, the remainder is 15,000 cubits and the rent of the land, according to this line, amount to R60,000, which I, Major S. G. Knox, Political Agent of the precious Imperial English Government in Kuwait, on behalf of the precious Imperial English Government, promise shall be paid yearly in advance to Shaikh Mubarak-us-Subah, ruler of Kuwait, and to his heirs after him, as long as the precious Imperial Government desires the aforesaid lands. But it is clearly understood and agreed upon between me, Major S. G. Knox, Political Agent of the precious Imperial English Government in Kuwait, on behalf of the precious Imperial English Government and Shaikh Mubarak-us-Subah, ruler of Kuwait, on behalf of himself and on behalf of his heirs after him, that should the precious Imperial English Government no longer desire to lease the lands aforesaid, they have the right to inform Shaikh Mubarak-us-Subah, or his heirs after him, of their decision at any time they wish and that, after such intimation, the rent ceases and land will return to Shaikh Mubarak-us-Subah, ruler of

Kuwait, or to his heirs after him, but if the precious Imperial English Government should have any desire for land other than these lands of Shwaikh, such as the lands enumerated in the sixth paragraph below, it will be by way of rent by consent with Shaikh Mubarak-us-Subah, ruler of Kuwait, or his heirs after him.

Fourthly.—There is included in the aforesaid rent, without other rent or demand of any kind, the right to all land, above ground or under sea, between the two sides, the east and the west, produced in the north-west direction to three fathoms of sea-water at the time of the lowest tide opposite to the north-west boundary and it is lawful for the precious Imperial English Government to build and construct between the aforesaid limits any building of any kind, coal-sheds, harbour works, etc.

And, also, it is lawful for the aforesaid English Government to put down buoys and do all works needful for the ease of the ships from the open sea to the Bander Shwaikh such as, *inter alia*, the construction of lighthouses and beacon in Kuwait territory, as may at any time be found to be necessary.

And, also, it is lawful for the aforesaid English Government that they should lease the lands in part or in whole for a fixed term of years or in perpetuity to English subjects or to the subjects of British India—I mean the people of India or to the subjects of Shaikh Mubarak-us-Subah, ruler of Kuwait—I mean the people of Kuwait, at their perfect will and desire.

Fifthly.—And, further, in consideration of the rent detailed, Shaikh Mubarak-us-Subah, ruler of Kuwait, on behalf of himself and on behalf of his heirs after him confirms his former promise that, neither he nor his heirs after him, will grant, sell, or lease to a Foreign Government, and in this is included the Ottoman Government, or to the subjects of any Foreign Government, any of his or their land within Kuwait boundaries or around it without the permission of the precious Imperial English Government.

Sixthly.—And, also, Shaikh Mubarak-us-Subah, ruler of Kuwait, on behalf of himself and on behalf of his heirs after him, is bound in this paper that he and they will give to the precious Imperial English Government the right of pre-emption in sale or lease of the lands detailed below :—

Firstly.—The lands which lie adjacent to the lands leased at a distance of 2,000 cubits in any direction from the nearest boundary of the leased lands, but to the subjects of Shaikh Mubarak—I mean the people of Kuwait—to them shall be a right of pre-emption, stronger and prior to that of the English Government in this land only.

Secondly.—The entire island of Shwaikh and its surrounding foreshore: only the fishing nets are to Shaikh Mubarak-us-Subah.

Thirdly.—The entire island of Warba, situated near the Khor Abdulla, and its surrounding foreshore.

Fourthly.—All the lands, and the foreshore in the direction of Ras Kathama to a distance of two sea-miles, I mean 8,000 cubits, in any direction of Ras Kathama : if the precious Imperial English Government should have any desire in that place, then it will be on lease, separate from the lands of Shwaikh, at a rent that shall please Shaikh Mubarak-us-Subah, ruler of Kuwait, or his heirs after him, and there shall be to Shaikh Mubarak-us-Subah, ruler of Kuwait, and to his heirs after him a house, near the house of the precious Imperial English Government, should the aforesaid Government desire the lands and the house which shall be to Shaikh Mubarak-us-Subah, ruler of Kuwait, and to his heirs after him, shall be a square, each side of which shall be 300 cubits long, the total 1,200 cubits long, and to the subjects of Shaikh Mubarak-us-Subah, ruler of Kuwait, the land which does not oppose the desire of the aforesaid English Government and, if it should be necessary, Shaikh Mubarak-us-Subah, ruler of Kuwait, and his heirs after him will leave to the aforesaid English Government a road to the sea, within their limits, the breadth of which shall not be less than ten cubits.

Seventhly.—In explanation of the preceding paragraph, whenever anysoever may come and desire to buy or to take on lease the lands, detailed in the sixth paragraph above, either in part or the whole, every time before that Shaikh Mubarak-us-Subah, ruler of Kuwait, or his heirs after him, accept the offer of the buyer or the lessee, it behoves and is incumbent on Shaikh Mubarak-us-Subah, ruler of Kuwait, or his heirs after him, that they should inform the Agent of the English Government in Kuwait or the Consul-General of the precious Imperial English Government in Bushire, and that they should give to the aforesaid friend a full opportunity not less than three months, that he may consult higher authority and decide whether the precious Imperial English Government wishes to buy or to take on lease the aforesaid lands or no.

Eighthly.—If the opinion of the aforesaid English Government is fixed on the purchase or the lease of the lands sought for in accordance with the offer and conditions of the purchaser or the lessee, the offer of the aforesaid English Government will be accepted without further talk or demand and the demanded lands will be sold or leased to the aforesaid English Government on these conditions.

Ninthly.—And it is clearly understood and agreed upon between the two parties and I, Major S. G. Knox, Political Agent of the precious Imperial English Government, am duly authorised on behalf of the precious Imperial English Government to promise, and do hereby promise, that the town of Kuwait and its boundaries likewise belong to Shaikh Mubarak-us-Subah, ruler of Kuwait, and to his heirs after him, and that all Shaikh Mubarak's arrangements in the matter of customs, etc., and all his arrangements at the present day shall remain in the hands of Shaikh Mubarak-us-Subah, ruler of Kuwait, and to his heirs after him and that, in the matter of the Shwaikh lands and of the lands which the aforesaid English Government may hereafter rent from Shaikh Mubarak-us-Subah, or from his heirs after him, the aforesaid English Government will not take customs on anything in all the lands which they may rent or in which they may dwell within the limits of Kuwait.

Tenthly.—In consideration of the above promise, Shaikh Mubarak-us-Subah, ruler of Kuwait, on behalf of himself and on behalf of his heirs after him, promises that they will not collect customs dues on goods imported or exported by the subjects of the aforesaid English Government—I mean English subjects and people of India and other than them of the subjects of the aforesaid English Government—at a rate in excess of 4 *per centum* per invoice value of goods at the port of export. Should, however, Shaikh Mubarak-us-Subah, ruler of Kuwait, or his heirs after him, at any time find it necessary to increase the rate of customs beyond 4 *per cent. ad valorem*, Shaikh Mubarak on behalf of himself, and on behalf of his heirs after him, promises that such an increase shall be levied on the subjects of the aforesaid English Government only after the consent of the precious Imperial English Government has been duly asked for and obtained to such increase.

Eleventhly.—And, further, Shaikh Mubarak-us-Subah, ruler of Kuwait, on behalf of himself, and on behalf of his heirs after him, promises that the rate, levied on goods imported or exported by the subjects of the aforesaid English Government to or from Kuwait territories, shall not exceed the rate levied on goods imported or exported by his subjects—I mean the people of Kuwait—to and from Kuwait territories.

Twelfthly.—It is further clearly understood that Shaikh Mubarak-us-Subah, ruler of Kuwait, has accepted this rent especially from the precious Imperial English Government and that, as for others than it, Shaikh Mubarak-us-Subah would not accept from among all the Powers: though they should give him more than this rent, Shaikh Mubarak-us-Subah would not allow them to possess authority in his dominions and, as for the precious Imperial English Government, he is grateful to them, and their generosity is upon him and that he will not consent that a Power, other than them, shall interfere, though they gave him more than this rent, and he hopes for the permanence of the care of the precious Imperial English Government and its kindness on him and on his heirs after him, and the precious Imperial English Government has honoured me with the special permission that I may assure Shaikh Mubarak-us-Subah, ruler of Kuwait, on behalf of the precious Imperial English Government that the aforesaid English Government does not wish to interfere in the affairs of Kuwait except for the profit of the people of Kuwait and the increase of trade and knowledge and friendship between the English Government and the people of Kuwait and, as regards Shaikh Mubarak-us-Subah and his heirs after him, the desire of the precious Imperial English Government is that the friendship and agreement between the English Government and the Shaikh of Kuwait may be perpetual.

And finally, Shaikh Mubarak-us-Subah, at the express wish of the precious Imperial English Government, promises that this agreement shall be kept absolutely secret until such time as the precious Imperial English Government gives permission for its disclosure.

And I, Major S. G. Knox, Political Agent of the precious Imperial English Government in Kuwait, on behalf of the precious Imperial English Government, have accepted each and all of the terms set forth in this agreement, and, therefore, I have affixed my signature this eighth day of Ramthan, 1325 H., corresponding to the 15th day of October 1907 A.D., and to what I say God is the best witness and protector.

S. G. KNOX, *Major,*
Political, Agent, Kuwait.

No. 6 (a).

No. 345, dated the 29th July 1911.

From—Captain W. H. I. Shakespear, Political Agent,
To—Shaikh Mubarak-us-Subah, Ruler of Kuwait.

(Regarding pearling concessions.)

After compliments. And after it must be within Your Excellency's mind that five years ago there arrived a stranger here who wished to take a concession to take sponges (a thing which comes out of the sea) and at that time Your Excellency did not agree and it was good what you did. And in these days it is possible that persons will come who will seek, like that, their own profit and the Resident at Bushire has written to me that I should inform Your Excellency that it may be in your discernment because it is possible there may be loss from this to the Shaikhs and their people, especially if they (the persons) should obtain a concession for the diving for pearls and because of this the Resident mentions that if anyone should come and seek a concession from the Shaikh for anything, Inshallah, His Excellency the Shaikh will inform us and take our advice before he completes the affair.

This is what was necessary to state to Your Excellency and may you be preserved.

Dated the 29th July 1911, equivalent to 2nd Shaaban 1329.

No. 6 (*b*).

TRANSLATION OF A LETTER FROM SHAIKH MUBARAK-US-SUBAH, RULER OF KUWAIT, TO CAPTAIN W. H. I. SHAKESPEAR, POLITICAL AGENT, REGARDING PEARLING CONCESSIONS, DATED THE 2ND SHAABAN 1329 (29TH JULY 1911).

After compliments. We have received with the hand of friendship your letter dated the 2nd Shaaban 1329, equivalent to 29th July 1911, and in it you stated of a stranger who five years ago asked from us a concession to take sponges and at the time we rejected his request and that in this time came to you intimation from His Honour the Resident at Bushire mentioning that in these days possibly will come people seeking their own profit and from this profit will arrive loss to us and to our people and advising us not to agree to them before asking for his (Resident's) opinion. I am exceedingly grateful to the beloved of all (Resident) and as is known to Your Honour I do not seek profit without your consultation in every circumstance and I will do nought except it agree with your view and the view of the precious Government. In the expectation from Your Honour that you will reassure him (Resident) and present my thanks to him and may you be preserved.

Dated 2nd Shaaban 1329.

———

No. 7.

UNDERTAKING OF RULER OF KUWAIT WITH REGARD TO ESTABLISHMENT OF A WIRELESS TELEGRAPH INSTALLATION AT KUWAIT.

———

TRANSLATION OF A LETTER FROM HIS EXCELLENCY SHAIKH SIR MUBARAK-US-SUBAH, K.C.I.E., RULER OF KUWAIT, TO LIEUTENANT-COLONEL SIR PERCY COX, K.C.I.E., C.S.I., POLITICAL RESIDENT IN THE PERSIAN GULF. (ENCLOSURE IN RESIDENCY LETTER 1739, 6TH AUGUST 1912, TO FOREIGN DEPARTMENT), DATED THE 11TH SHAABAN 1330 (=26TH JULY 1912).

I have had the pleasure to receive Your Honour's communication dated the 27th Rajab 1330 (=13th July 1912) in which you have referred to the desire of the High and Imperial Government to have the telegraph in our town of Kuwait and (stated) that on Your Honour's return to Bushire, you found, as you expected, final instructions from the High and Imperial Government to inform us of their desire and to ask for our co-operation in this object and that the existence of the telegraph will be a source of ease to the High Government and our people.

I have personally informed Your Honour when I had the pleasure of your august interview, of my co-operation and concord in this and other matters, which are conducive to reform and which you consider to be agreeable to (our) welfare, in accordance with such orders as may be issued thereon by the High and Imperial Government and according to your august wishes.

The details will be explained to us by our friend Captain Shakespear, as ordered by you, when the work progresses, and we will also explain to him the manner which will tend to our ease. And we pray to God to crown all your efforts with success and to grant happy results, and enable us to obtain your satisfaction by word and deed.

We trust that your kind regards will endure and that you will accept my assurance of high esteem and continue to be preserved.

No. 8 (*a*).

TRANSLATION OF A LETTER FROM LIEUTENANT-COLONEL SIR PERCY COX, K.C.I.E., C.S.I., POLITICAL RESIDENT IN THE PERSIAN GULF, TO SHAIKH SIR MUBARAK-US-SUBAH, RULER OF KUWAIT, REGARDING OIL DEPOSITS AT KUWAIT, DATED THE 27TH OCTOBER 1913.

After compliments. And after with reference to the conversation which took place between us yesterday, if you see no objection therein I wish with your consent to inform the British Government that you are agreeable to the visit of Admiral Slade in order that he may inspect the places (showing traces of) bitumen at Burgan and elsewhere and that if there seems in his view a hope of obtaining oil therefrom, Your Excellency agrees not to give a concession in this regard to anyone other than a person nominated and recommended by the British Government.

This is what was necessary to communicate to you and may you be preserved.

Dated the 26th Zu-al-Kada 1331 (27th October 1913).

No. 8 (*b*).

TRANSLATION OF A LETTER FROM SHAIKH SIR MUBARAK-US-SUBAH, RULER OF KUWAIT, TO THE POLITICAL RESIDENT IN THE PERSIAN GULF, REGARDING OIL DEPOSITS AT KUWAIT, DATED THE 26TH ZU-AL-KADA 1331 (27TH OCTOBER 1913).

After compliments. With the hand of friendship we received your esteemed letter, dated the 26th Zu-al-Kada 1331 and in it you stated that with reference to the conversation which passed between us yesterday if we saw no objection therein it would be profitable to Your Honour to inform the British Government that we were agreeable to the arrival of His Excellency the Admiral—we are agreeable to everything which you regard advantageous and if the Admiral honours our (side) country we will associate with him one of our sons to be in his service, to show the place of bitumen in Burgan and elsewhere and if in their view there seems hope of obtaining oil therefrom we shall never give a concession in this matter to anyone except a person appointed from the British Government.

This is what was necessary and I pray for the continuance of your high regard and may you be preserved.

Dated 26th Zu-al-Kada 1331.

APPENDIX V

TERMS OF A FRIENDLY CONVENTION ENTERED INTO BETWEEN SHAIKH MAHOMED BIN KHALIFAH, INDEPENDENT RULER OF BAHRAIN, ON THE PART OF HIMSELF AND SUCCESSORS, AND CAPTAIN FELIX JONES, HER MAJESTY'S INDIAN NAVY, POLITICAL RESIDENT OF HER BRITANNIC MAJESTY IN THE GULF OF PERSIA, ON THE PART OF THE BRITISH GOVERNMENT, 1861.

Preliminary.—Considering the tribe disorders which arise and are perpetuated from maritime aggressions in the Persian Gulf, I, Shaikh Mahomed bin Khalifah, independent ruler of Bahrain, on my own part and on that of my heirs and successors, in the presence of the Chiefs and elders who are witnesses to this document, do subscribe and agree to a perpetual Treaty of peace and friendship with the British Government, having for its object the advancement of trade and the security of all classes of people navigating or residing upon the coasts of this sea :—

ARTICLE 1.

I recognise as valid and in force all former Treaties and Conventions agreed to between the Chiefs of Bahrain and the British Government, either direct or through the mediation of its representatives in this Gulf.

ARTICLE 2.

I agree to abstain from all maritime aggressions of every description, from the prosecution of war, piracy, and slavery by sea, so long as I receive the support of the British Government in the maintenance of the security of my own possessions against similar aggressions directed against them by the Chiefs and tribes of this Gulf.

ARTICLE 3.

In order that the above engagements may be fulfilled I agree to make known all aggressions and depredations which may be designed, or have to place at sea, against myself, territories, or subject, as early as possible, to the British Resident in the Persian Gulf, as the arbitrator in such cases, promising that no act of aggression or retaliation shall be committed at sea by Bahrains or in the name of Bahrain, by myself or others under me, on other tribe, without his consent or that of the British Government, if it should be necessary to procure it. And the British Resident engages that he will forthwith take the necessary steps for obtaining reparation for every injury proved to have been inflicted, or in course of infliction by sea upon Bahrain or upon its dependencies in this Gulf. In like manner, I, Shaikh Mahomed bin Khalifah, will afford full redress for all maritime offences which in justice can be charged against my subjects or myself, as the ruler of Bahrain.

ARTICLE 4.

British subjects of every denomination, it is understood, may reside in, and carry on their lawful trade in the territories of Bahrain, their goods being subject only to an *ad valorem* duty of 5 per cent. in cash or in kind. This amount once paid shall not be demanded again on the same goods if exported from Bahrain to other places; and in respect to the treatment of British subjects and dependants they shall receive the treatment and consideration of the subject and dependants of the most favoured people. All offences which they may commit, or which may be committed against them, shall be reserved for the decisions of the British Resident, provided the British Agent located at

Bahrain shall fail to adjust them satisfactorily. In like manner the British Resident will use his good offices for the welfare of the subjects of Bahrain in the ports of the maritime Arab tribes of this Gulf in alliance with the British Government.

ARTICLE 5.

These Articles of alliance shall have effect from the date of ratification or approval by the British Government,

Done at Bahrain this twentieth day of Zilkad, in the year of the Hegira 1277, corresponding with the thirty-first day of May 1861.

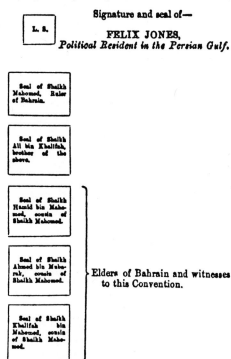

Signature and seal of—

L. S.

FELIX JONES,
Political Resident in the Persian Gulf.

Seal of Shaikh Mahomed, Ruler of Bahrain.

Seal of Shaikh Ali bin Khalifah, brother of the above.

Seal of Shaikh Hamid bin Mahomed, cousin of Shaikh Mahomed.

Seal of Shaikh Ahmed bin Mubarak, cousin of Shaikh Mahomed.

Seal of Shaikh Khalifah bin Mahomed, cousin of Shaikh Mahomed.

Elders of Bahrain and witnesses to this Convention.

Approved by His Excellency the Governor-General in Council on the 9th October 1861, and ratified by the Government of Bombay on 25th February 1862.

APPENDIX   VI

UNDERTAKING WITH THE BRITISH GOVERNMENT (Copy)

We the undersigned, Directors in the Persian Gulf of the
Dutch Reformed Church Mission in Arabia, recognizing the special
position of the British Government at Kuweit, hereby undertake -
in the event of our obtaining from Sheikh Mubarek with British
consent, a site in Kuweit, on lease or purchase, for the permanent
establishment of (*) our Mission - that while it will always be
our endeavour to carry on our work and arrange any little difficulties that may arise from time to time, with the Sheikh direct,
should we find ourselves unable to adjust our differences in that
manner, we will refer them for the arbitration or good offices of
the British representative alone, or , in his absence, of the
British resident in the Persian Gulf. The Kuweit establishment
will be entirely independent of the branch of our Mission at Busrah
and in no circumstances will we, directly or indirectly, seek the
intervention of Turkish Authorities, or of Consular officials
accredited to Turkish territory.

(Signed) Jas. E. Moerdyk
D. Dykstra

At Bahrein
 November 18th, 1910

(*) In this signed copy the word "our" has been substituted for
    the words "a Medical" of the original as submitted to us by
    the British Resident of the Gulf.

American Arabian Mission Historical Archives. New Brunswick, N.J.

APPENDIX   VII

ĀL-SABĀH RULERS OF KUWAIT

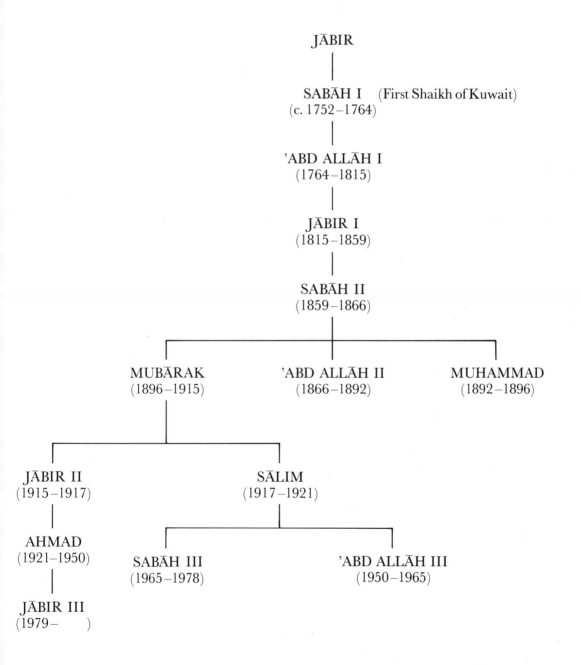

JĀBIR

SABĀH I   (First Shaikh of Kuwait)
(c. 1752–1764)

'ABD ALLĀH I
(1764–1815)

JĀBIR I
(1815–1859)

SABĀH II
(1859–1866)

MUBĀRAK   'ABD ALLĀH II   MUHAMMAD
(1896–1915)   (1866–1892)   (1892–1896)

JĀBIR II   SĀLIM
(1915–1917)   (1917–1921)

AHMAD   SABĀH III   'ABD ALLĀH III
(1921–1950)   (1965–1978)   (1950–1965)

JĀBIR III
(1979–   )

ĀL-KHALĪFA RULERS OF BAHRAIN

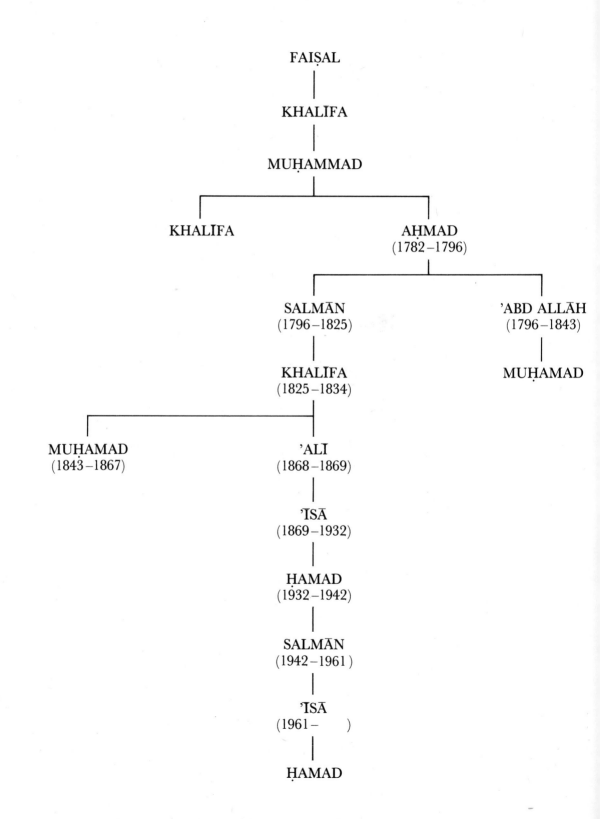

FAIṢAL

KHALĪFA

MUḤAMMAD

KHALĪFA

AḤMAD
(1782–1796)

SALMĀN
(1796–1825)

'ABD ALLĀH
(1796–1843)

KHALĪFA
(1825–1834)

MUḤAMAD

MUḤAMAD
(1843–1867)

'ALĪ
(1868–1869)

'ĪSĀ
(1869–1932)

ḤAMAD
(1932–1942)

SALMĀN
(1942–1961)

'ĪSĀ
(1961–   )

ḤAMAD

GENEALOGICAL TABLE OF ĀL-SUʾŪD AMĪRS

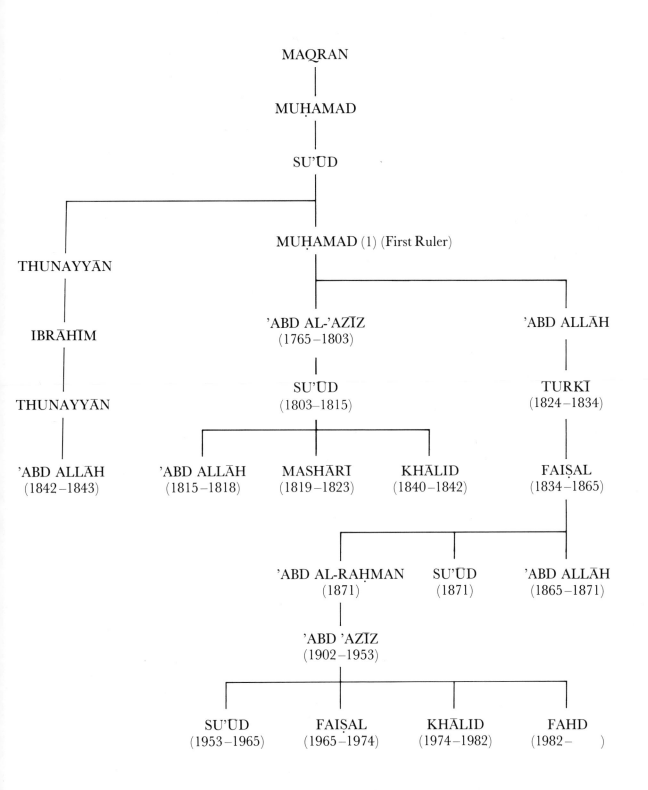

MAQRAN

MUḤAMAD

SUʾŪD

THUNAYYĀN

MUḤAMAD (1) (First Ruler)

IBRĀHĪM

ʾABD AL-ʾAZĪZ
(1765–1803)

ʾABD ALLĀH

THUNAYYĀN

SUʾŪD
(1803–1815)

TURKĪ
(1824–1834)

ʾABD ALLĀH
(1842–1843)

ʾABD ALLĀH
(1815–1818)

MASHĀRĪ
(1819–1823)

KHĀLID
(1840–1842)

FAIṢAL
(1834–1865)

ʾABD AL-RAḤMAN
(1871)

SUʾŪD
(1871)

ʾABD ALLĀH
(1865–1871)

ʾABD ʾAZĪZ
(1902–1953)

SUʾŪD
(1953–1965)

FAIṢAL
(1965–1974)

KHĀLID
(1974–1982)

FAHD
(1982–   )

GENEOLOGY OF THE BANĪ KHĀLID SHAIKHS
IN THE 17th AND 18th CENTURIES

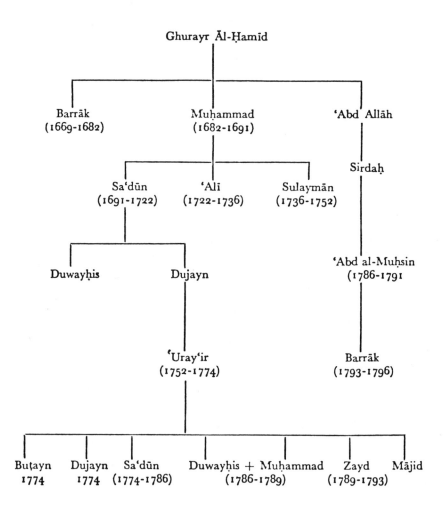

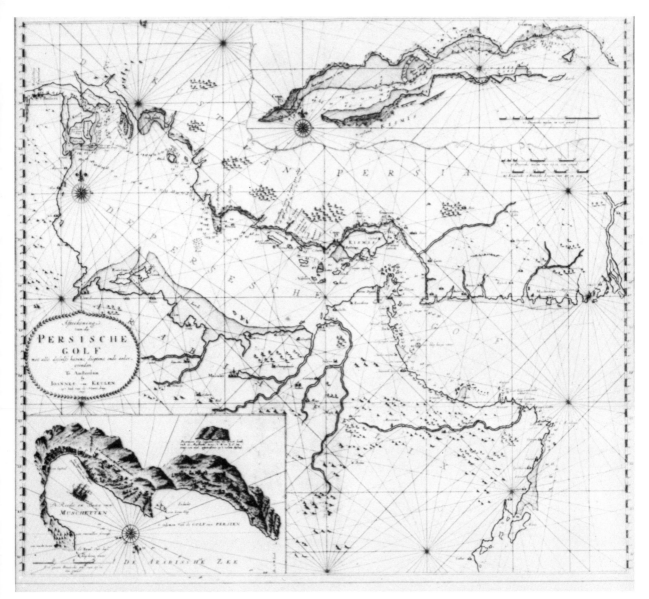

Dutch map of about 1660: Kuwait is shown as Grane.

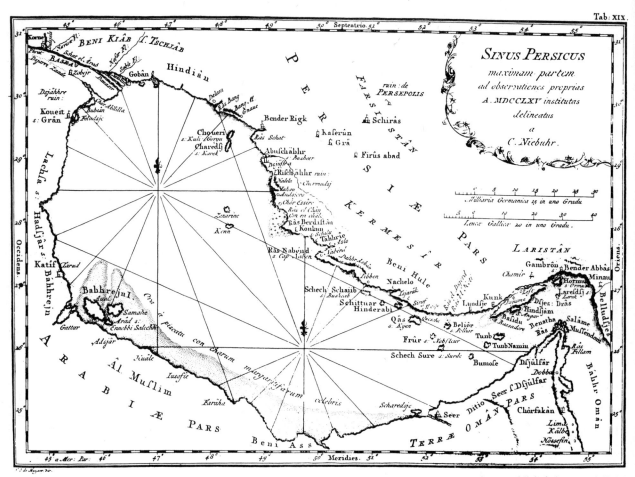

Carston Niebuhr's map of 1765.

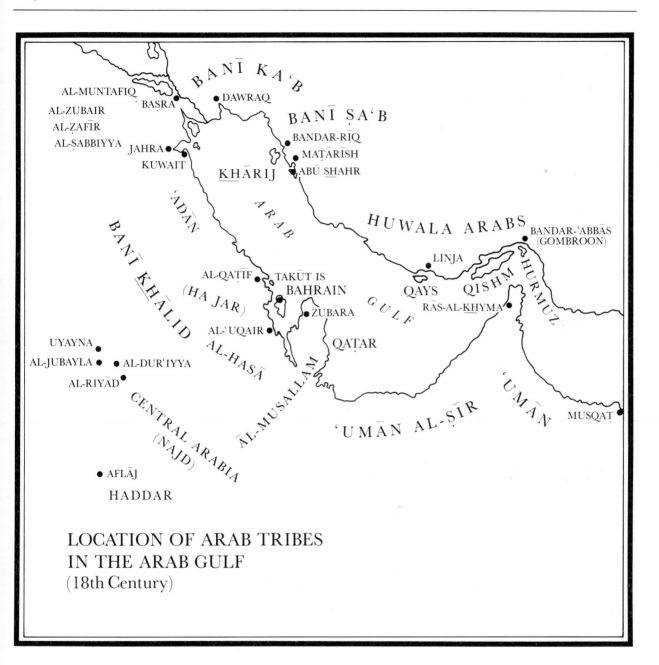

LOCATION OF ARAB TRIBES
IN THE ARAB GULF
(18th Century)

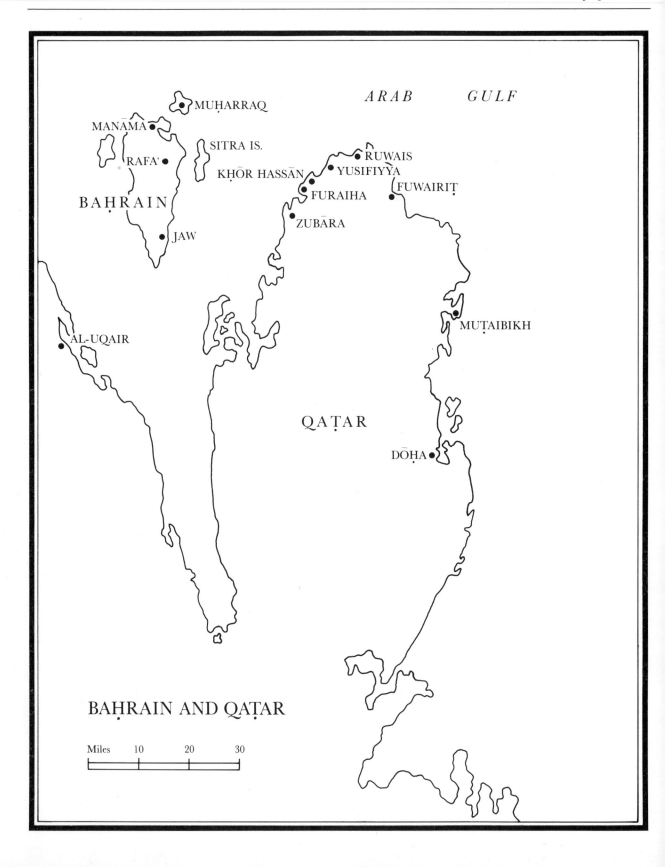

ARAB   GULF

MUHARRAQ

MANAMA

SITRA IS.

RAFA'

KHOR HASSAN

RUWAIS

YUSIFIYYA

BAHRAIN

FURAIHA

FUWAIRIT

ZUBARA

JAW

MUTAIBIKH

AL-UQAIR

QATAR

DOHA

BAHRAIN AND QATAR

Miles   10   20   30

Map to show the limits of Koweit and adjacent country – 1913

BIBLIOGRAPHY

Abu-Hakima, Ahmad Mustafa
History of Eastern Arabia, Rise and Development of Bahrain and Kuwait (1750-1800), Beirut, 1965.

ed., *Lam' al-Shihāb fī sīrat Muhammad ibn 'Abd al-Wahhāb*, Beirut, 1967.
Tārīkh al-Kuwait, vol. I, Part one, vol. I, Part two, vol. II, Part one, Kuwait, 1969 -

Admiralty, War Office, Intelligence Division
A Handbook of Arabia, Vol. I, London, May 1916. Vol. II, London, May 1917.

Aitchison, C. V. (ed.) *A Collection of Treaties, Engagements and Sanads Relating to India and the Neighbouring Countries: Persia, the Arab Principalities in the Persian Gulf and Oman.* Vol. XI, Calcutta, 1933.

Al-Dawud, M. A. *Al-Khalīj Al-'Arabī wal-'Ilāqāt Al-Dawliyya*, Cairo, 1961.

Ālūsī, Mahmūd Shukrī al-, *Ta'rīkh Najd.* Edited with notes by Muhammad Bahjat al-Atharī, Cairo, 1343/1924.

Amin, Abdul Amir *British Interests in the Persian Gulf*, Leiden, 1967.

An Account of the Monies, Weights, and Measures in General Use in Persia, Arabia, East India and China. London, 1789.

Anthony, J. D.
Arab States of the Lower Gulf: People, Politics and Petroleum. Washington, D.C., 1975.

'Aqqād, Salāh al-,
Le Premier état Sa'udite (1744-1818) Essai sur son histoire politique et réligieuse. These pour Le Doctorat d'Etat, Université de Paris, Faculté de Lettres 1956.

Ashkenazi, T.
"The Anazah Tribes", *Southwestern Journal of Anthropology*, New Mexico, 1948, pp. 222-39.

'Azzāwī, 'Abbās al-
Ta'rīkh al-'Irāq bayn Ihtilālayn, Vol. 6, Baghdād, 1373/1954.
'Ashā'ir al-'Irāq, Vol. I, Baghdād, 1365/1947. Vol. II, Baghdād, 1366/1948.

Badger, G. P.
History of the Imams and Seyyids of 'Oman by Salil ibn Razīk, from A.D. 661-1858, translated from the original Arabic and edited with notes, appendices and introduction containing the history down to 1870. Hakluyt Society, No. 43, London, 1871.

Bassām, Muhammad al-
Al-Durar al-Mafākhir fī Akbār al-'Arab al-Awākhir, British Museum M.S. Add. 7358.

Batrik, Abdel Hamid. M.El-
Turkish and Egyptian Rule in Arabia, (1810-1841), Ph.D. Thesis, London University, 1947.
Belgrave, Charles
The Pirate Coast, London, 1966.
Belgrave, James
Welcome to Bahrain, London, 1973.
Bidwell, R.
The Affairs of Kuwait, 1896-1905. Two volumes, London, 1971.

Brockelmann, Carl
Geschichte der Arabischen Litteratur, Vol. I, Leiden, 1943. Vol. II, Leiden, 1944. Supplementary Vol. I, Leiden, 1937. Supplementary Vol. II, Leiden, 1938.

Brucks, Captain George Barnes
"Memoir descriptive of the Navigation of the Gulf of Persia; with brief notices of the manners, customs, religion, commerce, and resources of the people inhabiting its shores and islands." in *Bombay Selections*, Vol. XXIV. Bombay, 1856.

Brydges, Harford Jones
An Account of the Transactions of His Majesty's Mission to the Court of Persia in the Years 1810-1811, to which is appended a brief History of the Wahauby, 2 Vols. London, 1834.

Buckingham, J.S.
Travels in Assyria, Media and Persia, including a Journey from Baghdad by Mount Zagros, to Hamadan, the Ancient Ecbatana, Researches in Isfahan and the Ruins of Persepolis, and Journey from thence by Shiraz, Bushire, Ormuz, and Muscat. Narrative of an Expedition against the Pirates of the Persian Gulf, with Illustrations of the Voyage of Nearchus, and Passage by the Arabian Sea to Bombay, London, 1829.

Burckhardt, John Lewis
Notes on the Bedouins and Wahabys, London, 1830.

Travels in Syria and the Holy Land, London, 1822.

Travels in Nubia, 2nd edn., London, 1822.

Busch, B.C.
Britain and the Persian Gulf, 1894-1914, Berkeley, California, 1967.

Calverley, Dr. Eleanor T.
My Arabian Days and Nights, New York, 1958.

Capper, James
Observations on the Passage to India, through Egypt and across the Great Desert: with Occasional Remarks on the Adjacent Countries and also sketches of the different Routes. London, 1784.

Carmichael, J.
"A Narrative of a Journey from Aleppo to Basra in 1751" in Carruthers' *The Desert Route to India etc.* Hakluyt Society, Second Series No. LXIII, London, 1929.

Carruthers, Douglas
The Desert Route to India, being the Journals of Four Travellers by the Great Desert Caravan Route between Aleppo and Basra, 1745-1751. Hakluyt Society, No. LXIII, London, 1929.

Chesney, F.R.
Expedition for the survey of the Rivers Euphrates and Tigris, 2 Vols., London, 1850.

Narrative of the Euphrates Expedition, London, 1868.

Chisholm, A.H.T.
The First Kuwait Oil Concession, A Record of the Negotiations for the 1934 Agreement. London, 1975.
Corancez, L.A.
Histoire des Wahabis depuis leur origine jusqu'a la fin de 1809. Paris, 1810.

Curzon, G.N.
Persia and Persian Question, 2 vols., London, 1938.

Danvers, F.C.
Report on the India Office Records Relating to Persia and the Persian Gulf. London, N.D.

Dayrani, Ibrahim B. Khalil al-
Kitāb Misbāh al-Sārī wa Nuzhat al-Qāri', Bayrūt, 1272/1855.

Dickson, H.R.P.
The Arab of the Desert, a Glimpse into Badawin Life in Kuwait and Saudi Arabia. London, 1949.

Kuwait and her Neighbours, London, 1956.

Dodwell, H.H.
The Founder of Modern Egypt: A study of Muhammad 'Ali. Cambridge, 1931.

Doughty, C.M.
Travels in Arabia Deserts, Cambridge, 1888.

Dujayli, Kazim al-
"Al-Shaikh 'Uthmān b. Sanad al Basrī" in *Lughat al-'Arab,* III, 180-186. Baghdad, 1331/1913.

Dutch Reformed Church of America
Historical Archives of the Arabian Mission, 1889-1965.

El Mallakh, R.
Economic Development and Regional Cooperation: Kuwait, Chicago, 1969.

El Sheikh, Riyad
Kuwait, Economic Growth of the Oil State, Problem and Policies, Kuwait, 1972/73.

Encyclopaedia Britanica, 1959 edition
Encyclopaedia of Islam, 1st and 2nd Editions.

Edwards, F.M.
"George Forster Sadleir (1789-1859) of the 47th Regiment, the First European to cross Arabia", in *Journal of the Royal Central Asian Society,* XLIV (1957), pp. 38-49.

Egyptian National Archives, Cairo
The Hijaz Files - Archival Material for the Period 1810-1840.

Faroughy, 'Abbas
The Bahrain Islands, New York, 1951.

Freeth, Zahra and Winstone, V.
Kuwait, Prospect and Reality, London, 1972.

Furber, Holden
"The Overland Route to India in the Seventeenth and Eighteenth Centuries", *Journal of Indian History,* Vol. XXIX, Part II, August 1951, pp. 106-133.

John Company at Work, a Study of European Expansion in India in the Late Eighteenth Century, Cambridge, U.S.A., 1948.

Griffiths, J.
Travels in Europe, Asia Minor and Arabia, London, 1805.

Hamza, Fu'ad
Qalb Jazīrat al-'Arab, Cairo, 1352/1933.

Hay, R.
The Persian Gulf States, Washington, D.C., 1959.

Haydar, Ali
The Life of Midhat Pasha, London, 1903.

Haydari, Ibrahim Fasih B. Sabghat Allah B. Muhammad As'ad al-
'Unwān al-Majd fī Bayān Ahwāl Baghdād wa Basra wa Najd. British Museum Ms.Or. 7567.

Hewins, R.
A Golden Dream, The Miracle of Kuwait. London, 1963.

Hulwani, Amin B. Hasan al-
Mukhtasar Ta'rīkh al-Shaikh 'Uthmān b. Sanad al-Basrī al-Musammā Bi Matāli' al-Su'ūd Bi Tayyib Akhbār al-Wālī Dawūd, Bombay, 1304/1886.

Ibn Bishr, 'Uthman B. 'Abd Allah
Kitāb 'Unwān al-Majd fī Ta'rīkh Najd, Makka, 1349/1930. British Museum MS. Or. 7718.

Ibn Durayd, Abu Bakr Muhammad B. al-Hasan
Kitāb al-Ishtiqāq, Cairo, 1378/1958.

Ibn Ghannam, Husayn
Kitāb Rawdat al-Afkār Wal-Afhām Li Murtād hāl al-Imām Wa Ta'dād Ghazwāt Dhawī al-Islām. Vol. I.
Kitāb al-Ghazwāt al-Bayāniyya wal-Futūahāt al-Rabbāniyya wa Dhikhr al-Sabab alladhī hamal 'alā dhalik. Vol. II, Bombay, 1919. The British Museum MSS are: Add 23, 344-5 and Add. 19,799; 19,800.

Ibn Manzur, Jamal Al-Din
Lisān al-'Arab, Vol. I, Bayrūt, 1374/1955.

Ibn Raziq, Humayd B. Muhammad
Al Fath al-Mubīn al-Mubarhin Sīrat al-Sādāt al-Bū-Sa'īdiyyīn, Cambridge Univ. Library MS. Add. 2892.

Al-Sīra al-Jaliyya al-Musammāt sa'd al-Su'ūd al-Bū-Sa'īdiyya, Cambridge Univ. Library MS. Add. 2893.

Sahīfat al-Qahtāniyya, Rhodes House, Oxford Univ. MS. Afr. S.3.

Ibn Sanad, 'Uthman
Matāli' al-Su'ūd Bi-Tayyib Akhbār al-Wālī Dawūd. Ber. Qu. 1338. This manuscript is now kept in the Library of Tubingen University, Germany.

Sabā'ik al-'Asjad fī Akhbār Ahmad Najil Rizq al-As'ad, Bombay, 1315/1897. British Museum MS. Or. 7565.

India Office Records
1. Factory Records, Persia and Persian Gulf. Vols. 14-130. 1703-1874.

2. The Agencies Records
a. Kuwait Agency 1904-1947, R/15/5
b. Bahrain Agency 1900-1947, R/15/2

Irwin, Eyles
A series of Adventures in the course of a Voyage up the Red Sea, on the coast of Arabia and Egypt; And of a Route through the Desert of Thebais, in the Year 1777. With a Supplement of a Voyage from Venice to Latichea: and of a Route through the Deserts of Arabia, by Aleppo, Baghdad and the Tygris, to Busrah, in the Years 1780, and 1781. Two Vols. London, 1787.

Ives, Edward
A Voyage from England to India, in the Year 1753, and an Historical Narrative of the Operations of the Squadron and Army in India, under the Command of Vice-Admiral Watson, and Colonel Clive, in the Years 1755, 1756, 1757; including a Correspondence between the Admiral and the Nabob Serajah Dowlah. Interspersed with some interesting Passages relating to the Manners, Customs. etc. of several Nations in Indostan. Also, a Journey from Persia to England, by an Unusual Route with an Appendix, containing an Account of Diseases prevalent in Admiral Watson's Squadron. A Description of Most of the Trees, Shrubs and Plants, of India, with their real, or supposed medical Virtues: Also a copy of a Letter written by a late ingenious Physician, on the Disorders incidental to Europeans at Gombroon in the Gulph of Persia. London, 1773.

Jenour, Captain Matthew
The Route to India through France, Germany, Hungary, Turkey, Natolia, Syria, and the Desert of Arabia, delineated in a clear concise Manner, with Distances, Time, Mode and Expence of Travelling. London, 1791.

Jones, Lieutenant J. Felix
"Extracts from a Report on the Harbour of Grane (or Koweit), and the Island of Pheleechi, in the Persian Gulf. Prepared in November 1839." in *Bombay Selections,* XXIV, Bombay, 1856.

Kahhala, 'Umar Rida
Mu'jam Qabā'il al-'Arab, Three Vols. Damascus, 1368/1949.

Karmali, Anistas Mari al-
"al-Kuwait" in *Al-Mashriq al-Bayrūtiyya*, X, Bayrūt, 1904.

Kelly, J.B.
1. "The Persian Claim to Bahrain" in *International Affairs*, Vol 33, No. 1, (London, 1957).

2. *British Policy in the Persian Gulf (1813-1843)*, Thesis for a Ph.D., London University, 1956.

3. *Eastern Arabian Frontiers*, (London, 1964).

4. *Britain and the Persian Gulf 1795-1880*, (London, 1968).

Kemball, Lieutenant A.B.
"Observations on the Past Policy of the British Government towards the Arab Tribes of the Persian Gulf." in *Bombay Selections*, XXIV. Bombay, 1856.

"Memoranda on the Resources, Localities, and Relations of the Tribes inhabiting the Arabian Shores of the Persian Gulf." in *Bombay Selections*, XXIV, Bombay, 1856.

Kumar, R.
India and the Persian Gulf Region, 1858-1907, London, 1965.

Landen, R.G.
Oman since 1856. Princeton, 1967.

Lam' al-Shihāb fī Sīrat Muhammad b. 'Abd al-Wahhab, British Museum MS. add. 23, 346.

Layard, A.H. (Sir)
1. *Early Adventures in Persia, Susania and Babylonia, 1887.*

2. *Nineveh and its remains, and discoveries in the ruins of Nineveh and Babylon*, 1853.

Lockhart, L.
Nadir Shah, a Critical Study Based Mainly Upon Contemporary Sources, London, 1938.

Loftus, W.K.
Travels and Researches in Chaldea and Susania, 1857.

Longrigg, S.H.
Four Centuries of Modern Iraq, Oxford, 1925.

Lorimer, J.G.
Gazetteer of the Persian Gulf, 'Oman and Central Arabia, Two Vols., Calcutta, 1915.

Low, Charles Rathbone
History of the Indian Navy (1613-1862), 2 vols., London, 1877.

Malcolm, John
The History of Persia from the most Early Period to the Present Time, Two Vols. 1st Edition, London, 1815.

Mansur, Shaikh
History of Seyd Said, Sultan of Muscat together with an account of the countries and People on the Shores of the Persian Gulf particularly of the Wahabees. London, 1819.

Mignan, R.
A Winter Journey through Russia, the Caucasian Alps, thence into Koordistan, 2 Vols., London, 1839.

Miles, Colonel S.B.
The Countries and Tribes of the Persian Gulf, Two Vols. London, 1919.

Moyse-Bartlett, H.
The Pirates of Trucial Oman, London, 1966.

Murray, H.
Historical Account of Discoveries and Travels in Asia from the Earliest Ages to the Present Time. Vol. III, Edinburgh, 1820.

Musil, Alois
1. *Northern Negd, a Topographical Itinerary*, New York, 1928.

2. *The Manners and Customs of the Rwala Bedouins*, New York, 1926.

3. *The Northern Hegaz*, New York, 1926.

4. *Palmyrena, A Topographical Itinerary*, New York, 1928.

5. *Arabia Deserta, A Topographical Itinerary*, New York, 1927.

6. *The Middle Euphrates, A Topographical Itinerary*, New York, 1927.

Mylrea, C.S.G.
Kuwait before Oil (MS). Memoirs of Dr. C. Stanley G. Mylrea, Pioneer Medical Missionary of the Arabian American Mission. Written between 1945 and 1951.

Nabhani, Muhammad B. Khalifa Al-
Al-Tuhfa al-Nabhāniyya fī Ta'rīkh al-Jazīra al-'Arabiyya, in Twelve Volumes.

Vol. I Ta'rīkh al-Bahrain, Cairo, 1342/1923.
Vol. IX Al-Basra, Cairo, 1342/1923.
Vol. X Al-Muntafiq, Cairo, 1344/1925.
Vol. XII Al-Kuwait, Cairo, 1368/1949.

Niebuhr, B.G.
The Life of Carsten Niebuhr, the Oriental Traveler, With an Appendix by J.D. Michaelis. Translated from the German by Professor Robinson. Edinburgh, 1836.

Niebuhr, Carsten
Description de l'Arabie, faite sur des observations propres et des avis recueillis dans les lieux me
Amsterdam, 1774.

Voyage en Arabie en d'autres Pays circonvoisins, Amsterdam, Vol. I, 1776, Vol. II, 1780.

Olivier, G.A.
Voyage dans l'Empire Ottoman et la Perse, 3 Vols., Paris, 1801.

Oppenheim, M.F. von
Die Beduinen Unter Mitbearbeitung von Erich Braunlich und Werner Caskel, Vol. I, Leipzig 1939; Vol. II, Leipzig, 1943; Vol. III, Wiesbaden, 1952.

Vom Mittelmeer zum Persischen Golf, durch den Hauran, die Syrische Wuste and Mesopotamien. Vol. I, Berlin, 1899; Vol. II, Berlin, 1900.

Palgrave, W.G.
Narrative of a years Journey through Central and Eastern Arabia (1862-1863), 2 Vols., London, 1865.

Parsons, Abraham
   Travels in Asia and Africa including a Journey from Scanderoon to Aleppo, and over the Desert to Bagdad and Bussora; A Voyage from Bussora to Bombay, and along the Western coast of India; A Voyage from Bombay to Mocha and Suez in the Red Sea; and a Journey from Suez to Cairo and Rosetta, in Egypt. London, 1808.

Pelly, L.
   "*A Visit to the Wahhabi Capital, Central Arabia*", Journal R.G.S., XXXV, 1865.

"*Remarks on the Tribes, Trade and Resources around the shore line of the Persian Gulf*", *Transactions of the Bombay Geographical Society*, XVII 1863.

Pelly and Colvill "Account of a Recent tour round the Northern portion of the Persian Gulf", in *Transactions of the Bombay Geographical Society*, XVII, 1863.

Philby, H. St. John
1. *Arabia*, New York, 1930.

2. *Arabian Jubilee*, London, 1952.

3. *Sa'udi Arabia*, London, 1955.

Philips, C. H.
The East India Company, 1784-1834, Manchester University Press, 1940.

Plaisted, Bartholomew
"*Narrative of a Journey from Basra to Aleppo in 1750*", published in Carruthers' *The Desert Route to India etc.,* Hakluyt Society, London, 1929.

Qinā'ī Yūsuf B. 'I
Safahāt Min Fārīkh al-Kuwait, Damascus, 1954.

Rashīd, 'Abd al-'Azīz, al-
Ta'rīkh al-Kuwait, in Two Vols. Baghdad, 1344/1936.

Raunkiaer, Barclay
Through Wahhabi Land on camel-back. London, 1969.

Rentz, G.S.
Muhammad ibn 'Abd al-Wahhab (1703/4-1792) *and the Beginnings of Unitarian Empire in Arabia.*
Dissertation submitted for the degree of Ph.D., in History, California University 1948 (microfilm copy).

Rihani, Amin al-
Mulūk al-'Arab, 2 Vols. Bayrūt, 1924-1925.

Ta'rīkh Najd al-Hadīth wa Mulhaqātuhu, Bayrūt, 1928.

Sadlier, Captain G. Foster
Diary of a Journey across Arabia from el Khatif in the Persian Gulf, to Yambo in the Red Sea, during the Year 1819, Bombay, 1866.

Saldanha, J.A.
Selections from State Papers, Bombay regarding The East India Company's Connection with the Persian Gulf, with a summary of Events, 1600-1800.
Calcutta, 1908.

Précis of correspondence regarding the Affairs of the Persian Gulf, 1801-1853, Calcutta, 1906.

Précis of Turkish Arabia Affairs, 1801-1905, Simla, 1906.

Précis on Commerce and Communication in the Persian Gulf, 1801-1905, Calcutta, 1906.

Précis of Nejd Affairs, 1804-1904, Simla, 1904.

Précis of Bahrein Affairs, 1854-1904, Simla, 1904.

Précis of Correspondence Regarding Trucial Chiefs, 1854-1905, Calcutta, 1906.

Précis of the Affairs of the Persian Coast and Islands, 1854-1905, Simla, 1906.

Précis of Katar Affairs, 1873-1904, Simla, 1904.

Précis of Maskat Affairs, 1892-1905, Simla, 1906.

Précis of Koweit Affairs, 1896-1904, Simla, 1904.

Précis of Mekran Affairs, Calcutta, 1905.

Précis on Naval Arrangements in the Persian Gulf, 1862-1905, Simla, 1906.

Précis of correspondence on International Rivalry and British Policy in the Persian Gulf, 1872-1905, Simla, 1906.

Précis on Arms Trade in the Persian Gulf, Simla, 1904.

Précis of Turkish Expansion on the Arab Littoral of the Persian Gulf and Hasa and Katif Affairs, Simla, 1904.

Précis of Persian Arabistan Affairs, Simla, 1903.

Précis on Slave Trade in the Gulf of Oman and the Persian Gulf, 1873-1905 with a Retrospect into previous history from 1858, Simla, 1906.

Sālimī, Nūr al-Dīn 'Abd Allāh b. Humayd al-
Tuhfat al-A'yān Bisīrat Ahl 'Umān, Vol. I, 2nd Edition, Cairo, 1350/1931. Vol. II, 1st edition, Cairo, 1347/1928.

Seetzen, Dr.
"Letters to Baron von Zach" in *Monatliche Correspondentz,* XI and XII, July-December, 1805, pp. 234-241.

Shamlān, Saif Marzūq al-
Min Ta'rīkh al-Kuwait, Cairo 1378/1959.

Stocqueler, J.H.
Fifteen Months Pilgrimage through untrodden tracts of Khuzistan and Persia in a journey from India to England through parts of Turkish Arabia, Armenia, Russia, and Germany performed in the years 1831 and 1832. Two Vols. London, 1832.

The Overland Companion: being a guide for the traveller to India via Egypt (London, 1848)

The Oriental Interpreter and Treasury of the East India knowledge. A Companion to the Hand-Book of British India. London, 1848.

The route of the Overland Mail to India, from Southhampton to Calcutta, London, 1850.

Sykes, P.
A History of Persia, in two vols. London, 1921.

Taylor, John *Consideration on the Practicability and Advantages of a more speedy Communication between Great Britain and her Possessions in India: with the Outline of a Plan for the more ready Conveyance of Intelligence over-land by the Way of Suez: and an Appendix, containing Instructions for Travellers to India, by different Routes, in Europe, as well as Asia.* London, 1795.

Taylor, Captain Robert
"Extracts from Brief Notes, containing Historical and other Information connected with the Province of Oman; Muskat and the adjoining country; the Islands of Bahrain, Ormus, Kishm, and Karrack; and other Ports and Places in the Persian Gulf. Prepared in the year 1818" in *Bombay Selections,* XXIV, Bombay, 1856.

Thomas, Hughes R.
Selections from the Records of the Bombay Government No. XLIII - New Series, Bombay, 1857.

Thornton, Edwards
A Gazetteer of the countries adjacent to India on the Northwest; including Sinde, Afghanistan, Beloochistan, the Punjab and the neighbouring states, 2 Vols., London, 1844.

Tuson, Penelope
The Records of the British Residency and Agencies in the Persian Gulf, London, 1979.

'Umarī, Yāsīn B. Khayr Allāh Al-Khatīb al-
Al-Durr al-Maknūn fī Ma'āthir al-Madiya min al-Qurūn. British Museum MSS. Add. 23312, 23313.

Vidal, F.S.
The Oasis of al-Hasa.
Arabian Oil Company, Arabian Research Division, New York, 1955.

Wahba, Hāfiz
Jazīrat al-'Arab fi al-Qarn al-'Ishrīn, Cairo, 1935.

Warden, Francis
"Extracts from Brief Notes relative to the Rise and Progress of the Arab Tribes of the Persian Gulf - Prepared in August 1819." in *Bombay Selections,* XXIV, Bombay, 1856.

"Historical Sketch of the Rise and Progress of the Government of Muskat; commencing with the year 1694-95, and continued to the year 1819." in *Bombay Selections,* XXIV, Bombay, 1856.

"Historical Sketch of the Uttoobee Tribe of Arabs (Bahrein) from the year 1716 to the year 1817." in *Bombay Selections,* XXIV, Bombay, 1856.

"Sketch of the Proceedings (from 1809 to 1818) of Rahmah bin Jaubir, Chief of Khor Hassan". in *Bombay Selections*, XXIV, Bombay, 1856.

Welsted, J.R.
Travels in Arabia, 2 Vols., London, 1838.

Travels to the City of the Caliphs along the Shores of the Persian Gulf and the Mediterranean, including a Voyage to the Coast of Arabia, and a Tour on the Island of Socotra. 2 Vols., London, 1840.

Wilson, A.T.
The Persian Gulf, Oxford, 1954.

Wilson, D.
"Memorandum respecting the Pearl Fisheries of the Persian Gulf", *Journal of the Royal Geographic Society,* III, 1833.

Wilson, H.H.
A Glossary of Judicial and Revenue Terms and of Useful Words occurring in Official Documents Relating to the Administration of the Government of the British India from Arabia, Persian ... and other Languages. London, 1855.

Winder, R.B.
A History of the Sa'udi State from 1233/1818 - 1308/1891. Ph.D. 1950 Thesis, Princeton University.

Sa'udi Arabia in the Nineteenth Century, New York, 1965.

INDEX